HOW TO BE A FAMILY

HOW TO BE A FAMILY

THE YEAR I DRAGGED MY KIDS

AROUND THE WORLD TO FIND

A NEW WAY TO BE TOGETHER

DAN KOIS

Little, Brown and Company

New York   Boston   London

Little, Brown and Company
Hachette Book Group
1290 Avenue of the Americas, New York, NY 10104
littlebrown.com

First Edition: September 2019

Little, Brown and Company is a division of Hachette Book Group, Inc. The Little, Brown name and logo are trademarks of Hachette Book Group, Inc.

The publisher is not responsible for websites (or their content) that are not owned by the publisher.

The Hachette Speakers Bureau provides a wide range of authors for speaking events. To find out more, go to hachettespeakersbureau.com or call (866) 376-6591.

Excerpt from "On Any Walk" reprinted with the permission of Ashleigh Young.
Maps by Harper Kois
Photographs by Alia Smith

ISBN 978-0-316-55262-2
LCCN 2019931306

10 9 8 7 6 5 4 3 2 1

LSC-C

Printed in the United States of America

Our own nostalgia is already here, the first of a series of autumn moods that will pile up, layer on layer, as she leaves her various younger selves behind.

—Brian Hall, *Madeleine's World*

I just want
four walls and adobe slats
for my girls

—Animal Collective

COSTA RICA
July – September

KANSAS
October – December

HOW TO BE A FAMILY

YOU'RE SCREWING UP

I didn't go to Iceland expecting to meet the perfect family. It was February 2016 and I was there to write a magazine feature about the country's geothermally heated public swimming pools, a simple municipal investment that had helped make the people there among the most content in the world. But then one subfreezing night at Vesturbaejarlaug, an outdoor pool in Reykjavik, I scampered across the frigid deck and hopped into the steaming family pool with Henry Henrysson and Regina Bjarnadóttir and their children. Elin and Emma splashed together while little Henry clung to his mom. My job as a magazine editor usually involves sitting in an office working on other people's stories, staring at my computer until my eyes cross, so this was not a typical day for me—but this was a typical evening for them, Henry and Regina told me: the whole family in the pool, a final swim before bedtime, pajamas at the ready in the dressing rooms. "The ritual helps the kids go to sleep, I think," Henry said. "The water calms them." This is a particularly Icelandic parenting strategy, I'd learned; I'd talked to many adults who could still summon the childhood memory of slipping their still-warm bodies between cool sheets.

Regina was the executive director of an NGO that built schools and waterworks in Sierra Leone and, also, sure, in addition, was a dead ringer for Jennifer Garner. Henry the elder was a philosophy professor so handsome he seemed like a lost member of the Skarsgård family. The children were a Mini Boden catalog come to life: Elin, twelve, extremely mature with impeccable English; Emma, seven, cute and enthusiastic; Henry, three, mischievous and charming. *National Geographic* had recently offered them a free cruise of Iceland's Westfjords in exchange for their giving a few lectures and mingling with Americans for a week. That is, the entire family had been certified by *National Geographic* as the kind of Icelandic natural wonder that tourists ought to experience.

After swimming, the family invited me to dinner at the café across the street. "Let me tell you a magical story," I said as we crunched through the snowy parking lot. The girls eagerly gathered near. "Say you have a snowstorm here in Reykjavik," I continued. Their mother translated quietly for Emma. "Perhaps almost a meter of snow."

"Yes," they said, nodding. This was a not-unfamiliar scenario. It was snowing now, though only a dusting, the flakes flickering past the street-lights.

"So if there was that much snow here," I continued, "would you go to school the next day?"

Elin crinkled her brow. "What does this mean?" she asked.

"I mean, would they cancel school?"

Elin laughed. A moment later, Emma laughed too, having either worked out the English or decided that if Elin was laughing, she'd better join her. "No, of course not," Elin said.

"Well," I said, "just before I came to Iceland, we had a storm like that in Virginia, where I live. And do you know how many days they canceled school for my kids?"

Elin's eyes were wide. "How many?"

"Seven," I said.

Their screams of disbelief echoed through the dark neighborhood. "I think that is too many days!" Emma said quite seriously. As the children chattered about this remarkable story, their parents took me aside.

"How do parents work?" Regina asked me. "How do you live?"

That was a good question. Even before the snowstorm, it had been a time of particular craziness in my house in Arlington, Virginia. My daughter Lyra, ten, and her little sister, Harper, eight, were navigating more difficult schoolwork, more complicated friendships, and shifting personal identities. I was managing employees for the first time as the editor of a section of a magazine, and finding it hard to balance the personalities and responsibilities involved. Alia, my wife, a First Amendment attorney, was working eighteen hours a day on the toughest case of her career, one that she worried was going off the rails in a state court proceeding that seemed wildly unjust. The stress of both our jobs, the sense of the general out-of-control-ness of things, was bleeding ever more regularly into our home life.

One night a few months before my trip to Iceland I'd been walking down the hallway to my bedroom when I saw that Lyra's light was still on. As usual, after putting our daughters to bed, I'd spent several hours at the kitchen table chipping away at the infinite mountain of work, chugging Diet Coke, tweeting. Alia was holed up in the office downstairs, writing a brief. It was eleven o'clock, much later than I would expect Lyra still to be awake. I peeked into her room to find her sprawled across her bed, staring at the ceiling. She turned to me as the door opened, her eyes wide.

"Hi, sweetie," I said. "What's up? Why aren't you asleep?"

She made a desperate gesture of overcapacity around her head. "I can't turn it all off!" she cried.

I knew the feeling. After rubbing Lyra's back and singing to her and turning out her light, I too lay in bed staring at the ceiling. Had I finished all the work I needed to do? (I remembered an email I'd intended to write, grabbed my phone off the bedside table, typed it, tapped Send.) Was Alia holding up—could I be doing more to help her out? (She was still downstairs.) Did I remember to send in that form for Harper's school? When was the quarterly tax payment due? Ah, did I forget to buy toilet paper? Why were my eyelids twitching like that?

Maybe the Diet Coke wasn't helping things.

Then came the snowstorm. Two feet in one day, resulting in seven days of missed school—a second, unscheduled Christmas vacation for our kids. But not for us! It was the kind of catastrophe for parents that wrecked weeks of planning and put us at the edge of panic every hour as we juggled the stuff we needed to get done with the task of keeping two bored girls occupied for the nearly two weeks they were stuck in the house. The snowstorm transformed me in my coworkers' eyes from a guy they could depend on into a guy who bailed on his responsibilities and disappointed them. We paid our wonderful babysitter, Alia's cousin, hundreds of extra dollars just so we could do distracted, not-very-good work during the day and then yell at our children after she left.

This act of God seemed to serve as the perfect crucible to reveal how broken our family life was. Our household operated like the nation's air traffic network: we functioned, but forever on the edge of catastrophe, knowing that one closed runway would set off a cascade of problems that would eventually overwhelm the system. When our children finally returned to school, we looked at the wreckage behind us and the future ahead of us. The all-hours working—the concern about whether Lyra and Harper were happy, healthy, learning the most, getting the best—the certainty that somehow, despite all the advantages we were lucky enough to possess and pass on to them, we were fundamentally living the wrong life. It seemed to me, nearly every day, that we were doing *being a family* wrong.

My children had wonderful opportunities, full schedules, and enriching experiences. Yet working our days and nights away as we did, my wife and I rarely spent time with them, and the time I did spend with them often left us all anxious, as I tried to connect through my own distraction and their complaints about screens they couldn't watch or shit I couldn't buy them. Of course, often they were loving and grateful and kind—but then I was so beside myself with annoyance and frustration that I didn't see it. Above all our life as a family felt as though it was flying past in a blur of petty arguments, overworked days, exhausted nights, an inchoate longing for some kind of existence that made more sense. Our family wasn't broken or dysfunctional, but we were in an unhappy rut, one that seemed of our own making but was also tied to the busy, hyper-competent parenting culture that surrounded us in Arlington. We could have gone on as we were, and after eighteen years, our kids would be...what? What would we be parenting them into? Two smart, kind women, I hoped, but also blinkered people from the burbs, unable to deal with adversity, without much of a sense of the world outside the path we'd cleared for them.

As the cohost of a parenting podcast, I heard every day from listeners that the only thing that made them feel worse than the amount of time they spent away from their kids was the poor quality of the time they spent with them. The secret belief that, despite living in relative comfort and freedom, you're fundamentally screwing up parenting is the tie that binds pretty much all the parents I know. The friend who was so driven to distraction by her daughter's screen obsession that she posted pleas to Facebook begging for advice, and the other friends who just commented, "God, I wish I knew." The podcast listener who wrote in infuriated by his children's ungratefulness, who wished his kids could see what the real world was like just once, how fortunate they were to live the lives they did. Once an old college friend told me, "Well, I hardly ever see them, but at least when I do we drive each other crazy!"

Very little of the time I spent with my kids was *quality* time, which to me meant facing a challenge together, talking about the world together, enjoying one another's company in some kind of rewarding way. Like so many ideals, or even fantasies, of good parenting, this vision of what our time together *should* be invaded and darkened the time together we actually had. Sometimes, during my regular phone call to Alia while I walked to get lunch in downtown DC—often the only conversation we would have until after kid bedtime—we both confessed how overwhelmed we felt, giving comfort to each other but no solutions. There *were* no solutions. On afternoons that I needed to pick the girls up, I ducked out of conversations with coworkers and apologized for putting off my final tasks but *still* always ran late, getting stuck in traffic or on a balky Metro train. I'll never forget the afternoon that, already behind schedule to get Harper at basketball practice, I pulled out of the garage, looked left, looked right, and then drove directly into a pedestrian in chinos, knocking him over.

"What the *fuck?*" he shouted, leaping to his feet.

"I'm sorry!" I cried through the open window. "It was my fault! I'm so sorry!"

He slammed the hood of our Honda. "What the fuck is *wrong* with you?" he yelled. Half a block later, I had to pull over because I couldn't see the road through the tears.

So what could we do? Should I quit my job, move us off the grid, join a commune? Some kind of life upheaval seemed necessary to break us out of the trap we'd put our family in, but the shape and scope of such a change was beyond me.

Settling at a table with the happy Henrysson-Bjarnadóttirs at a café across the street from the pool, I wondered if I'd been thinking too narrowly about my American family and our American life. I'd never even considered, for example, how swimming in a hot tub with my kids each night might change us. What if my general ignorance about the rest of the world wasn't just a symptom of our family malaise but a cause? Other cultures raise their children in manners wholly alien to me; they organize their lives differently, value different qualities in their kids, measure success in different ways (or don't measure it at all).

In the café, I asked Henry and Regina if they and their kids had spent much time overseas, and I learned that, thanks to both Regina's job and the family prioritization of travel, the children had been to more countries than I, a grown adult, ever had: Guyana, Panama, Grenada, Rwanda, the Netherlands, Turkey. "I really love traveling," Elin said brightly. In fact, the family was considering moving to Sierra Leone for a year or so. "Some people are going to think we're crazy," Henry admitted, "but many of my friends are adventurous."

I asked Elin how she would feel about such a move. "Well, I'm at a very difficult age, of course," she said, and I laughed out loud because the only young woman less awkward than clever, poised Elin Reginasdóttir was, like, Malala. She shrugged to acknowledge the absurdity of her statement and then continued: "I'll miss my friends, but I'm excited for the trip. I think it will be *amazing*."

I'd finished my beer and ordered another, despite the wary glances Henry and Regina kept giving each other. I told them about how my wife and I felt like we were grasping for some other, completely different way of life. "I often wish something like that as well," Henry said. ("You *do?*" I gawped.) "If I could choose one place for our family to live, it would be Holland," he added. "I think Holland is the most successful country."

Soon, beautiful Henry and Regina and Elin and Emma and Henry climbed in their car to drive home. I walked across town to my hostel, the snow now coating my beard, mulling over everything I'd seen and heard. What if Alia and I took the leap so many parents dream of— ditched our overstuffed, incomprehensible lives and went in search of a better way?

We weren't perfect like the Henrysson-Bjarnadóttirs, but I liked our family. Alia and I had met on the first day of freshman year in Chapel Hill, North Carolina, on a sand volleyball court outside our dorm. Our meet-cute was Alia telling me that just because I was a guy didn't mean I was allowed to stray out of position and steal plays that my female teammates could make just fine. We traveled in the same circle of friends, bonded over improv comedy and music, flirted through a psychology class, and finally, after an epic senior-year road trip to Graceland, started dating. Within twelve months of graduation we were engaged; it just seemed pointless, we thought, to wait to get married when it was evident to us and everyone we knew that we were right for each other. We were the first of our friends to get married; I was in grad school and she was in law school.

Did we talk about children? I hope so, though I don't remember. Alia recalls me telling my mom on the phone about our engagement and assuring her that this girl did indeed want to have kids someday. We certainly weren't going to have them right away, though; we were so young! We'd both had pretty comfortable childhoods, each of us the less-troublemaking sibling in a two-child family. I grew up in the suburbs of Milwaukee; my parents' divorce when I was in eighth grade unsettled my adolescence, but it remained clear through my childhood that I was a priority in both my parents' lives. Alia was raised in a weird hippie neighborhood forty-five minutes south of DC; her parents were quirky and loving and the exact level of strict-yet-kind that we later struggled to achieve in our own parenting. (Our kids definitely don't have the healthy terror of disappointing us that Alia had of disappointing her mom.)

After getting married, we lived in Honolulu and then in New York City, where many of our college friends had also ended up. Alia worked for a big firm, and then, as soon as she could, joined a small First Amendment boutique outfit, defending newspapers and magazines against libel suits and battling the government for access to public records. I made my way, eventually, to journalism, writing and editing about movies and books. We established traditions, had adventures, developed inside jokes. Feel free to ask me in person for the very, very long story behind why, whenever one of us drops something in the kitchen, the other one automatically says, "You're screwing up."

We'd adopted a dog in Hawaii and brought her with us to New York, where we doted on her, singing endless verses of a song of Alia's invention called "Dora Is a Dog":

Dora is a dog
She is not a frog
She is not a log
She doesn't drink eggnog

...and so on. We referred to Dora, *to her face,* as our "practice kid." So when we'd managed to keep her alive for five years, we decided: Time to have the actual kids. Alia went off birth control, came home one night from a court date in Buffalo, and announced, "I'm pretty sure I'm ovulating"; nine months later, in 2005, Lyra was born.

Lyra revealed herself early as someone who organized the events around her into narratives, inventing stories and questing to understand the motives behind people's actions and words. Harper, born two years later, viewed the structures and tasks the world required as delightful puzzles to solve, and she tirelessly practiced the things that seemed important to her: walking, doing cartwheels, dribbling a basketball, baking cookies. Dora abdicated her firstborn position, bearing the countless indignities of a big dog's life with small children. Lyra's babysitter wanted Lyra to ride Dora like a horse. As a toddler, Harper spent quite a bit of time trying to stick her finger in Dora's butt. Those first years were nearly impossible, as they are for most parents, but we survived them by thinking of ourselves as a team. We had each other's backs. "Esbu," Alia and I would whisper to each other, a sweet nothing we shared when some person outside our little circle disappointed us in some way. It was an acronym for *everyone sucks but us.*

We fled New York in 2009 and headed down to the DC suburbs. Our choice made sense even as we disappointed ourselves by giving up the bustle and diversity of the city for a placid house in Arlington. But we were exhausted from raising small kids and getting priced out of the city; many of our friends were moving away, and Alia's parents lived close to our new home, in Prince George's County, where Alia had grown up. They were A+ grandparents, engaged, supportive, and minimally meddlesome, and we were desperate for help.

And that's where we were seven years later, in a brick ranch on a busy street, the proverbial worst house in a nice neighborhood. We'd refinanced to expand the galley kitchen and build a porch, upon which I liked to sit and watch baseball on summer nights. The girls had their own rooms next to our room and pined for an upstairs like their friends' big houses had. Dora, now sixteen years old and retired, roamed the backyard, pursuing her passion, squirrels. We didn't have a fancy coffee machine or a smart fridge but we *did* install a soda fountain that pumped out Diet Coke like at McDonald's. After a number of lonely years, we'd finally assembled a group of close friends in Arlington, and I'd found a job at a magazine I loved. But in other ways, things were harder than ever. Alia's parents, facing sudden health problems, were about to move away; we felt less and less at home in a neighborhood becoming Manhattanesque in its wealth; Alia was overworked and stressed out. And I, like Lyra, couldn't turn it all off.

That night in Reykjavik, I called Alia as I walked home through the snow. "Hold on," she said. "Harper, please wait, I'm on the phone with Daddy." In the background, Harper, just home from school, was asking for more screen time. "Did you get good stuff for the story?" Alia asked me.

Yeah, I said, but what I *really* wanted to talk to her about was the crazy idea we'd sometimes batted back and forth, a kind of parenting vision quest, a bananas dream to dump everything for a year and try out life somewhere far, far away. "I think we should just do it," I said. "I think we should, like, get the hell out of our parenting bubble."

In the background of the phone call, I heard Lyra and Harper shouting at each other about some bullshit. "I have to go," Alia said. "I have to finish this brief and get them to not kill each other. So, you know, I'm in."

If we could go somewhere else for an entire year, where would we go? A tropical paradise where we sat on the beach all day? The damn South of France? A new city that offered more family support, a more sane idea about balance? No single culture has completely solved these issues, of course. (Even Henry Henrysson dreams of someplace else!) We wanted to find a place that would challenge the aspects of our parenting we already struggled with. So over the next few months we researched, talked to friends, peered unhappily at our savings account balance. At night in bed, we discovered that when you're too tired for sex you can get a pretty great endorphin rush just from hearing your partner speak aloud the name of a country you could maybe move to. "Argentina?" Alia would say, and I'd moan with delight.

The more we spun out dreams of our 2017, the less able we were to find a single country that had everything we wanted. There were so many countries that could transform so many different parts of our family life. Surely we would never have this chance again, so couldn't we try a sample platter of global parenting? That's how we settled on *four* new homes. First we'd take our slothful, screen-addicted kids (and slothful, screen-addicted selves) to New Zealand, a country whose parenting philosophy revolves around outdoor recreation and adventure. Then we'd seek order in the Netherlands, the country where everything works and where the children are supposedly the happiest in the world. We'd search for a simpler, more beautiful life in Costa Rica, a country that prizes *pura vida* and whose population of native Ticos was swelling with American retirees and families looking for paradise on a budget. And to finish the year off, we'd return to America, but not to Arlington. Instead, we'd settle down in Hays, Kansas, near the precise geographic center of the United States, joining old friends who'd fled the East Coast for a small town, to learn whether what we'd been desperate for all along was a kind of smaller, more "authentic" American life—or if such a thing even existed anymore.

We weren't presumptuous enough to imagine that we could parachute into a city for three months and *truly* understand all there was to know about it. We wouldn't magically become Dutch or Tico or Kansan. But we could model our family life after the lives we saw around us, practicing curiosity and open-mindedness, trying out ways of interacting we might never have thought of. And as a journalist, I could uncover a perspective bigger than what most families would experience by reporting and researching, interviewing other parents, educators, and academics.

I had a whole list of questions I wanted to ask in each place. But for Alia and me, the question was simpler: Could the two of us set aside our relentless quest to make sure our children had every material and educational advantage, and instead focus for twelve months on caring for all our hearts and souls? The more we talked about our plan, the more it seemed like a chance to substantially change our lives—to learn from other places and bring those lessons back home. Or bring them wherever! Perhaps we'd return to Arlington and stay, finding a way to live there sanely. But perhaps the experience would change our outlook so profoundly that going back to our lives in Arlington would be intolerable. Maybe we'd move to a small town, or Central America, or the other side of the world. Part of the shivery delight of dreaming of such a trip was dreaming of the entirely different life you might live on the other side of it.

And maybe we'd *need* to completely change our life, because it became clear pretty quickly that we might not have any money left when the trip was over. We'd drawn up a complicated yearlong budget that was 50 percent incredibly specific well-researched numbers and 50 percent laughable guesses. ("How much do you think we would spend on Diet Coke per week in New Zealand?") Our proposed budget was predicated not only on us economizing, convincing our bosses to let us work remotely, dipping into our savings, and maximizing credit card points but also on the theory that I could get a publisher to pay me to write a book about our experiences, an assumption that seemed like both a tantalizing possibility and a truly bad idea.

Should I write a book about my family? (It's moot now, I wrote the book, here it is, you heroically bought it or shamefully borrowed it from a friend, but Alia and I really discussed it a lot at the time.) I dispensed pretty quickly with the principle that one's own family ought not to be fodder for public consumption; that ship had sailed years before, when I started telling stories about my own bad parenting on a podcast. But there was the very real possibility that I would end up sounding like a total choad. What kind of choad? There were so many! The self-congratulatory Superdad who co-opts the domestic labor of women everywhere and wears it like a cape? The coastal elitist who thinks that he's got some right to weigh in on people living *real* lives in *real* places? Take your pick. Whatever kind of jerk you can think of, it's a kind of jerk I would definitely feel like at least once during our year's travels.

The dream of chucking it all and starting a new life somewhere far away is one of the foundational fantasies of upper-middle-class parenting. Of course, there's a level of privilege in being able to worry that my extremely fortunate children are fortunate in the wrong ways. But one of the biggest failures I saw in my own parenting was that I hadn't managed to give my children a sense of their own advantage—that they were growing up incurious about the world and ignorant of their place in it. This is the exact issue that, unchecked, would lead them to thoughtlessly perpetuate that privilege throughout their adulthoods. I wanted to find a way of life for our family that involved truly connecting with the world around us as well as with one another.

It was almost summer, and soon we had to decide whether or not we were gonna do this thing. Alia had returned from a several-week-long trial in Florida; the news site she had been defending against a vindictive billionaire had lost its case and was on its way to dispiriting bankruptcy. She was exhausted from months of late nights and worried about the future of a country she saw turning against values she'd spent her career protecting. She was also pretty sure that Lyra had grown a couple of inches in the weeks she'd been gone; Lyra had hit puberty and, as Alia had as a child, was nearing her adult height at the age of eleven. Alia and Lyra were dead ringers for each other, in fact, with Harper a smaller, more elfin collection of the same traits: dark hair, dark eyes, brilliant smile, brows for days.

As a parent, Alia's a snuggler and a nurturer, warm and funny. She's calmer than me, more likely to give an upset or angry child a sympathetic response, less likely to lose it. (That means, though, that when she does yell, it *really* registers with them, unlike when I do.) But she's also a worrier. In *Peter Pan,* J. M. Barrie wrote movingly of mothers and the emotional caretaking they do for their children:

> It is the nightly custom of every good mother after her children are asleep to rummage in their minds and put things straight for next morning, repacking into their proper places the many articles that have wandered during the day. If you could keep awake (but of course you can't) you would see your own mother doing this, and you would find it very interesting to watch her. It is quite like tidying up drawers. You would see her on her knees, I expect, lingering humorously over some of your contents, wondering where on earth you had picked this thing up, making discoveries sweet and not so sweet, pressing this to her cheek as if it were as nice as a kitten, and hurriedly stowing that out of sight. When you wake in the morning, the naughtiness and evil passions with which you went to bed have been folded up small and placed at the bottom of your mind, and on the top, beautifully aired, are spread out your prettier thoughts, ready for you to put on.

It's a lovely metaphor, but Barrie ignores, or leaves unspoken, the real effects on parents that this kind of hands-on emotional effort can have. For of course this work—walking through experiences with children and highlighting the beauty of the world and helping them understand the bad things in life—doesn't actually happen when kids are asleep; instead, it's a set of constant conversations, each of which has as much of an impact on the parent as it has on the child. As a mom, Alia is wonderful at offering the mixture of comfort, context, and sympathy such moments require. But all those discoveries that were not so sweet, I thought, rose to the top of *her* mind, leading her to occasional anxious nights talking and thinking about the kids. (I'm sure my frequent unwillingness to admit when I'm similarly uncertain doesn't help things.)

We're the kind of couple who talk through even tiny decisions, looking for agreement, so needless to say, this *big* decision was one we chewed over for hours every day, in texts and emails and late-night conversations out on the porch. Alia had hung Christmas lights around the porch, giving the space a dorm-room ambience that, I was convinced, encouraged crazy ideas. "What should we do?" I asked her one typically muggy Virginia night after the kids were in bed. "We can economize and work while we travel but we would definitely come back broke, or maybe seriously in debt."

In our marriage, Alia is the more cautious one, more concerned about money, less likely to take a big personal or professional leap. Which is why I was so struck by her response, struck the way our kids are when she shakes off her usual persona and hollers at them. Think of ourselves twenty years from now, Alia suggested. Would we say, *Oh gosh, good thing we didn't make a possibly foolish financial decision,* or would we say, *We had the chance to change our lives forever, and we didn't do it because we were ten thousand dollars short?* That hot night on the porch, each of us fortified by a glass of wine, we looked at each other and started laughing.

We did it. We overturned our lives. We were screwing up, probably. But we wanted an adventure. We wanted our kids to see that there were other ways to live. We wanted to figure out how to be a family.

I could write a book, if the world needed such a boring book, about the logistics of planning a four-country journey. Alia, who is very good at getting shit done, kept a running to-do list of dozens of items, and her first task was to find us houses in four different countries. Meanwhile, I dug into the local schools. Private school was off the table, considering the expense, and also the idea seemed antithetical to what we were trying to learn from the trip. We considered homeschooling. We did! But (a) if we wanted to make a lot of friends fast in these four new homes, the connections offered by school were an easy way to do that; and (b) as much as it might have goosed sales, a quadruple murder-suicide was not how I wanted my memoir to end. Alia was concerned the girls might fall behind, particularly in math. I argued that everything would be *fine,* it wasn't like they were in *high* school—their grades didn't matter, they were smart, they'd catch up.

There were visas to apply for and principals to Skype and neighborhoods to Google Street View and houses to rent and embassy events in DC to crash so we could ask everyone if they would be interested in helping us learn more about the country to which we were about to move. (Hot tip: Kiwi Happy Hour, Friday afternoons in the basement bar at the New Zealand embassy, is super-fun.) We had to figure out who we could ask to take our beloved Dora while we were gone despite her failing health, and then we had to deal with our beloved Dora becoming immobile and incontinent, and then we had to put our beloved Dora to sleep. Then we had to cry for a week while also purging and packing our possessions, finding a renter from whom we could recoup some of our mortgage payment, and incorporating as a small business absurdly called GloboParents, LLC.

The first people we had to tell about the trip, of course, were our children. Just kidding! First we had to sweet-talk our bosses. My magazine's editor in chief and the managing partner at Alia's firm were very nice, saintly in fact, assuring us that we could work part-time while we were gone *and* that we'd be welcomed back when we returned. This was a lucky break, and we tried not to feel guilty about it, given the seventy-hour weeks we'd put in over the years. That helped us balance our budget while also giving us hope that we wouldn't be out on the street when the trip was over.

Then I had to tell our Arlington friends, conversations that were trickier than I expected. We are very close with a group of other parents on our block, a typically Arlingtonian mishmash of Republicans and Democrats, civil servants and lawyers and entrepreneurs and toilers at nonprofits. What they all had in common was that they were living the precise life—right down to ZIP+4—that had driven us to undertake our entire adventure. By traveling around the world looking for a different way to be a family, weren't we explicitly saying that our current way of being, and theirs, was, at its heart, flawed?

I think it went okay? I downplayed the likelihood of a permanent departure from our neighborhood, especially after our friend Ashley made it clear that if we didn't come back, we were dead to her forever. And the truth was, I didn't know if we were leaving for good! I wasn't sure if our trip would lead us to rebel against our Arlington life or crave a return to it; as difficult and stressful as it was, it was also comfortable in many ways, and we couldn't deny that the friends we'd made, after years of feeling friendless and alone in the suburbs, gave us tremendous happiness.

But we were close enough to these friends that we'd already talked with them many times about the treadmill on which we often felt trapped, and most of them confessed a similar desire to shake up some aspect of their lives, even if they didn't know how. In the end I felt that I had their blessing to go on this trip, to think hard about our future, and to write this book. All they asked was that I, in the words of Ashley's handsome husband, Kevin, "make us look good."

Like many sandwich-generation fortysomethings, we had parents whose lives were as complicated as those of our kids. Both my dad and Alia's dad had dementia, which had arrived for each of them just after retirement. My father was still quite capable; Alia's father, farther down his path, was close to being entirely absent. They both had wives caring for them (in my dad's case, his third wife; for Alia's dad, her mom), although the same summer we announced our trip, Alia's dad's awareness and temperament took a sharp turn, and by the end of the year he was in long-term care. We felt a lot of things all at once: guilt that we'd be gone during difficult times, worry about those we were leaving behind, gratitude for the moms and brothers and sisters-in-law who would be picking up the slack.

But for several years, Alia and I had discussed how our fathers' surprise diagnoses—both men around the age of seventy, both in otherwise fantastic health—had made much more concrete our inchoate desires to change our lives. To see both our fathers and their wives curtailing ambitious late-life plans to focus on seeking treatment and maintaining routine was a reminder that we might not have the decades we'd counted on to do the exciting things we'd always wanted to do. We no longer felt willing to wait for adventure to become convenient.

We did eventually tell our kids. (We couldn't tell them first because they couldn't keep a secret to save their dang lives.) "So, guys," we said on a drive down to North Carolina in July. "Can you put your iPods down for a second? We want to have a family meeting. Family meeting!"

Alia and I like to have family meetings. Harper enjoys calling the roll. Lyra cannot deal.

"Daddy?"

"Here."

"Mommy?"

"Present."

"Lyra?"

"Ugggghhhhhhh."

"Harper? Present. Okay."

"So, girls," I said. Alia and I made eye contact and I giggled foolishly. "You know how sometimes we talk about how it would be exciting for our whole family to just travel around the world for a while?"

"Oh no," Lyra said from the back seat, a note of hysteria in her voice.

"Oh yes," I said.

"We're doing it," Alia added.

"For all of 2017!"

The girls screamed. Even listening to the recording I made of this moment on my phone, I have trouble accurately characterizing this scream. It included some disbelief, a bit of excitement, a bit of silliness. One hears in it not a small amount of rage. Pour all those ingredients into a 2009 Honda CRV and light on fire.

After the girls eagerly discussed it for about five minutes, though, their attention flagged. We'd told them we had a lot of decisions to make and we wanted them to help us make them, but it was clear they were having trouble conceptualizing the journey as a real event in which they would actually participate. It was months and months away!

Over those months and months, their responses to the trip and to our frenzied planning mirrored their personalities. Lyra, now eleven and entering sixth grade, dealt with the upheaval in her life mostly by ignoring it, focusing even more deeply on the online communities she was allowed to participate in for precisely one hour of her day and on the books that occupied all the other hours. She was starting middle school, a big worry that overrode many of her other worries, especially as her two best friends at the school had recently moved away. She was a loner, happy to read or write or ride a scooter up and down the driveway, lost in thought. From time to time she would bemoan her lack of friends, but her absolute shunning of any potentially uncomfortable situation—she even ran out of the room to avoid seeing awkward misunderstandings on TV—meant she would rather drop dead than invite a friendly kid over.

What Lyra hated most of all was to be made to do things. If she was pursuing an idea of her own, she could be devoted, but if she was busy in her head, she was uninterested in what others thought she should do. And so it was that her resistance to our upcoming trip came most often when we asked her to perform some small task—sorting through a shelf or two of books to see if there were some she could donate to charity, say. Unexpectedly, she would fly into a fury. I found it baffling, but as far as Lyra was concerned, her whole life was people demanding that she do things, and this new plan had broken the camel's back. "And on top of everything," she would sometimes say, "you're making me go on this stupid *trip* I don't even *care about* and you didn't *ask me*."

It was true, we hadn't asked her. Parents make a lot of unilateral decisions on behalf of their children. But no matter how confident I felt that this decision was a wonderful one for which our kids would forever be grateful, these arguments with Lyra shook me. (More than they shook her, apparently; shortly afterward she would be perfectly civil.) One reason we'd wanted to take this kind of trip *now* was that our kids were the perfect ages, old enough to get a lot out of the trip and remember it but young enough that we wouldn't wreck their teenage years. But Lyra was already knee-deep in puberty, already acted like a teenager; what if we were too late and we were about to screw her up?

Other times, though, Lyra surprised us. She liked to tell new people we met about the epic journey we were about to go on, and once when I picked her up at school she introduced me to a classmate as "the reason I get out of a whole year of the hell that is middle school."

For her part, Harper, who had turned nine and entered fourth grade, *loved* to help us prepare. Participating in and learning what she considered adult skills had always been a priority in her life; she was the kid who, through several days of diligent practice at age six, taught herself to wink. As she got older, it became clear to her that being *the one who helps* was a way of differentiating herself from Lyra, which made Harper even hungrier to pitch in. And so our preparation for the trip was a smorgasbord of opportunities for Harper to accomplish the kinds of little tasks she delighted in. Need someone to put fifty-cent price stickers on various household items before the garage sale? Harper's your gal.

Detail-oriented Harper worked her way into understanding the trip by asking question after question about our itinerary. And not just "Which country are we visiting first?" but "How many hours is our flight from New Zealand to the Netherlands?" (Answer: Twenty-four hours, split over two flights, with a stop in Dubai.) She was particularly fascinated by our flight across the international date line, when we would go from Honolulu to Auckland, and hearing her trying to explain to her friends how an entire day would just disappear was how I knew the trip felt real to her. But with that realization came the bitter understanding that she really *was* going to have to say goodbye to all those friends, to Caroline and Maddie and Shira and Morgan and Nora and Ellen and . . .

Lyra's friendships, though close, were few, and already existed to a large extent online, where she would find Sophie in a Roblox game or Lindsay on a Hopscotch message board. Harper's friendships were analog, dependent on playdates and sleepovers in which girls would turn cartwheels in the basement and giggle in the bedroom. And so her December became a cavalcade of tearful goodbyes, each of which seemed to sand off just a little bit of Harper's usual good cheer. "Remember," I would tell her, "this trip is just a chance to make *even more* friends," and she would brighten a bit—though once she reminded me, "Yeah, but then I'll have to say goodbye to *them* too."

For the summer and fall preceding the 2016 election, friends had made very funny jokes about how our trip was perfectly timed, wouldn't we be happy to escape the first year of the Trump administration, ha ha, how we laughed. Those jokes were particularly apropos as the first country we were visiting, New Zealand, was a frequently mentioned destination for ironic Trump-fleers as august as Supreme Court justice Ruth Bader Ginsburg.

Donald Trump's election changed the complexion of our trip quite a bit. Suddenly we were an object of envy for our liberal friends, not for the life change we were trying to make but because we were *really doing it,* getting out of Trump's America. But we *weren't* really doing that, we hastened to tell them. We were not abandoning our country in its time of need! From the road, I would be editing politics pieces for the magazine. Alia would be vetting stories and defending FOIAs for newspapers and websites that were working to ferret out the truth. If we couldn't be protesting in the streets of Washington, we vowed, we would be faces of reason and kindness out in the world, Americans doing our best to explain our country and its bad choices. I suspected that I'd be given plenty of opportunities to talk about President Trump on our travels.

The odd new political climate just added to the sense of unreality and insanity in our lives through December, the pressure getting more and more intense until, finally, on December 29, 2016, it was over. Our house was empty. Our flight was hours away. I'd composed a complicated autoreply for my work email and had nothing left to deal with in my inbox. The four of us stood in our empty living room and stared at one another.

Our giggles echoed off the bare walls. There's where our dining-room table had been. That's the hallway once lined with photos of the kids. After we took a family selfie, Alia and the girls headed out to the rental car, now loaded with five big suitcases, and I walked through the house turning off every light.

At the bottom of the hill I pulled a U-turn around the median and headed back up our street toward the airport. Our house, as we passed it, was totally dark.

"Bye, house," Harper said.

"Will we have internet on the flight?" Lyra asked.

Alia:

When we told friends about our one-year trip, everyone responded with excitement and enthusiasm. But every once in a while, I'd be pulled aside for a cautious word or sent a surreptitious text. "And how do *you* feel about this?" people asked. "Are you on board with this trip?"

In 2009, when we moved from New York City to Arlington, I was very apprehensive. I loved Inwood, our neighborhood in Manhattan — its parks, its many cultural traditions, its neighborhoodiness, its location as the first stop on the A Train, which meant that you always got a seat going downtown. I loved the idea of raising our girls in a place with so many different types of people, music, food, and experiences. I loved the bodega down the block and Lyra's preschool just across the river. I loved being in the city where movies always opened first and where we could see plays long before anyone else knew about them. (I got to see Mindy Kaling play Ben Affleck in a weird pop-culture satire at PS Something-or-Other in the East Village!)

But I didn't love not having a washing machine. Or a place to keep a vacuum cleaner (we just swept the rugs). Or the fact that we had two small children with no family help nearby. (It always seemed like everyone we knew could just drop their kids with Grandma while they went and did awesome NYC stuff while we were stuck paying twenty dollars an hour for babysitting.) Arlington was near my parents, was at least somewhat more affordable than New York, and had good neighborhood public schools where we could just send the kids without having to embark on New York City's insane process that starts with intelligence testing for four-year-olds. We bought a grill! We were surrounded by other families with kids! We could park the car without circling the block seventeen million times to find a space! (I could not bring myself to get a minivan, though, as practical as I realize they are.)

These things made life more comfortable and easier, but also more boring and homogenous. Over time, I worried that the comfort that Dan and I were providing for ourselves was depriving our children of the experiences and challenges we wanted them to have. Would our children grow up to be citizens of the world if they spent most of their childhoods in a place where everyone was more or less just like them?

But to say that this was the reason I was "on board with this trip" would be leaving something out. Yes, I wanted my children to have new and diverse experiences. But I also wanted *myself* to have new and diverse experiences. I had been in the same (often stressful) job for nearly fifteen years. I had recently turned forty. Our marriage hadn't experienced a seven-year itch, but I think I was maybe experiencing one in my relationship with Arlington. I needed and wanted to do and learn something new. Plus it seemed like it would be super fun! I *liked* traveling and travel planning. I *liked* exploring different cultures. I *liked* the idea of taking a year to work less and live more. And I liked the idea of our little family forming its own travel team.

So when friends asked me, candidly, how I *really* felt about the trip, I said, candidly: "I'm really excited. Come visit us!"

Frequently Asked Questions About Our Trip Around the World, for Those Who Demand Greater Logistical Detail

How did you find places to live?
In New Zealand, the Netherlands, and Costa Rica, Alia found Airbnbs we liked and then negotiated long-term deals with the owners. Hays, Kansas, did not have any Airbnb listings, so our miracle-worker friend Catherine, who lives there, called every house that had sat on the market for more than six months until she found an owner willing to rent to us for a three-month lease.

What was your favorite of the four countries?
New Zealand.

What was the actual schedule?
The trip took place over the calendar year 2017. We were in New Zealand from January until mid-April (summer into autumn in the Southern Hemisphere). We were in the Netherlands from mid-April until early July. We were in Costa Rica from mid-July through September. We were in Kansas in October, November, and December.

What did you do about your house while you were gone?
We rented it out to a very nice family who were building a house elsewhere in north Arlington and needed a place to live for the endless months of construction. Their rent *almost* covered our mortgage, though not quite.

Did the kids go to school?
Yes. They attended school in New Zealand for first term, February 1 to April 13. In the Netherlands, it was the final term of the school year, May 8 until July 5. Though in Costa Rica we made them attend Spanish classes for a month, we otherwise considered our time there "summer vacation." Needless to say, we made the kids return to school the *instant* we got to Kansas, on October 4, and they continued until Christmas break.

Did you work?

Yes. As we traveled in 2017, I cowrote a cultural-history book called *The World Only Spins Forward* with a friend who lives in New York and wrote a profile of a film director for a magazine. I also did the work of *this* book: interviews with academics, neighbors, and officials, plus daily writing on our activities and experiences. And finally, I worked quarter-time for Slate, the online magazine where I've been on staff for several years, assigning, editing, and writing stories about culture, politics, and parenting. This provided a very modest steady income (and health insurance).

Did Alia work?

Yes. She hashed out a deal with the law firm where she'd been a partner to get paid for her work by the hour, as opposed to getting a salary. This gave her much-needed flexibility, though it meant her income was extremely variable. Some weeks she worked a lot; other weeks there was no work to be had.

Did the kids work?

No. They didn't earn a dime. Can you believe: They actually *cost* us money?!

So how did your income compare to a typical year?

We earned somewhat less than half as much as we did in a typical year. We knew going in that we would have a lot less money, overall, in 2017. The explicit trade-off we were making was less money, more time with our children.

So did you have enough money for this trip?

Kind of. The budget we worked out before the trip was balanced, though what does *balanced* mean when a budget contains as much guesswork about costs and earnings as ours did? In our case, it meant that we dipped into our savings when things ended up (as they always do) costing more than expected. We used a lot of credit card points and frequent-flier miles, which really helped.

Did you ever just flat-out run out of money?

Yes. One time, all our credit card bills were due the same day, so I had to get someone to text me a photo of a paycheck in New York so I could print it out at the Hays Public Library and then take a photo of the printout to deposit it on my mobile banking app. Another time I had to write a chapter of this book very, very quickly in order to get the money that allowed us to purchase plane tickets to get from the Netherlands to Costa Rica. See if you can figure out which chapter it was!

Was the trade worth it? Less money for more time with the kids?

Oh, man. Great question.

ISLAND BAY

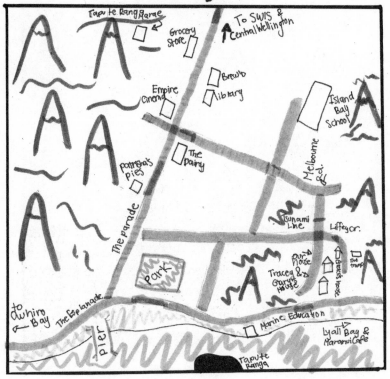

NEW ZEALAND

January – April

STEVES

On our first day in New Zealand, Lyra picked up, from a shipping container turned funky free library on the Auckland waterfront, a tatty 1957 hardcover of *Kids Say the Darndest Things!* I thought it was a little on the nose, but she loved it. For weeks a cackling Lyra retold these mod tots' bon mots, many of them revolving around the light comedy of absentminded dads who leave the parenting to their wives while they "watch the fights in the parlor," et cetera. It was in that gender-normative spirit that I, that first day in New Zealand, handed off the kids to Alia and set off to buy a car.

The theory was this: We needed a car to drive the length of the North Island from Auckland to our eventual home, Wellington. But renting a car in New Zealand for the three full months we'd be here, starting in the peak of summer vacation season, would be crazily expensive. Better, I'd proclaimed sagely, to buy a used car your first day in the country, drive it until you leave, then sell it on your way to the airport. All you spend is the very slight devaluation that comes from owning a car for a couple of months, basically. Maybe if you play your cards right, strike a couple of great deals, you *earn* a little money along the way! Honestly probably this is exactly what would happen. Jeez, maybe I should buy *two* cars.

So that's why, while Alia and Lyra and Harper traipsed around beautiful Auckland eating ice cream, discovering L&P (New Zealand's tastiest beverage), and watching an *amazing* juggler on a unicycle, I slathered on sunscreen and took a cab to the Greenlane neighborhood near One Tree Hill. There I walked down busy Great South Street visiting car dealership after car dealership. It was just as scenic as any city's neighborhood where all the car dealerships are. The clock was ticking; it was Saturday morning, and tomorrow we were due at the house we'd rented on the Coromandel coast.

After a long morning's search I narrowed my prospects down to two cars that seemed plausible if somewhat beyond our hoped-for price range, each from a different dealership, each shown to me—in what felt like fate—by a guy called Steve. Steve 1, a Simon Pegg lookalike who'd come to New Zealand from Essex more than a decade ago, wanted to put me into a Subaru wagon, the only car at his Subaru dealership more than five years old. Jolly, shorts-clad Steve 2 had, among the dozen cars packed into a lot roughly the size of our house in Virginia, a great 2008 Volvo with a lot of room in the boot. I decided to give each Steve's car a road test and then buy from the Steve I liked the best.

At 1:00 p.m. Steve 1 took a photo of my Virginia driver's license and handed me the keys to the Subaru. "I've never driven on the left side of the road," I said. "Do you want to come along?"

"Nah, you'll be all right," Steve 1 replied; he pointed me toward a quiet residential neighborhood behind the dealership and told me to call if I got lost.

Eight minutes later, I called. "Are you lost?" he asked, laughing. He stopped laughing when he heard I had broken his car.

Back in the showroom, Steve 1 looked just like Simon Pegg does when Nick Frost has done something daft. "But how did you blow *two* tires?" he asked.

"I don't know," I said unhappily. "The road narrowed and there was this big decorative curb and, like, I just misjudged it." In truth I had driven those entire eight minutes in a state of panic, talking out loud to myself like a lunatic: "Okay, stay left, stay left, okay, you're turning left, look right, you're turning into the closest lane, *look out,* okay, stay left..." The windshield-wiper switch was where I expected the turn signal to be, so every time I wanted to make a turn, my already high level of anxiety was heightened by a surprise *whapwhapwhap.* And then: *thunk.* I'd parked the crippled car in front of a KFC on Great South Street and trudged two sweaty blocks back to the Subaru dealership, where I explained to Steve 1 and his fellow salesmen—all wearing crisp suits—just what I'd done. My face was red from sunburn and shame.

They were very nice to me, far nicer than they needed to be. The car couldn't be fixed until Monday and therefore was no longer the solution to my problem of needing a car that day. Not only had I broken Steve 1's car, I couldn't buy it. I gave my credit card number to cover the repairs and walked out, leaving a downcast Steve 1 regretting he'd ever met me.

So now it was two o'clock. Most dealerships closed at four. So did all the rental-car places I'd identified as backups. I was down to one option, the Volvo on Steve 2's tiny lot—which was, I realized as I approached it, right next to the KFC. Steve 2 was a bluff Kiwi in sandals who was as sunburned as I was but who appeared to have been that way his entire life. "Have you ever taken out a right-side-drive car?" he asked. I ignored the forlorn Subaru in my peripheral vision and said, "Nope, first time!"

"How about a driving lesson?" Steve 2 asked.

"Sounds great!"

"The key," he said from the passenger seat as I very, very, very carefully drove through One Tree Hill, "is to focus on the *middle* line, not all those parked cars along the side. That'll keep you from veering too close to the curb."

"Wouldn't want to do that," I said through gritted teeth.

Steve 2 told me he sold a lot of cars to foreign visitors. "Just last week I sold a car—oh, look out—to these Germans, young guys, and they barely knew how to drive!" He shook his head. "I just hope they're not did."

"Did? Oh, *dead*." I knew this from *Flight of the Conchords*.

My test drive was wildly successful, not only in that I liked the car but in that I did not crash it. But *God,* was it hard. I got better at driving on the left side over our three months in New Zealand, but I never really felt comfortable. I want you to imagine for a moment that you've been typing on the same kind of keyboard every day for, like, your whole life—it won't be hard, as it's probably true—and then one day you have to type on a keyboard with all the letters reversed. And you have to sit on the opposite side of your desk from where you usually do. And your desk is traveling along winding mountain roads with sheer cliffs on one side and the raging sea on the other. And even a tiny typing error on your new mirror-image keyboard might lead to the fiery death of you and everyone you love. Imagine!

It was three o'clock. I made an offer; Steve 2 accepted. Given that I was likely to crash pretty often—because of either my own incompetence or that of other foreigners to whom the Steves of New Zealand had recently sold cars—it seemed good that I'd be doing it in a Volvo. As I filled out various neat New Zealand forms, Steve 2 stood in the window of his office trailer and marveled at the Subaru marooned on the pavement by the KFC. "How do you blow *two* tires like that, I wonder," he mused. "You'd have to really hit something hard."

"Hmmm, yeah," I said.

"Ah, there's a tow truck now to take care of that Subaru," he observed. He opened the sliding glass door of his trailer and stepped onto the porch. "Whose car is that?" he called down the street.

"It's ours, mate," replied the guy climbing out of the truck, who was, I realized to my horror, Steve 1, dressed in his suit and everything. He ambled toward Steve 2's lot as the tow-truck driver maneuvered behind the Subaru. I was miserable. Never had I imagined my Steves meeting.

"Well, who did that to the tires?" asked Steve 2.

"A customer on a drive. American bloke."

"No!" exclaimed Steve 2. He turned to me and said, "Did you hear that? It was another American on a drive who busted up that Subaru!"

Steve 1 was just steps away. I mouthed, *It was me*. Steve 2's eyes went as round as a cartoon character's. "It was *you?*" he cried just as Steve 1 stepped onto the porch, saw me, and shouted, "It was him!"

Steve 2 turned back to Steve 1, grinning. "Well, he didn't crash *my* car," he said.

It would be simplistic to describe New Zealand as a slightly off-kilter mirror-image America, though my adventures on the wrong side of the road point out the most literal way that's the case. Even its stars are reversed; as a British character notes upon his arrival in the Southern Hemisphere in Eleanor Catton's novel *The Luminaries,* the only constellations he knows are inverted, like "Orion—upended, his quiver beneath him, his sword hanging upward from his belt."

But it is true that in making New Zealand the first stop on our journey, we were starting with a place that we eyed, hopefully, as America-but-a-little-bit-different. It wasn't a huge stretch to imagine a comfortable sort of life for English-speaking people in a comfortable English-speaking country.

The way in which New Zealand might affect our day-to-day lives, we hoped, had less to do with sweeping change and more to do with shifting our priorities. We knew that Kiwis, surrounded as they are by natural beauty, value outdoor adventure in a way that our family never has. And so we wanted our life in New Zealand to be filled with hikes, rafting trips, kayaking—experiences that would immerse us all in nature and begin to transform us from a family that views a short walk through the park as an arduous task into a family that enjoys such activity, somehow.

And although the popular American view of New Zealand is of a country of jolly white people—some short like hobbits, some stout like dwarves, some tall like elves—in fact, New Zealand is rapidly becoming one of the most diverse countries on earth. Recent influxes of South Asians and Chinese, among many other races, have added new colors to a nation already rich in immigrants from across the Pacific Islands. And of course there's New Zealand's first people, its Aboriginal Māori, about whom I knew very little but whose culture, I understood, permeated "mainstream" New Zealand to an uncommon degree. Admittedly, this understanding was mostly based on seeing the country's Olympic rugby team performing the haka before matches, but living as I did in the Washington, DC, area, I had a pretty clear sense of the level of disrespect with which a sports team *could* treat native people.

And so Alia and I hoped that among the many other experiences we'd have in New Zealand, we might have a chance to engage with, befriend, and spend time with people whose cultures, religions, and skin tones differed from ours. This was a bit hypocritical, in that the mostly white life we experienced in the Virginia suburbs was entirely our own doing. Like many parents, we'd abandoned a cheek-by-jowl existence in the city for an easier life in the suburbs, one that was also whiter than the life we'd left. But that made the notion of a small city like Wellington, which promised livability *and* diversity, even more appealing.

By the time we got to Wellington, on a beautiful sunny day in mid-January, we were hungry for a place to call home. The house Alia had found south of downtown was perfect. Spacious and sun-facing (chilly Wellingtonians prize their northern exposures), it was nestled a third of the way up a hill from the center of a neighborhood called Island Bay.

The island in the bay that defines Island Bay, Tapu te Ranga, breaks the waves sweeping up from Cook Strait; as a result, even though the water at the beach is very cold, the calm bay harbors a number of fishing boats. Indeed, just forty years ago, Island Bay was a fishing village filled with Italian and Greek immigrants. In recent years its proximity to the city, ocean views, and sturdy if drafty turn-of-the-century houses have helped transform Island Bay into a haven for bohos a bit surprised to have become bourgeois; our neighbors included graphic designers, a documentary producer, heaps of homebrewers, and two well-known (for poets) poets.

Bronwyn, the café owner whose house we were renting—"I thought I'd give living with my boyfriend a try," she told us, "which was quite a surprise to him"—had twin boys Lyra's age; it was their rooms (and impressive arsenal of Nerf guns) that our girls took over. As Bronwyn gave us a tour of the house that first sunny day, it quickly became clear that—unlike some Airbnbs I've stayed in that were decorated, if at all, as neutrally as possible—Bronwyn's house exhibited her oddball aesthetic, mixing antlers, illuminated Virgin and Child portraits, Day of the Dead imagery, and 1960s pinups. Above our bed was a gorgeous, absurd painting of a buxom swamp woman sporting only a loincloth and a beehive hairdo reclining on a moss-covered branch. She was intimidating but also, c'mon, a bit inspiring. Bronwyn used the image for her Facebook profile photo.

After giving us the tour and glasses of wine, Bronwyn excused herself—"I'm going surfing this afternoon, looks like the weather's about to go to shit"—but mentioned that the neighbors might stop by. Less than five minutes later, with a "Hello there!," Tracey and Gary walked through the front door, bearing really quite a lot of beer and snacks, and without any ado sat down at our new dining-room table, under the antlers, and chatted with us for two happy hours. Their teen-age daughter and son stopped by as well and offered babysitting (from Trinity) and a secondhand scooter (from Grainger).

"What do you think?" Alia asked me that night.

"I love them," I said. "How do we get them to be our friends?"

"I think maybe they already *are* our friends."

The next day we took the bus downtown to join in the Wellington Women's March. In just a few weeks traveling around New Zealand, we'd been amazed at the extent to which Kiwis had a granular under-standing of the current American political situation. Lyra, meanwhile, had taken to beginning each conversation with a new person "Sorry about Trump." Due to New Zealand's position at the far right of the time zones, we were first in the world to march—a point several speak-ers connected to the country's being the first to give women the vote, in 1893. It felt good to be connected, even in protest, to the country we had left; it felt good to march alongside our new countrywomen. We saw Wellington's steel-and-stone downtown from street level and pointed out to our girls the Māori-language signs with their *wahines* and *whānaus*. It was gray but warm that afternoon, low clouds hugging the city's hilltops.

The day after the march I woke an hour before my alarm to the sound of howling wind and branches knocking against our bedroom window. By midmorning, a cold, driving rain was roaring through the valley, the hills just a mile away obscured by waves of water. The roof of our dreamy rental house had a leak; we set up a couple of bowls in the kitchen. The *drip, drip, drip* accompanied my worried check of the weather app on my phone. It would be like this all day, I learned, except for the parts of the day it would be worse.

We'd been warned about the weather in Wellington, of course. It was the windiest city in the world, sure. But we'd thought, *Come on, it's sum-mer. No matter how bad it gets, it'll still be summer!* But this was something else, an October nor'easter in the middle of the Southern Hemisphere's equivalent of our August. Tracey next door texted me: *Even for Wellington weather, this is real shit.* We couldn't leave the house and it wouldn't be bedtime for eleven hours. Was it the snowstorm all over again? Lyra walked into the dining room, saw me looking worriedly at my phone, and said, with a comedian's perfect timing, "Can I get online?"

But somehow the day's slow unfolding was pleasant, not torturous. We had morning tea and then, later, afternoon tea. We found Bronwyn's covered woodpile, built a fire in her wood-burning stove, and watched a couple of episodes of not-bad TV. We thought about going through some of the math worksheets the kids' American teachers had sent along, but that didn't seem very fun. Instead I taught Lyra how to edit videos, and Alia made a stop-motion movie with Harper. Lyra even deigned to play a game with the entire family.

Over our weeks of travel, I'd already seen a slight shift in Lyra's treatment of her sister, and in their relationship to each other. Lyra, transplanted into an entirely new environment, seemed to feel a bit more free to act like a kid than she had in some time. She was goofier, more willing to play along with nonsense, and Harper, a craftswoman of artisanal nonsense, had moved to dominate that market. Taken away from our house, from Arlington, they had shifted from acting as rivals to being cautious allies, partners out in the big wide world. If sometimes the common enemy against whom they were united was me—well, hearing them plot and giggle in one or the other's room made that feel okay.

But still, they were ready to make some friends, and so were we. School was about to start. Wellington's wet windy summer was under way. Our job was to become Kiwis, so we rolled up our sleeves to get to work. Then we rolled our sleeves back down—it was like fifty-two degrees out there.

CHAPTER I

Number 8 Wire

The first thing that surprised us about living on Melbourne Road was the neighborhood tramp.

A decade old at least, ramshackle and rusty, the trampoline had been installed at some prior date in a front yard a block over, on Liffey Crescent. Reports differed on its origin. Some claimed it was a gift from a long-ago resident's cousins in the country; others said that several neighbors had pooled funds to buy it.

What was certain was that the neighborhood tramp was comically unsafe. It had no sides. It was perceptibly canted so that jumping kids tended to drift out toward the edge, where, again, there were no sides. The rails, once covered in padding, were now "protected" by foam pool noodles attached with duct tape. I was told that once there'd been a sign on the tramp that read JUMP AT YOUR OWN RISK, but it had blown away in a strong wind.

And positively *everyone* used the neighborhood tramp. Kids in Island Bay ran around in packs, and when they came back from buying ice pops in town or finished playing rugby in the yard, those packs of kids wound up at the trampoline. Older kids, like our teenage neighbors Grainger and Trinity, remembered doing the same in their primary- and intermediate-school years.

Our children, who were used to trampolines existing only in the yards of school friends whose parents loved them, leaped at the chance to leap, although they did it in manners befitting their divergent personalities. Harper fell in with a gaggle of girls her age—Grace, Millie, Bailey, Lucy—and spent sunny afternoons sproinging and chattering. Lyra carried a book up to the trampoline on her own later in the day; if it was full, she'd wander and read until the crowds cleared and she could bounce in peace.

Now, I'm sure there are shared trampolines in some towns in America, probably located in cul-de-sacs in which the bonds of neighborly trust and free-spirited play hold fast. But when I told this story to friends in the States, every one of them, to a person, immediately asked about liability. Who would put a *trampoline* in her *front yard* for *anyone to use?* Surely some kid would break his arm on it and then his parents would sue the parents who supplied it, and that would be the end of the neighborhood tramp, not to mention the end of neighborhood comity in general.

But this was my first exposure to a public policy in New Zealand that had a concrete effect on the way parents parent. Personal-injury lawsuits are essentially nonexistent in this adventure wonderland, thanks to the Accident Compensation Corporation. The ACC (Te Kaporeihana Āwhina Hunga Whara, in Māori) is a government-run scheme that pays for any injury stemming from an accident, no matter whose fault it is. Slip and fall on your neighbor's icy sidewalk? The ACC will pay for your medical care. Get in a car accident that takes you out of the workplace for years? The ACC will cover that.

So no one's getting sued over the neighborhood tramp, even if somebody does break his arm. The ACC isn't perfect. It removes some market incentives for workplace and product safety, for example. But the ACC and its philosophy of "no fault, no winners, no losers" contributes to a general sense in New Zealand that accidents happen and that blaming others for those accidents doesn't help matters. "In America there's fear of kids getting hurt and all the money repercussions of that," Anna, an artist from the Northland neighborhood of Wellington, told me. "I would never consider getting sued by someone else's parent for something."

In conversations and interviews, I heard parents and experts valuing one quality above all in Kiwi children—not obedience or caution but *independence.* "It's a *Man Alone* thing," the Auckland education researcher Stuart McNaughton told me, referring to the 1939 novel by John Mulgan still viewed by many as essential to understanding the "Kiwi character." "Getting on with stuff, taming a difficult environment, getting hurt in the process. If they're gonna have an accident, they're gonna have an accident—it'll probably do them good."

"You do hear a lot of stories about American helicopter parenting," said Kirsty, a consultant in Northland. "But your whole job as a parent is to push your kid away and make sure they can be a fully functioning adult. The way you do that is you give them ever greater opportunities to take chances."

Not every parent behaves that way, of course; Wellington has its share of overbearing parents hovering over their kids, striving for perfection, and making everyone else feel bad, a type that Alia and I were familiar with. In as green a place as New Zealand, that parenting superiority can manifest around issues of "natural" child-rearing. Author Emily Writes, the parenting editor at the news site the Spinoff, satirizes those crunchy Kiwi parents expertly in her book *Rants in the Dark:*

> Are you using a white noise app?
>
> Oh really? *tilts head to the side* We use organic white noise. We prefer not to expose her to chemical and unnatural white noise.
>
> Do you use blankets?
>
> *tilts head to the side*
>
> Oh, we don't. We just blow on her. Yes, all night. It seems a more respectful way to parent than using artificial sheets of thread.

But the vast majority of parents we met were just... very chill. When Alia asked Gary his parenting philosophy, he thought for a moment, drinking his beer, and then said, "Benign neglect?"

There are downsides to this focus on raising tough, independent kids. "It took New Zealand a long time to ban corporal punishment," McNaughton mentioned; the country's "anti-smacking" statute wasn't made law until 2007, and the nation still suffers high rates of child abuse.

"It took us a long while"—until 1989—"to get seat belts mandatory for kids in cars." New Zealand is still learning to balance a cultural desire for parents and kids to just *get on with it* with the community's responsibility to ensure that families who need support and protection get it.

But one practical result of this focus on independence is that in many neighborhoods, ours included, kids roam the streets in a way that seems straight out of a bygone era. In Wellington, most kids start taking the bus on their own when they're ten or eleven; Lyra rode her scooter or took the city bus the three kilometers to school pretty much every day. Even though moms and dads sometimes complained to me that kids were *too* sheltered and protected in New Zealand compared to how things were in *their* day, it was not at all uncommon in Island Bay for a group of nine-year-old girls to decide on their own to scooter over to the Parade, buy some kind of horrible lollies at the dairy, then end up at someone's house. If that happened in our neighborhood in Arlington, it would require multiple parental texts and at least two chaperones. Tracey pointed out that the small size of New Zealand, the sense that everyone's only two degrees of separation from everyone else, helps quite a bit. "There's always eyes on," she said. "Trinity and Grainger learned pretty early that there's nothing they could do that I wouldn't hear about."

About a month into our stay, though, a minor dispute tugged at the fabric that held our neighborhood together. Around seven thirty on a Saturday night, Lyra, Harper, and Lucy who lived across the street came running in, all positively heaving with injustice, and said that a woman on the next block had kicked them off the tramp. They were *enraged*.

"Was it because you were jumping too late?" Alia asked. The kids had received requests in recent days to please restrict trampolining to the hours before seven o'clock. While that seemed a little silly, especially during the summer when it stayed light until almost nine, I sympathized with the woman in whose yard the tramp was installed. I'd heard tell she'd rented the house unaware that the trampoline in her yard was designated for the use of everyone in Island Bay, including, I was sure, drunk teens at one in the morning.

"No!" Lyra said. "She said the tramp's only for people who live on"—she waved her hand—"that street over there."

"Liffey Crescent," Harper clarified.

Lyra goggled at Harper. "How do you *know* that?" she demanded.

"But my mum's told me," Lucy added, "that the tramp is for everyone in the neighborhood to share."

The next day, around lunchtime, Lyra, Harper, and Lucy discussed the situation and decided to go back to the tramp. "Are you going to be polite to the woman who kicked you off?" Alia asked. "Maybe tell her you're sorry for jumping too late but that you think the tramp really is for people in the whole neighborhood, not just her street?"

"No," they said. "She was mean." A grown-up was wrong, and they were *not* going to be nice to her.

Now, if I'd been in Arlington, my first impulse might have been to head over there and try to have a friendly chat with the grown-up in question. But the idea of walking to Liffey Crescent and solving my kids' problems for them felt very... American. Real Kiwi parents let their kids figure things out themselves, preferably while the parents were drinking a nice Tuatara lager.

Over the next few months, the trampoline was the cause of steady, low-level neighborhood warfare, much of it delivered straight into the lap of poor Fiona, the woman who lived behind us and whose yard Melbourne Road kids cut through to get to Liffey Crescent and the tramp. Fiona knew the mean grown-up, was friends with her, and she found herself torn between her belief that indeed the tramp *was* intended for everyone to use and her loyalty to the friend whose aggrieved complaints about kids jumping and shouting after seven o'clock were usually justified. (Not *always* our kids! But, er, often.)

One weekend the kids reported that the tramp was broken. We heard a lot of different stories about how that came to be; the word from Fiona was that the woman was upset about it but that Fiona herself was a little relieved. "Maybe it's meant to be knackered for a while," she said. "That'll give her a bit of a break."

"And you too?" I asked. She raised an eyebrow. Within days, Eddie down the street had fixed the tramp, and the skirmishes began anew.

For weeks the weather was just awful. I simply couldn't understand how people could say it was summer when one morning I was literally blown off my feet on my way to an appointment. Alia planned scenic excursions around Wellington that were made pointless when we couldn't see anything through the blowing rain. Evening activities consisted mostly of the four of us huddling under blankets watching Netflix, the woodstove burning fiercely. "Our Bummer Summer," moaned the front-page headline on the local paper.

On the first nice afternoon in weeks, a brilliant warm Friday in February, Bronwyn rang the doorbell to her own home. (It was an actual clang-a-lang bell, dangling from the porch roof underneath the colorful bunting that everyone in New Zealand hangs everywhere.) "Fi's doing drinks in the yard," she told us. "You want to come over?"

I pulled all the beer we had out of the fridge and carried it up our back stairs, through the gap in the fence, and down Fiona's stairs to their back porch. At this point we hadn't yet met her, but Fiona welcomed each of us with a kiss to both cheeks and added the beers to the impressive array already on her table. After a bit, her husband, Regan, arrived home on his bike, changed out of his gear, and put some Pixies on the stereo; down the table, neighbors were discussing the band's upcoming show in Wellington. "Are you going?" Regan asked me, and I gave the only correct answer, which was "No, Kim Deal isn't even in the band anymore."

Regan nodded. He was small and soft-spoken with a dry sense of humor that contrasted with his wife's more exuberant style. "Bron said you're writing a book?" he asked.

"Yeah, about parenting around the world," I said.

"Ah, so it's good you're talking to us," Regan said, and turned to his wife. "Where are our children?" he asked.

"To New Zealand parenting." Bronwyn laughed, raising her glass.

Over the next few hours a steady flow of neighbors and friends and also Bronwyn's gardener stopped in, accompanied or sometimes preceded by their children. ("Is my dad here yet?" one little girl asked. "He said he's coming over." Sure enough, ten minutes later, there he was.) Fiona and Regan ferried a constant stream of snacks from the kitchen; each new arrival brought something, craft beer or a chilled sauvignon blanc or, in Eddie's case, a very large bottle of gin. The kids, which included ours as well as Bronwyn's twin boys, appeared at the table, stole snacks, then disappeared to jump on the tramp or play with the neighborhood cats or organize a game of football or—who knew what they were doing, really. Not us. Eventually Eddie declared himself clearheaded enough to go pick up some pizza so the kids could have a proper dinner.

This kind of impromptu, ad hoc get-together is not *uniquely* Kiwi—we've experienced glorious summer afternoons in Virginia where all our neighbors were serendipitously available, no travel soccer games or piano recitals—but it is *definitively* Kiwi. "There are some cultural memes here around the idea of inviting over some mates and chucking some stuff on the barbie," our neighbor Gary acknowledged. "The weekend's here, the sun's out, come on over." This is particularly true in Wellington, a city whose bummer summers lead residents to treasure, and make full use of, the nice days when they do arrive. "Wellingtonians never make plans for a specific date," Pip, a novelist, told me. "You just do things when you have the chance. You may not feel like swimming, but come on, it's sunny, we're all going to the beach."

Even on non-sunny days, Wellingtonians take real joy in get-togethers both planned and unplanned. Within a week of our arrival, Alia had been invited to join two book clubs: a feminist book club for which Alia reread *The Feminine Mystique* and a standard book club of the sort where no one reads the books. The members of the standard book club invited themselves over to our house for a New Zealand Cuisine Night, the women bringing supposedly distinctive Kiwi party food like onion dip. "Invented in New Zealand!" its chef said, at which everyone nodded with great pride, citing a recent report on the radio that rescued from obscurity the woman who'd invented "Kiwi onion dip" in the early 1960s. (In fact, onion dip was invented in the 1950s in America and the recipe was printed on Lipton soup packets by 1958.)

Americans we met marveled at the net of social connection that was built at these get-togethers and which then propagated throughout Wellington day-to-day life. "Everyone knows everyone," said Schamet, a yoga instructor who'd moved from America to New Zealand with her Kiwi husband fifteen years before. That net of social connection tends to keep people on good terms through the years. "I've always thought it was weird that my husband is still really good friends with most of his exes," Schamet told me. "I'm not friends with *my* exes! But the longer I've lived here, that's how everyone is." In America, Schamet said, "There's so many people that relationships can be left to wither."

Schamet was one of several American expatriates I met who'd stuck in New Zealand—not just the millionaires whose South Island doomsday bunkers were written up in *New Yorker* profiles but everyday Yanks who'd found family life in New Zealand more fulfilling than what they'd left back home. Take Harlene, a psychology professor who came to Dunedin in the early 1990s with her husband and a seven-month-old. "The main draw for us in staying here was about parenting," she said, citing the balance she could find in her career and home life. A quarter of a century later, Harlene was a vice chancellor at the University of Otago, and both her daughters had graduated from American universities and returned to Dunedin to live their lives.

The social connections among parents in neighborhoods don't develop solely from proximity; several New Zealand early-childhood institutions also work to forge those bonds. For example, there's Plunket, the mostly government-funded child-health organization that delivers free pre- and postnatal care to all New Zealand mothers and their children to age five. The organization also sets up playgroups among families with similarly aged children, a service that, sure, benefits middle-class moms on maternity leave but that is also, the director of Plunket told me, a godsend to low-income immigrant parents in Auckland who might otherwise struggle to make connections in a new city.

There's also Playcentre, a parent-run education cooperative that's a touchstone in New Zealand, inspiring devotion and eye-rolls in equal measure. Parents who join Playcentre attend workshops in early-childhood education and commit to working there a few days a week. It's not day care; you don't drop your kid off. Instead, you attend with your child, and with other parents and their children, and play together.

You can imagine the type of hyper-engaged, nonworking parent who might become a devotee of such a place; Playcentre has a bit of a reputation in New Zealand for harboring "superior, know-it-all mums who are going to judge your parenting choices," as Auckland photographer Sonya Nagels wrote in an essay on the Spinoff. But that wasn't Nagels's experience. Her community of Playcentre parents cooked and delivered meals to her house when her second child was born. "You go through so much in those formative years," she told me, "and so you create a tight bond with the people in that Playcentre. And you really become an auntie to the other children there."

There are also all the familiar ways that parents get to know each other: You live next door or you meet at the park or you share a laugh at a school function or you stand next to each other on the sidelines at football. But the existence of structures and organizations in Kiwi society that help to accelerate the process of making adult friends is incredibly valuable. I remember, when we were living with our tiny children in our tiny apartment in New York City, how hard it was to make new friends, and how grateful Alia and I would have been for such a kick-start. Even once we moved to Virginia, it took years and years for us to make friends we considered close.

Of course, it didn't help that we were working all the goddamn time. Who can host the neighbors when you're not home from the office until eight fifteen? There, too, is where Wellington life improved on Virginia life. Early at that get-together in Fiona's backyard, I was surprised when Fiona looked at her phone and said, "Ah, it's odd that Regan's not home yet." It was barely six o'clock!

Sure, there are some Kiwis who work long hours with unpredictable schedules. In our three months there, we met a total of one of them, a digital artist at Peter Jackson's special-effects company WETA who had to leave early from a school dinner to return to work on a secret project that I assume was, I dunno, the third *Avatar* sequel. Even among our

Island Bay cohort, packed with high achievers in the kind of creative industries that in America tend to produce workaholics who overidentify with their jobs, people generally left the office at a reasonable hour most nights, didn't bring work home with them, and never worked on weekends.

In our day-to-day life, we adopted this same very humane schedule. Once the kids ate their avocado toast or delicious Kiwi yogurt for breakfast and scootered away to school, I went to my spot in the bay windows in the living room and handled the emails that had piled up overnight. I found it mildly discombobulating to be editing stories about the chaos in the United States—Donald Trump had recently been inaugurated and people protesting his travel ban were flooding airport arrivals terminals—while looking out over the peaceful wooden houses of Island Bay and the blue sea beyond. Alia spent her mornings grocery shopping, planning the next leg of the trip, or hiking the paths that wended their way through the hills above our house. When she had work vetting news stories, they usually came in after lunch—evening on the East Coast, when reporters needed their next-day stories reviewed but local lawyers just wanted to go home. We strove to finish our work by five o'clock, which was pretty easy, given that by then it was one in the morning in New York, so no one was really checking up on us. Then we'd spend the endless high-latitude evenings with the kids exploring the city, walking the neighborhood, or, when the weather was bad, playing cards and watching TV in the woodstove-heated living room. The only thing that foiled these plans was that sometimes I would stay up too late, and then all of a sudden at midnight in Wellington, it was morning in America, and the emails would start pouring in.

"We guard our nonwork time pretty zealously," said Sally, a child psychologist in Auckland. "I think we work to live more often than we live to work." A recent study by the Australian educational nonprofit ASG bears this out. More than eight hundred New Zealand parents and caregivers were asked how they made decisions about prioritizing their time and energy. "In many countries—Australia, for example—economic resource is a contributing factor for such decisions," the ASG researcher Sivanes Phillipson told me. "But New Zealander parents, in our initial analysis, won't even consider finance as one impact. They consider their own preferences and expectations—that's the deciding factor for how much time they spend on certain things." A New Zealand estate planning firm, Perpetual Guardian, recently made international news by moving the entire company to a four-day, thirty-two-hour workweek after a trial period demonstrated that staff were more productive and happier working less.

Is this devotion to work/life balance and humane working hours the case for everyone in New Zealand? Absolutely not. Recent immigrants are more likely to work at all costs, and low-wage or low-skill employees often are not in control over their own schedules. A recent study found that Māori and Pacific Islanders are also more likely to be poorly paid than white New Zealanders, or Pākehā. But over and over, I met professionals in (mostly Pākehā) Island Bay who'd had to decide between earning more income and working fewer hours and had chosen the latter. For many parents, that's possible because of a remarkable New Zealand law, passed in 2007, that allows any employee, no matter how long he's worked at a company, to request a flexible schedule or a reduction of hours and requires the employer to seriously consider that request.

" 'Seriously consider,' sure," I scoffed when Kiwis told me about the law. In America, I assured them, many employers would "seriously consider" laughing long and hard at such a request. Or such accommodations would take the form of the part-time arrangement Alia had once made at her firm, in which she was paid a lower base salary but, due to the vagaries of litigation, often had to work just as many hours as she did before.

But in New Zealand, I kept hearing from parents who'd made those requests and had them granted. The TV producer who'd gone to 80 percent time. The web developer who took every Tuesday off, and his wife, the museum copywriter, who worked three days a week. The university professor who'd worked part-time through her children's school years and who did not see her earnings and potential dry up; in fact, she was now the head of her department. Indeed, according to statistics provided by the New Zealand government, in 2016, 99 percent of requests for flex- or part-time schedules were granted in some form.

"I work half-time," explained Jennifer, a senior lecturer in the University of Auckland's medical school (and another American who stayed in New Zealand after she had kids). "I go to conferences, and the number of American women who say, 'Gosh, that sounds like heaven.' It's not so hard! You teach fewer classes, you do less research, you get paid half as much. But it's a completely alien concept to them!"

I guess it hardly needs explaining *one* reason why Americans are hesitant to take part-time roles: You work fewer than forty hours, and there goes your health insurance. In New Zealand, of course, as in nearly all Western democracies except the United States, that's not a concern. New Zealand's health-care system, a single-payer government-run plan augmented by some private insurance, is by no means perfect, but it certainly allows parents to make life and career decisions without fearing that bad news from their doctors might wind up bankrupting them. I met two moms whose children had recently been diagnosed with chronic health problems—one with epilepsy and one with diabetes—and they both stressed how grateful they were to live in a country where all those specialist visits and medications and tests were paid for. (Both worked for themselves, not for companies.) "We gripe and moan about things falling through the gaps," one told me, "but at least we have gaps to fall through." Lyra injured herself when she wiped out on a scooter one morning, and the bill for the doctor was twenty New Zealand dollars. (We paid zero New Zealand dollars because her scooter accident was covered by the accident-compensation scheme.)

For those Kiwis who feel they can't make flexible arrangements work in their current jobs, there's always the option of chucking it aside and trying something new. That's a pipe dream for many Americans, who once again must worry about losing their health insurance, but in New Zealand, people just go ahead and do it. Take our neighbor Fiona, who told me, "My whole job was built because I wanted to work around the kids." A few years ago, shortly after her maternity leave ended, Fiona was on a walk with a teacher friend and the two started discussing their dream work/life scenarios. "We thought, *What can we create that would allow us to actually live the way we want to?*" When they got back to Fiona's house they jotted down a plan that eventually became Natty, a design workshop that makes cute tea towels and gift cards in Berhampore, which is a five-minute bike ride from Island Bay.

The trade-off, of course, is money. Compared to Fiona's former job in marketing, Natty isn't a huge money-earner. ("Be sure to add *yet,*" her husband, Regan, implored me.) But that's a decision the couple feels comfortable with. And if Natty becomes successful enough ("*When* it becomes successful enough"—Regan) that it takes up most of Fiona's time, Regan anticipates that he'd step back from his civil service job.

New Zealand is packed with establishments like Natty, tiny independent storefronts and home-based operations. Harper's confusingly named friend Aalia invited Harper over for the afternoon and they spent the day bopping around the sandwich shop her mom ran in Newtown. Island Bay's Parade, like the main streets of every neighborhood in Wellington, was made up mostly of small businesses: the one-woman pie shop, the mystifying crystal gallery, the two cafés, the greasy takeaway with the best fish and chips I've ever eaten. The only franchises were the Unichem pharmacy and Hell Pizza, part of a national chain that advertises itself as "666 percent New Zealand–owned."

Kirsty works as a consultant from her Northland home, a move she made a few years ago after a lot of careful grooming of a variety of government clients. "I used to work full-time," she told me, "and I felt like I was having a nervous breakdown trying to make that work." She felt empowered to modify her career to fit her family's life in part, she said, because of where she lives. New Zealand has a very do-it-yourself, number 8 wire culture, she told me, a reference to Kiwi ingenuity I heard again and again. (Number 8 is the gauge of fence wire used by sheep farmers to fix anything on the ranch.) "The people who came here in the nineteenth century, they just had to make it, because they couldn't buy it."

If you're fixing your fence with number 8 wire, you're not too concerned about whether it performs at peak level. You just want it to keep the sheep in. That's the attitude many parents I spoke to took toward their jerry-rigged work situations, their four-day jobs or cobbled-together consultancies or not-yet-making-money design workshops. It's an attitude that's totally foreign to my American brain, the brain that insists that my job is my identity. New Zealanders want to make enough money to live their lives, but many of them don't care about excelling. "It's looked down upon here to be really, really successful," Kirsty said matter-of-factly. "It's okay to be middling!"

I was not convinced that New Zealand's acceptance of mediocrity was quite my cup of tea. Sure, U.S. parents could be overly intense, but what does it do to a kid to grow up around people who don't seek to excel? Indeed, New Zealanders like to talk about the country's tall-poppy syndrome, a reference to the Kiwi habit of criticizing any fellow citizen who's become a big deal. (It's the tallest poppy in a field that gets its head chopped off.) At lunch, Anna and Kirsty discussed how Kiwi parenting most differed from that of Americans. "When my daughter says she wants to be in the Olympics, I tell her that's pretty unlikely," Anna said. "In America they say, '*Absolutely*, honey! You're a*mazing!*'"

"No one does that here," Kirsty confirmed. "If you do, the second you leave the room, people say, 'Fuckin' hell, she's really up herself.'"

Anna laughed. "Here we just tell our kids, 'You're a dog just like all the other dogs.'"

We saw this reluctance to push kids in the schools Lyra and Harper attended. In some ways this was great; the debate over redshirting that consumes parents of kindergarten-age children in Arlington, for example, was completely absent in New Zealand. No one would dream of waiting an extra year to place a child in school, because in New Zealand, kids just start school on their fifth birthday, whenever that is. But the teachers' lack of high expectations also made us nervous. Harper's school applied the endless energy of nine-year-olds toward creative tasks—launching projects to improve local water quality, for example—so I found myself able to over-look the fact that she didn't seem to be learning much math. And Lyra's coursework at SWIS, her intermediate school, also seemed fairly unrigor-ous. She loved it! Alia worried about both of them falling behind (a worry that proved justified, as they struggled in math when we returned to the States). New Zealand's schools, by traditional measures, are not any more successful than ones in the United States; both countries score roughly the same in the Organization for Economic Development's (OECD) survey of educational quality by nation—they're right in the middle of the pack.

But I'll say this for an embrace of mediocrity: for adults, there's much less of a stigma attached to failure. "It's understood that people change careers, and if they don't succeed in something, that's considered normal," said our neighbor Eddie. A CV with a few gaps in it, many Kiwis told me, wouldn't raise the red flags I would expect it to in the United States. This made it much easier for parents, including many moms I met, to reenter the workforce after caring for small children.

Nearly all of Lyra's and Harper's classmates' parents worked. In two-parent families, what did that mean about the childcare balance? I'll admit that reporting this kind of thing is tricky. Time-use surveys suggest that the United States' gender imbalance in childcare in heterosexual two-parent families is roughly the same as New Zealand's. And I certainly met plenty of families in which it was the women who had downshifted their careers and who performed the majority of domestic and childcare responsibilities. Yet I also met Eddie, who worked four days a week and cochaired the Island Bay School's parent-teacher association with another dad. And Gary, whose 80 percent schedule made him the parent most able to ferry kids to after-school football practice. Across our peer group in Wellington, I saw devoted fathers for whom the schedules and responsibilities of their children were not mysteries and who were fully involved in domestic life.

Now, is that rare in America? Even among my loudly feminist friends, I see far fewer fathers than mothers cleaning the house, scheduling playdates for kids, and volunteering at school. When I was a room parent in Lyra's first-grade class, I was the only dad in a sea of moms; when emails go out for group gatherings or birthday parties, I'm often the only male name among the addressees. Yet for all my attempts to carry my weight, I know I fall into some of those same traps; once Harper, writing about her parents for a school project, listed my hobby as "watching baseball" and Alia's as "cleaning."

"Traditional" masculinity is still prized in rugged, outdoorsy New Zealand. "You still get gender imbalance," our next-door neighbor Tracey noted. "I would not want to say there is not a massive degree of sexism present in New Zealand, like everywhere." The country still has one of the highest rates of domestic violence in the industrialized world. And certainly children who express gender in ways outside the norm can struggle, even in crunchy Wellington; Emily Writes wrote movingly about the teasing her young son endured for his love of tutus. But I saw the definition of *masculinity* evolving, for many fathers, to include caregiving, not just economic support. Gender roles shift and evolve more freely in New Zealand, Tracey mused, a country that prides itself on being a kind of laboratory for social innovation. "People of any gender who choose a different path can do so much more easily here."

New Zealanders may excel at spontaneous sociability, but they also know how to plan a blowout. I ended up accidentally hosting one myself in early February: Bayvana, an Island Bay celebration of homebrewing. After we'd rented our house from Bronwyn, she mentioned that every February she cohosted this big beer fest in the driveway, and would I mind if the tradition continued? This was a bit of a surprise, but a welcome one, not unlike the fluffy gray cat who, we learned on our first day, lived with us. I graciously agreed to allow fifty neighbors to bring the beer they brewed in their basements to our house so I could drink it, and just like that, I was on the organizing committee.

On the big day, drinking would begin in our driveway at noon and would migrate to another house in the neighborhood around four. I ran speakers out with an extension cord and played loud music as dozens of strangers—new friends!—assembled in my driveway, bringing with them growlers, bottles, and, in one case, a full keg. Jolly, bearded Quintin grilled lamb, fat spitting on his apron and the beer he held in his free hand; Bronwyn flipped quesadilla after quesadilla. Kids wandered in and out, grabbing snacks and then going across the street to Lucy's house or into ours or to the trampoline. I never worried, because every fifteen minutes Quintin or Bronwyn would produce some new snack and the kids would serendipitously assemble, like pigeons at a picnic.

Somehow I had become convinced that this eight-hour beer crawl was a kind of test of my ability to become a Kiwi dad. If *they* could drink all day and still effectively parent, why couldn't I? So I paced myself, laying down thick base layers of snacks and sipping saison and hefeweizen and a quite delicious sour beer. I sipped and I sipped. The sour, it turned out, was something like 12 percent ABV, so when Bronwyn said she was surprised to hear me playing "Single Ladies" on the speakers, I might have taken a bit of a hectoring tone as I explained that while the Commonwealth might have its queen, in America *our* queen was *Beyoncé* and soon *we* would put her on *our* money. When the time came to walk the half a mile to the second house of Bayvana, I found myself trudging alongside four other dads and attempting with my very thick tongue to explain Donald Trump. I was, I'm sure, very respectful. In my memory, the dads were all called Barry, they were all tan and tall, and not one had a beer gut despite the evidence that they were far more used to drinking all day than I was.

By five o'clock I could barely keep on my feet. I'd made the same inane statements about American politics to like ten people, I was absolutely stuffed with abalone fritters and grilled lamb, and I was tanked. Without even saying goodbye, I stumbled down the hill, where I ran into Helen on her way up. I asked if she knew where my kids were. "Harper's at our house," she said. "I don't know where Lyra is."

"Great," I said, parenting. "Great." Within a block I had to pee so badly I was sort of half shuffling, half hunched over. Somehow a chilly, windy day had turned tropically muggy. As I galumphed my way home, groaning audibly at the discomfort in my bladder and my general drunken sweatiness, I found one word running through my head: *stumblebum*. "Stumblebum," I said out loud to distract myself. "Fuuuuuuuuuck."

On the way up the final hill to our house I passed the bright blue tsunami line on Melbourne Road, the marker painted on every street near the coast that delineates the elevation above which you're meant to retreat if there's a long or strong earthquake. I expect that, to the objective observer, I appeared wobbly enough to be undergoing my own personal seismic event. This inspiring tale of assimilation ends with me falling into my house, desperately putting off demands from Lyra (who'd returned home hours before) to know where I'd been, peeing with such relief that I had to lean against the wall, then going straight to bed. Alia was already asleep. We could try all we wanted to parent like Kiwis, but we couldn't drink like them.

CHAPTER 2

Te Aroha

Was I really about to commit this unthinkable act with the principal of my child's school? Everything was moving far too quickly, but I was next in line, and everyone in front of me had done it, so: I clasped his hand, put my other hand on his shoulder, and leaned in, in, in, toward his face. My forehead and nose gently knocked against his. I felt his breath upon my lips; I breathed out and knew he could feel mine. I was too close to his face to see him clearly but I could discern his eyes were open too. I had never met him before.

Who was the last person you put your face that close to? Your spouse or partner? Your child? Imagine your breath mingling with that of a total stranger, and then imagine disengaging, moving down the line to the next stranger, and touching noses with her too. And again and again, with teachers and parents and fifth-graders.

The hongi—a word often translated as a "sharing of breath"—is a traditional Māori greeting that once upon a time symbolized a stranger's welcome into a hapu, a community. You clasp hands with the person, lean in, and gently push your forehead and nose against his. Do your best not to concuss yourself or your partner. As with other Māori cultural traditions, the hongi is now incorporated into many civic occasions, as when Secretary of State Hillary Clinton hongied during her official welcome to Wellington. You can see her on YouTube; like many people engaging in an unfamiliar ritual, she looks a bit silly, but the experience of being inside a hongi is quite profound.

The hongi was the final beat in the powhiri—pronounced "*po*-furry," kinda—the welcome ceremony that both our girls' schools performed for the benefit of their new students the first day of the school year, which in New Zealand begins in February. At South Wellington Intermediate and at the Island Bay School, a collection of older students and staff sang and spoke to the year sevens and year ones and transfers and imports, mostly in te reo Māori (the Māori language). Perry, the principal of Harper's Island Bay School, stood before us and welcomed us in a clear, strong voice, the ten consonant sounds of Māori ricocheting off each other in the school's gymnasium. I found myself mesmerized by his handsome, bearded fluency as he delivered his mihi, a ritual introduction. By all of us coming together today, he told us, we join together as one. When he was done speaking, he picked up a goddamn guitar and *strummed*—as if to cement my crush—while we all sang the simple song whose lyrics a teacher had photocopied for us that morning:

Te aroha	Love
Te whakapono	Peace
Te rangimarie	Faith
Tatou e.	To us all.

Sati, the father of a first-year student, stood up. His head was shaved; he wore a flowered shirt and a rāpaki, a dapper linen ceremonial skirt.

Lyra:

On my first day at SWIS, I was a bundle of nerves. All I could do that day was watch other kids talk and shake in my shoes as I imagined approaching them. I thought that they would simply snort at the sight of the quaking seventh-year desperately attempting to make a witty quip and introduce herself.

That was not what happened.

I didn't take a deep breath and approach a group of giggling girls with a confident smile that day. Instead, a girl separated from her laughing friends and introduced herself to me. *To me.*

She didn't become one of my longtime friends, as she wasn't in any of my classes, but I didn't forget her gesture. She wasn't alone and

His left arm was a sleeve of tattoos. In te reo he told us: This day is sacred. Our energy is sacred. I don't even have the words to encapsulate how sacred this moment is. He turned to the parents and older students: Thank you for your hospitality. We are one family now. When he explained to me later what he'd been saying, all I could think was *Thank God I took off my hat.* I felt, in the moment, as if I'd been granted membership into a community, and I would pitch in to defend the hapu if called.

Then we went upstairs to the staff room for a cuppa.

The Māori activist Tame Iti has advocated hongiing even those you do not like, which in his case means Pākehā—white—politicians: "You hongi your enemy because it is better to have eye-to-eye contact with them—to know their shape, their form, their smell, and their thinking." Lyra's and Harper's teachers were not my enemies—*not yet!*—but in hongiing them I still found myself startlingly aware of their shapes and forms, and, it seemed to me afterward, the hongi gave me a sense of their thinking too. In Arlington, teachers—often wary and exhausted from charged encounters with moms and dads who demand only the best for their children—tend to build a bit of a barrier between themselves and parents. They reveal little of their own lives for fear of some parent objecting to a misunderstood Facebook post. They hold us, understandably, at arm's length. I couldn't imagine even patting a teacher at Discovery Elementary on the back, much less grasping one by the shoulder and touching my nose to hers.

friendless like me, desperate for someone to talk to. She had people who she liked and who liked her. She approached me just because I was scared and alone. She approached me just because she was kind. *Kind* is a magical word.

So many people in New Zealand are smart and loyal and funny and brave. But the most important trait they have is kindness. So many of them are kind. And when they have become blurs in my mind, when I can no longer remember their names or the way they laughed, I will remember their kindness.

The powhiri sanctified the school year, marked its opening with solemnity, gave the coming months a shape. Never before in my adult life had the first day of school held the kind of momentousness that I remembered from childhood, that sense of an era changing underneath me, accentuated for kids because they are always, every year, named and knighted with a new title. *Now you are a fifth-grader.* That's how the powhiri felt.

Our children's schools in Wellington were markedly different in many ways than the schools they went to in Arlington. Some of those ways were representative of New Zealand education as a whole; others were quirks of the well-funded urban schools at which they happened to land. Harper called her teachers by their first names and didn't wear shoes in the classroom; Lyra wore a uniform every day, though that uniform consisted of ugly athletic shorts and an uglier polo shirt. After years spent with increasing amounts of homework from their American teachers, both were delighted to find that in New Zealand, they had nearly no homework at all. Lyra's class took a three-day camping trip and Harper's went snorkeling in the ocean.

But the incorporation of te reo and of Māori cultural traditions in school was striking and in stark contrast to the way that most American schools treat Native Americans; even in progressive Northern Virginia schools, our kids' exposure to native culture consisted of memorizing the names of a few Virginia tribes and learning about trade. Māori culture in schools is emblematic of the role Māori culture plays in New Zealand, even in majority-Pākehā settings. Here's a statement that most people in New Zealand would agree with, even if grudgingly: New Zealand's treatment of its native peoples has been significantly better than America's or Australia's. Does that mean that New Zealand's history is free of colonialist exploitation? No way; the first few centuries of Aotearoa's interaction with Europe were a cavalcade of atrocities and betrayal, from the destruction of Māori tribes thanks to the introduction of disease and firearms, to the countless violations of the Treaty of Waitangi as British settlers stole Māori lands, up through the mid-twentieth century, when Māori students were caned for speaking their own language in school.

But that same Treaty of Waitangi—signed in 1840 by envoys of the British Crown and dozens of Māori chiefs and fiercely debated ever since, in large part due to suspicious discrepancies between the English-language and te reo versions—became a crucial tool of the Māori renaissance in the second half of the twentieth century. Activists used the inconclusive language of the treaty to petition for the return of lands and the redress of grievances, leading to reparations settlements with individual tribes and coalitions of tribes and, perhaps even more important, contributing to a shift in public perception of the value of Māori tradition and the responsibilities of the entire country in perpetuating it. "Much of our generation of Pākehā takes it as given that Māori culture *is* New Zealand culture, and it's important to respect and understand it," Veronica, a civil servant in Wellington's Brooklyn neighborhood, told me. "That wasn't true of our parents' generation."

You see that respect and striving for understanding all over New Zealand in the spread of te reo vocabulary into "mainstream" language; it's quite common for Pākehā New Zealanders to refer to their *whanau* (family) at home or their *mana* (authority) at work. (The Māori activists I spoke to view this not as an unwelcome appropriation by foreigners but as their culture reasserting its primacy.) Social interactions, too, reflect Māori influence, and these are not limited to the formal rituals that are often adopted by schools and workplaces; the grace-like thanks given for food and companionship before even the most pedestrian of office meetings. When one is introduced to a New Zealander, even casually, it's likely to result in a friendly interrogation as to one's hometown, one's neighborhood, one's common friends. Rarely did I meet a new person in Wellington who didn't, in the end, know someone in Island Bay; Kiwis I met would often name people they knew who lived in Washington, DC, and then look at me expectantly. "We always seek out connections with the people we meet, people they know who we know," the

University of Auckland professor Irene De Haan told me. "Two degrees of separation: That's a very New Zealand thing to do. It's partly because it's a small country, but it's also because that's what Māori do."

Right now, Māori readers will be rolling their eyes at the cheery biculturalism expressed by the liberal Pākehā I spoke to. I don't mean to misrepresent the degree to which racism remains in New Zealand. As I heard over and over again from both Māori and Pākehā New Zealanders, there's still a wide disparity between white and nonwhite income, standard of living, and cultural influence. Māori children are more likely to live in poverty, grow up in abusive homes, and wind up in the criminal justice system. These disparities have always started early. "We know Māori students and Māori families have not had good experiences in New Zealand schools," Hineihaea Murphy, a Māori education consultant, told me. "We know Māori achievement in schools has not been good." They may no longer be rapping children's knuckles for speaking te reo, but teachers still discriminate against Māori students. "Even teachers who don't realize they are expecting less of Māori students often do so," said Zhu Yao, a PhD student researching gifted education in New Zealand.

But despite a dogged cadre of older Pākehā stubbornly maintaining that the New Zealand of their childhoods was the "true" culture of the islands and despite the structural disadvantages still faced by Māori and Pacific Islanders, New Zealand is remarkably diverse and getting more so, especially in its North Island cities, where intermarriage has been the norm for decades. Auckland is by some measures the most diverse city on earth, mixing a historically large Māori and Pacific Islander population with a recent influx of East and South Asian immigrants. Wellington, though more European-dominated, still feels vibrantly multicultural. (Its progressive spirit means the city's welcome can spread beyond race into gender. I met several parents of transgender or gender-fluid teenagers who had moved to Wellington at least partly because, in this city, their children felt happily unremarkable. "Here, people are just like, 'Ah, sweet as,'" said one.)

Alia and I have lived in diverse places (Honolulu, New York) and depressingly monocultural ones (Whitefish Bay, the Milwaukee suburb where I grew up, known derisively as White Folks' Bay). Our children were born in New York, but they have no memories of living anywhere but very, very white North Arlington — a situation that's no one's fault but our own. Alia and I are the ones who self-segregated when we left New York, sacrificing a diverse environment for the lure of "better schools," as defined in one specific way. It didn't escape my notice that we were avidly seeking international diversity after making a set of educational and life-style choices that had mostly eliminated diversity from our American lives.

In Wellington, wonderfully, even though the girls attended high-decile (affluent) schools, their classmates were a mix of Pākehā and Māori, Samoan and Indian, Australian and European. Most important, it seemed to me, all those kids were being taught, plainly, that New Zealand was not simply a white society — that Māori traditions and language were intrinsically, crucially Kiwi and that to be a citizen of this country meant understanding and adopting them. "We're recognizing as a country the importance of cultural capital," Hineihaea Murphy said. "It's had a dramatic effect on the Pākehā population of New Zealand." Pointed out Quintin, a market specialist at New Zealand's state-owned electric company and a father of three: "Māori life is the only actually unique thing about being in New Zealand!" He and other Māori I spoke to talked about their culture not just as personally important but as a treasure worth preserving for the good of the nation.

Māori bicultural education starts even before primary school, John O'Neill, director of the Institute of Education at Massey University, told me. "It's deeply embedded in the philosophy of Te Whāriki, the early-childhood curriculum." In primary school, which is similar to American kindergarten through sixth grade, daily classroom activities and rituals incorporate Māori culture in ways large and small, from children practicing a ceremonial introduction called a mihi to a focus on ecology and community. (Harper learned a lot of te reo, but that snorkeling trip to the ocean just meters from her school, where she and her classmates identified native fish and rays, was in its own way a deeply Māori experience.) Lyra's intermediate school — the equivalent of American seventh and eighth grades — did far less with te reo, though the language was a popular elective and certain classroom standards and rules carried over. Children were not to sit on desks or tables, for example, a restriction derived from Māori taboos and common in New Zealand schools since the 1970s.

The government has recently set a goal of getting all New Zealand schools to offer te reo instruction by 2025 and having 20 percent of the country speaking the language conversationally by 2040. This plan is aided by dozens of Māori immersion schools scattered across New Zealand; one I visited in Wellington's Wilton neighborhood was about half Māori students and half Pākehā. But even parents of kids in non-immersion schools espoused an earnest desire for families to be more connected to what they viewed as the authentic heart of their homeland. It was an echo of what I'd heard from one mom at Harper's school, another American transplant, who told me wistfully that "every day they learn to be grateful and thankful for everything they have. Every morning at breakfast they thank the food for existing."

Of course, New Zealand students aren't all kumbayaing every day. There are plenty of high-decile, mostly white schools where the attention paid to Māori culture is tokenist at best. And there's broad disagreement, still, among New Zealanders—especially older Pākehā—about the extent to which Māori tradition ought to inflect mainstream culture. In recent years, a movement to make formal te reo study compulsory in all schools has faced stiff opposition from politicians and some parents. Just read the comments on any Stuff.co.nz story about te reo or Māori

---

Harper:

This is my mihi, I learned it in school, this is how you traditionally greet someone for something big in Māori. What I'm saying is like "welcome" in the *tēnā koutou* part and then I'm telling you the mountain and the river that were the closest to me when I grew up, then it's telling you my mum, my dad, my last name, my sister's name, and my name, then it's telling you where I grew up, then *nō reira, tēnā koutou tēnā koutu tēnā koutou katoa* means goodbye.

politics and you'll see there is still a vocal segment of the population that believes, as John O'Neill put it, that "having different services and supports for an ethnic group is inverse racism." Quintin, who's Māori, mentioned his experience attending a parents' meeting at his children's Catholic school where they discussed the possibility of mandating te reo. "Why are we even talking about this!" one mother protested. "Island Bay is not a Māori community, it's an Italian community." Quintin, as he was telling me the story, chuckled. "Now," he said, "I don't like to get into arguments about who was here first or anything, *but...*"

In New Zealand I saw television commercials that employed Māori myths and traditions for the purpose of selling precooked sausages; I watched sporting events that opened with the national anthem sung in te reo. "The crowd sing without looking at the words, with proper pronunciation and with gusto," said Alice Patrick, an education consultant who helped oversee the development of the New Zealand curriculum guidelines for te reo learning in English-language schools. "That means something!"

It means something especially because of the outsize role that sports — sorry, *sport* — plays in Kiwi culture. It seemed to me that sport was the closest thing to religion in a place without much of a tradition of churchgoing. About 35 percent of New Zealanders say they attend church at least once a month, compared with 69 percent of Americans who attend

Tēnā koutou, tēnā koutou, tēnā koutou katoa
Ko Miners Hill te mounga
Ko Potomac te awa
Ko Alia taku māmā
Ko Daniel taku pāpā
Ko Kois te whānau
Ko Harper tōku ingoa
Ko Lyra te kiriāhuā
Nō Virginia te ahau
Nō reira, tēnā koutou tēnā koutou tēnā koutou katoa.

about as frequently. On a recent New Zealand census, 173,000 respondents objected to even being asked about their religion, and 53,000 described themselves as "Jedi." "New Zealanders are basically pantheistic," Tracey told me.

But the All Blacks, New Zealand's national rugby team? The country shuts down when they play. The game itself, martial and rugged, occupies an exalted position in the culture. (No less a leading light than director Taika Waititi—a guy not known for being uncritical about his home country—told me, "Ah, man, it's the greatest sport in the world.") However, for many, rugby's high status has long had to do with the way the sport represents certain aspects of idealized manhood still prized by some New Zealanders.

Much of the All Blacks' popularity, of course, comes from their success. They've won the past two Rugby World Cups, matters of great pride in a country where boosterism runs rampant. Fans of other sports teams have less to get excited about; Gary, a soccer fan, eagerly recapped for me the New Zealand men's performance in the most recent World Cup they'd qualified for, in 2010. "We did not lose a game in that World Cup," he boasted. "The only team not to lose a game." (The All Whites tied three times and were eliminated.) That enthusiasm extends to every sport in which New Zealand competes; perhaps the Kiwiest day I spent in Wellington was the day I attended a test cricket match between South Africa and New Zealand (the Black Caps) at the Basin Reserve, a broad and beautiful green dropped plumb into the middle of the city. The lawns around the pitch were full of jolly Kiwis taking the day off work to cheer on their team. I ate delicious food, drank a lot of beer, and didn't really understand a single thing that happened on the pitch.

Unsurprisingly, sport plays a major role in New Zealand family life. Most every child plays a couple of sports, and many families' school-year schedules revolve around their kids' practices and games. Trinity and Grainger, next door, played football, floorball, netball, and probably some other imaginary sports as well. "Sport definitely drives our schedule," Tracey acknowledged. "I think we're pretty comfortable with that. It's finite."

Those were familiar sentiments to us; in Arlington, competitive travel leagues had taken over youth sports culture. Kids as young as nine tried out for leagues that had them practicing three times a week, playing seemingly year-round, and competing in tournaments in Norfolk, New Jersey, and Charleston. Their parents spent their weekends driving, staying in hotels, and shouting on the sidelines. (*"Esbu,"* we hissed when travel-sports obligations caused parents to cancel a playdate or a weekend away.) All over America, it seemed, devotion to travel teams was leading to childhoods spent on the road; one survey revealed that half of such parents spent between a hundred dollars and five hundred dollars per month on travel sports, and 20 percent spent a thousand dollars a month or more!

And the growth of kid-sport specialization meant that for children whose parents *weren't* willing to invest that kind of time and money, sports were sometimes out of reach. We heard annoying stories of casual players unable to make school teams because they were outclassed in tryouts by kids who'd been training for, like, the Olympics; meanwhile, Harper's rec soccer team disbanded because too many players moved to the more advanced travel league. Harper wanted to try out for travel soccer too, and she never quite understood why the topic got such a firm *no* from us every time she raised it.

Yet I didn't find youth sports quite as oppressive in New Zealand as I had in Arlington, even though Grainger, for example, did play on an all-star football team that had him spending days in far-flung North Island towns. In part this was because children's relative lack of homework meant people could get together after sports practice was over. But it also had to do with the way *everyone* played sports. Not Lyra, of course — she's retired from sports, she likes to say, though even she ended up swinging a cricket bat in a friend's backyard. But basically everyone else played, because everyone was allowed to play. "There's a huge emphasis on sport as something that everyone can do, and should do," explained Harlene, a university administrator in Dunedin. In America, where she grew up, she said, "You have to have your child in summer programs so they'd be good enough to get on the team. But here, there's a team for everyone, and everyone plays everything. If sixty kids want to play net-ball, you have six netball teams. And if you have ten more, you form a seventh."

Netball? Yup, Harper, who in Arlington played every sport we let her sign up for, played netball, despite none of us knowing what netball even was. Netball (definitely a real sport) is played by women in Common-wealth countries around the world. New Zealand has a six-team semipro-fessional netball league; the national team is the Silver Ferns and they've won the absolutely not-made-up Netball World Cup four times. Think of netball as basketball but without dribbling or as ultimate Frisbee with a ball instead of a disk. Rather than prizing one-on-one ball-handling skills, netball rewards movement away from the play, as the person holding the ball must get rid of it within three seconds and cannot run or dribble. The basket is really high up in the air, really small, and has no backboard, so scoring can be low. It seemed incredibly fun to play and was sure fun to watch, as Harper and I learned when we drove over to the big sports com-plex in Kilbirnie to watch Tracey's adult netball team play a game. In a real thrill for Harper, her teacher Steph was also on Tracey's team, and we cheered them both on despite their team getting beaten pretty decisively. "Ah, that team's a bit young, aren't they?" asked one of Tracey's gasping teammates of their rosy-cheeked, twentysomething opponents.

Yes, Harper's teacher played league netball. In fact, many adults we met had their own substantial athletic commitments, from football with local club teams to netball leagues to mountain-biking buddies to regu-lar surfing dates. Once again, sports were an activity *everyone* was expected to do, grown-ups included. As a guy who's spent his whole life basically trying to get people to play sports with him even though he's not very good, I found a country that wanted all its residents to play whether they were good or not very appealing. In our months there, I played a lot of pickup basketball at the sports complex with a bunch of young men who, in a phenomenon that's unique in my experience, called three-second violations on themselves.

Lyra, to her great relief, found that sports didn't play much of a role in her intermediate-school schedule, though unlike her middle school in

Arlington, which had done away with recess, SWIS did feature a substantial amount of outside time. (Unlike Harper's school, SWIS didn't *require* adorable hats in the fierce New Zealand sun, only recommended them strongly.) I visited SWIS for a morning and observed Lyra's class in action; despite intermediate school generally being considered quite arduous compared to primary school, I found her school day alarmingly chilled out. Kids worked together on projects, sprawled out on the floor; the class did word puzzles together; I even got to witness a movie-quality bit of mischief when one boy took advantage of the teacher being called out of the classroom to sneak into her desk and liberate the mobile phone she'd confiscated earlier. Whether a particular child did any actual learning in class seemed, in my short visit, to be mostly a matter of personal preference.

The highlight of the first term at SWIS was the outdoors trip, a three-day retreat at a camp in the central North Island. The trip was an example of EOTC, education outside the classroom, long a priority in New Zealand schooling. "All Kiwi kids used to do out-of-school camps," explained John O'Neill. "It was an annual event. You'd go to one of the bays on the South Island or this place or that place. It was just part of the standard experience." These days, parents sometimes bemoan the fact that their children's trips are less arduous than the ones they used to go on; Lyra's excursion was essentially a visit to the equivalent of a pleasant YMCA camp. But ambitious treks still happen; in secondary school, O'Neill's children did the Tongoriro Alpine Crossing, a nineteen-kilometer tramp at altitude and one of New Zealand's Great Walks.

Harper would miss her school's outdoors overnight, which took place in November, but her class did have its own adventure to prepare for: a snorkeling trip to Island Bay, reflecting the marine ecology theme around which the entire first-term "inquiry-based" curriculum revolved. I volunteered to chaperone the trip, only to learn that chaperones were expected to bring their own wet suits in order to snorkel with the kids. Now, I like snorkeling, but the very idea of owning my own wet suit was patently absurd. "Is there a way I could help that *doesn't* include snorkeling in freezing-cold water?" I asked Steph.

"On the snorkeling trip?" she replied dubiously. "Errr...we do need a few people to stand at the shore keeping an eye on everyone. Perhaps you could do that?"

So on a sunny and warm morning we all hiked down the road to the ramshackle Marine Education Center, where fit parents and cheerful staffers awaited, snorkels at the ready. I was handed a whistle and a clipboard. "Now, you'll blow the whistle to get everyone's attention if needed," said one of the ecologists who worked at the center. "And here we've got everyone's names, so you're to check everyone in and out of the water."

Fully wet-suited, Harper and her buddy Bailey strapped on their snorkels, checked in with me in matching Kiwi accents—"Bailey?" "Yis!" "Harper?" "Yis!"—and then stepped into the bay. Harper shrieked as she felt the water and then immediately said, "Dad, you should do this, with the wet suit you can't even tell how cold it is."

"I'm good here," I said and gave the thumbs-up to whoever's wet-suited mom was accompanying the girls into the sea. I walked along the windswept beach, clambering over rocks, as a couple of dozen nine-year-olds in bright red suits floated along the shore. At one point one of the marine center's staffers waved a bunch of kids over to see something particularly exciting. Everything about this seemed improbable—this brilliant morning; the South Pacific waves rolling in; lumpy Tapu te Ranga island, the sun bright on its flanks; these kids out in the world without a parent even signing a permission slip. Most improbable of all was my kid, my Harper, swimming with her friends, playing her netball, learning her mihi, speaking in her aspirational Kiwi-inflected accent.

Lyra had enjoyed her school's outdoor adventure, which consisted, as far as I could tell, of kids messing about just as they did at school, only in a field. Would she appreciate a wilderness excursion that required her to actually be in the wilderness? Harper loved her snorkeling trip, mostly because she got to do it with her friends. How would she feel about an adventure she shared with only her parents? And what about Alia and me? I was not exactly Mark Trail. I wouldn't even put on a wet suit! But even now, as our time in New Zealand was coming to a close, we were collecting supplies—borrowing packs from neighbors, buying weird dehydrated food—and planning an adventure of our own. We, the Smith-Koises, were going to go tramping like real Kiwis.

I blew the whistle at the appointed time and the kids made their way out of the water, pulling off their fins and chattering about what they'd seen. "Dad!" Harper called. "We saw an eagle ray!"

"It was huge!" exclaimed one boy. "It was bigger than me!"

"Really?" I asked. That seemed unlikely—this kid was really big. "Aren't they poisonous?"

"Dad, we learned about eagle rays—they can be, like, two meters wide," Harper said.

"Well, hold on, everyone, I need to check you all in," I said, pulling out my clipboard. "Millie?"

"Kia ora!"

"Aalia?"

"Yis!"

"Oliver?"

"Kia ora."

"Asher?"

"Here!"

"Harper?"

"Kia ora!"

"Bailey?"

"Kia ora!"

CHAPTER 3

On Any Walk

O let me sing the song of the Smith-Kois family's one previous journey into the wild, the occasion on which we let the grandeur of the earth overwhelm our senses and lift our spirits. It was the trip when we got so bored by bison.

We traveled to Yellowstone National Park one glorious August week. The park was alive with sunlight and flowers; the worst of the wildfires were over but smoke still smudged the horizon. Just a few miles into Yellowstone, we pointed, shouted, pulled over for the herd of bison snuffling along the road. By our family's second day in Yellowstone, the kids no longer looked up from their iPods when we passed a herd, so inured were they to their wild majesty, etc. By day three, my only interaction with bison was to yell at them from the driver's seat when they impeded my path. Our immunity to bison mirrored our family's generally unsatisfying response to the natural world, a response that came into sharp focus at Yellowstone, a place we sometimes enjoyed but often just endured. Or, rather, a place we sometimes enjoyed while often enduring one another.

We weren't exactly roughing it on this trip. We weren't camping in tents or sleeping in our car; we were staying in Park Service cabins. But the singleness of purpose one must adopt in nature—you may hike or swim or boat, but really, you are there to *be in beauty,* that's it, there's no miniature golf—was a poor match for parents who were just discovering how little time they'd previously spent simply existing side by side with their kids.

Kids, it turns out, are annoying to adults. I didn't understand this when I was a kid. I thought I was wildly entertaining, a laff riot. Of course, I was not. And while my annoyingness was perhaps exceptional in degree, it was not unique. All kids are annoying. Kids lack impulse control and perspective. They cannot let a moment's discomfort or the tiniest indignity pass without complaining loudly, and they do not care if anyone else's discomfort or indignities match or exceed theirs. They are constitutionally incapable of patience. They ask stupid questions, don't listen to the answers, and then ask the questions again. They are solipsistic, greedy, and profoundly ungrateful for everything they have. They are frequently covered in food or snot or, on the worst days, food *and* snot.

And adults? Don't get me started on *adults*. Adults are, if possible, even more annoying to kids than kids are to adults. Adults think they're so wise, but actually they're *not*. When something's wrong, instead of fixing the thing that is wrong, they just tell kids about how the thing that's wrong doesn't really matter! Instead of just giving kids the things they want, they make irrelevant comments about how the things are expensive or unhealthy or dangerous. Or they say, "Maybe later." Why be duplicitous, adults? Don't say "maybe later" when what you mean is "no." Just because they're bigger and earn money, they get to tell kids what to do. Everything about the adult-kid relationship is unfair.

So anyway when you put adults and kids together in the same place with no internet to distract them, things can get pretty disputatious. This is not to say that the trip to Yellowstone was awful or that we completely failed to experience the Great Outdoors. There were long stretches of time in which we enjoyed one another's company, held aimless conversations, sat at the edges of waterfalls or meandered down trails. (Through every one of these moments, however, I was able to devote only 75 percent of my attention to enjoying the experience, as the other 25 percent was devoted to remaining constantly prepared for the appearance of a bear on the trail. Would the bear come from behind us or ahead of us? How would I distract the bear as the rest of my family escaped? What exactly would it feel like as the bear removed each of my limbs? Would my children remember me fondly, as the dad who saved them from a bear, or resentfully, as the dad whose dumb decision to go to Yellowstone meant they had to watch him be eaten by a bear?)

It's only to say that perhaps my dreams for the Yellowstone trip were a bit out of reach. I dreamed of a journey during which my children would be filled, now and then, with awe at the beauty of the earth on which we live and in which they would embrace, now and then, the adventure and accomplishment of setting off on a trail, traveling its length, and reaching its end. Instead, in order to achieve even the shortest hike through the woods, Alia and I had to develop a system of bald bribery: For every mile that our children successfully hiked without whining, they would each receive a key chain. "You can't expect us to *never* whine," Lyra said reasonably. "That's impossible when we're doing something boring like hiking."

So what would happen in New Zealand, a country that is not only generally accepted as the most beautiful in the world but also one where diving into that beauty is a national preoccupation? Vacation, for most Kiwis, revolves around the outdoors. For summer vacation, from Christmas to February, Kiwis tramp along a Great Walk, or tent near a stream, or drive a campervan from forest to forest, or rent a bach — a beach house — on the coast. (At Alia's feminist book club, one mom suggested Alia was exaggerating when she said that "everyone" in New Zealand goes tramping or camping on vacation; when Alia then asked which of the attendees do, in fact, go tramping or camping on vacation, each and every woman raised her hand.)

According to a New Zealand Department of Conservation survey, 80 percent of New Zealanders visited at least one DOC site in 2016. Compare that to the United States, where recent gains in National Park Service attendance are due substantially to international visitors. A 2008–2009 survey revealed that only 47 percent of Americans could remember visiting any National Park Service site in the previous *two* years, and that included bogus "national parks" like the Smithsonian and the Freedom Trail in downtown Boston.

But the difference between Kiwis' relationship to the natural world and Americans' goes beyond the simple choice of where one vacations. Most New Zealanders, both rich and poor, live surrounded by a kind of splendor that most Americans can't comprehend. (Yes, the Pacific Northwest is beautiful. So is Maine. Hawaii is great. But c'mon.) Take Wellington, the city where we lived for three months. To look at a Google map of Wellington is to note, perhaps, that it has a lot of parks, and that many of its roads are twisty. But to *be* in Wellington, to drive those hairpinning roads or walk through the town's green belt, is to understand that the city is nestled among dozens of deep valleys, the result of the confluence of two significant faults running deep beneath its streets. (Let's leave aside for now the catastrophe that will occur, tomorrow or five hundred years from now, when those faults finally unsnag and let rip.)

Each valley appears filled from the bottom with houses, as if they'd been poured from a jug in the sky. The houses pile atop one another, each securing its own narrow slice of the view across the valley or to the water; their driveways and front walks, switching back and forth across cliff faces, can feel like daredevil trails. (A few forgo steps and have small funiculars from the garage to the front door.) Where the valley walls become too sheer even for ambitious Wellington builders, the cliffs erupt into tangled bush, every shade of green you can imagine, every paint-sample card at once. Tall pines that appear imported from a Scandinavian fairy tale jostle for space with palm trees and knotty scrub. Then lining each ridge, at the very top, is one last set of houses, an exclusive row of homes big by Wellington standards but smaller than your average North Arlington McMansion.

The city is surrounded on three sides by the South Pacific, cold even in summer, and many of the city's neighborhoods are defined by their relationship to the bays carved out of the land like bites from an apple. From Wellington's southern suburbs, the bays, on sunny days, are a vivid greenish blue, the color of a jewel, the white flecks of wind-driven waves like facets. The deeper Cook Strait is a thin navy-blue line at the horizon, as straight as a seam. The mountains of the South Island, about forty kilometers away, are invisible in the mornings but appear, like Brigadoon, as the ocean mist burns off. In the red evenings they glow in shimmering profile as the sun sets behind them. One night, driving along the water, I turned a corner and there appeared before me a sunset so luridly beautiful that I immediately pulled over to the side of the road to take a photo. The two cars behind me also pulled over, as did, moments later, a Wellington city bus that disgorged its passengers onto the gravel path, phones held out in supplication.

Whatever, you don't need to read an ode to New Zealand's beauty—you saw *The Lord of the Rings*. But living every day steeped in Wellington's crenellated splendor, in Auckland with the sun winking off the harbor, or with the South Island's alps at their backs, Kiwis understand that the world exists and ought to be lived in. In our time in Wellington we saw neighbors surfing, mountain biking, rowing across the harbor. Kids were sent to the beach on sunny afternoons or when the adults at a cocktail party had had enough of them. One neighbor, a doctor, was paid by patients from time to time in live five-pound crayfish. Another neighbor liked to free-dive for paua, enormous New Zealand abalone with rich meat and rainbow-slicked shells, and bring them to us to cook.

And on a basic moment-to-moment level, Kiwis simply seem more attuned to the natural world. Quick—do you know what direction the wind is coming from today? A Wellingtonian would know if it's a southerly or a northerly and what that implies for ocean temperature and whether your planned barbecue's likely to be rained out. On multiple occasions, I witnessed Kiwis as young as eight point to some random-ass bird in a tree and tell me its name, its cultural importance, and its level of scarcity. "Ah, that's a saddleback! He's got that mark because Maui got angry at him and grabbed him. They're quite rare." The only birds *I* can identify on sight are affiliated with baseball teams.

Alia and I set ourselves a goal upon our arrival in New Zealand: we would overcome our apprehension of the outdoors and embrace nature as real Kiwis do. We'd start slow, with some short hikes around places we visited on the North Island. We'd build up our strength and tolerance while also somehow magically making our children enjoy walking through the bush. And then we'd finish by taking on one of the New

Zealand Great Walks, the nine splendid multiday tramps all Kiwi out-doorspeople strive to complete.

We spent our first week in New Zealand on the Coromandel Penin-sula, a sunbaked collection of natural wonders so close to one another, it's as if they've been laid out by the tourism board. Our nights were spent watching *The Lord of the Rings,* but it became clear that each day would begin, at Lyra's behest, with a trip to the Tairua Library. At first we welcomed such stops as chances for her to check out books—she was, per usual, roaring through four or five a day—but soon we noted that in fact she spent only a couple of minutes grabbing books off the shelves; the rest of her visit she hunched over her iPod, using the library's free Wi-Fi. I was sick of her daily entreaties for more time online, had been sick of them for years, but I found them particularly galling here. Why did she want to be on the same old internet when every day we were going someplace brand-new?

So one morning we skipped the library and headed up the coast to our initial outdoor challenge: the hike to Cathedral Cove. A gorgeous beach on the east coast of the Coromandel, Cathedral Cove is defined by a dramatic white sandstone arch that divides the beach in two, fram-ing a vista of sapphire-blue ocean and bright green cliffs. To get there, you can either hire a water taxi or hike about two rolling kilometers from the busy car park at the top of the bluff.

We hiked. The New Zealand sun beamed down on us through the ozone hole, ruthlessly seeking out the thin stripes at our wrists and the backs of our necks where we hadn't completely sunscreened and toasting them a glowing pink. Considering that we started at the top of a cliff and our goal was to get, eventually, to the bottom, the track went uphill sur-prisingly often, a fact that did not go unnoticed by our children, attuned as they are to any infinitesimal change in their level of comfort. Over the course of our one-hour trek, Harper delineated a hierarchy of walking terrain: "Walking a flat path is best. Walking downhill is the second best. Walking uphill is third." Lyra added that fourth was plummeting off a cliff, "but it's close."

So was there whining? Yes. I was once a whiner; I was the kid whose mother played loud music in the car so she couldn't hear him ask if we were there yet. And so when my kids whine, I empathize with them—I know how satisfying it is to complain bitterly about stuff that sucks. Whining offers a blessed, momentary relief from growing discomfort, much like a deep fart, which it also resembles in how unbearable it makes you to be near.

On Whining

The pitch of the average whine is a B above middle C, but played on an oboe that's a quarter-step flat.

The whine comes not when we are least expecting it but when we are *most* expecting it, and it is more irritating for its lack of surprise. Each time our children rise to the occasion, we are freshly disappointed. The application of whatever a child's trigger might be sets off a countdown clock in a parent's head, like the timer on a cartoon bomb. We imagine what the whine will sound like before the child even knows she is unhappy. That's why the whine is in its way worse than, say, the shout of dismay at a sudden calamity. Even before the child takes the breath, we've been hearing the expression of discontent she is about to make. To the child, the whine is the first straw. To the parent, it is the last.

In systems design, a *single point of failure* is a location within a system—a router, a segment of code—the failure of which will take the entire system down. Those who use the system become acclimated to that design flaw, making sure to avoid overtaxing, say, that particular router. We parents know our children's single points of failure. For one kid, it's being hot—the moment a bead of sweat pops on a forehead, the parent braces herself. For another, it's a certain kind of homework problem or the frustration of a task not going the way it was supposed to. We know our children's psyches intimately, have spent countless hours observing and analyzing them, and so we know the overload of a child's SPOF leads, inevitably, to system shutdown.

It took a lot for me to change, in my late teens, into someone who just tries to make the best of things, who tries silently to improve everyone's lot rather than complain about it. Even now I hear the whines I could be whining inside my head, more plentiful each year as more things go wrong with my body. And that's why, I think, my children's quite age-appropriate whining upsets me so; they are young and hale and flexible, while my physical state is one of accelerating decay. My

---

Research shows that whining peaks in children between the ages of two and four, but every parent knows that it continues well into tweenhood. In adolescence the whine is often replaced by the sulk or the simmer, the dissatisfaction swallowed or, more likely, tucked away for later use. This is part of becoming an adult.

We wish to whine but cannot because we are the parents. Our whining happens in texts to one another, in commiseration with parent friends on Facebook, or late at night, just before sleep, when we let our guard down and allow ourselves to collapse into frustration. When things are the hardest it can feel as though we are carefully taking turns, considering: Whose turn is it to complain tonight?

We know the volume of our children's whines, their contours, their angles of descent. We have heard the whines so often that the sound lives in our heads like a ringtone.

Is whining involuntary, like a reflex? In some ways it seems like that must be the case. Whining can be thought of as the body's response to a stimulus, a spontaneous act rather than a considered one. Yet the wide eyes with which so many whines are delivered — imploring, beseeching eyes — feel so intentional that it is easy to view the whine as a calculation and to respond to it not with the understanding that one's child has accidentally done something annoying but instead with the anger that one's child is being deliberately manipulative.

Do not reward whining, parenting books instruct us. *If whining yields results, children will learn to continue whining in order to get what they want.* But we can go months responding to whining with

---

back hurts all the time—it hurts when I'm, like, eating ice cream—and *they're* bitching to *me* about walking up a hill?

There was whining about the heat. There was whining about the bugs. There was whining about shoes—they hurt, they didn't fit, why hadn't we made them wear socks. ("Why didn't you put on socks?" I asked. "I didn't *knooooooooow.*") And there was whining each time the path turned uphill. "It just means that on the way back, it'll be *downhill,*" I said as cheerfully as possible. ("But it's uphill *nooooowwwwwww.*")

"Why do you have to whine so much?" I asked at one point.

"You whine all the time," Harper retorted.

I was offended. "I do not!"

"You whine about us whining," she said with the air of someone who'd just perfectly poached an egg.

stone-faced constancy, and yet the whining doesn't cease. Some parents have convinced their children that adult ears literally cannot hear whining, but their children still, enduring discomfort or uncertainty, whine, and the parents are left performing a pageant of unhearing while their children keen, red-faced.

The idea that adult ears cannot hear the whining of children is not only an invention; it is the opposite of true. We *really* hear whining. A 2010 study revealed that the sound of whining focused listeners' attention more effectively than neutral speech and even caused an increase in galvanic skin response, a sign of emotional arousal. The same researchers found in a separate study that whining is even more effective than the sound of infant cries in distracting subjects trying to solve simple math problems.

No one ever hears, though, a child whining from another room. That is because children do not whine without an audience, the person who might remedy the problem that caused the whine. A frustrated child gathers her frustration, carries it with her to the room where you are, and presents it to you as a gift.

If a child falls in the forest, does she make a sound? No.

After about an hour we took the stairs down the final leg to the beach ("Downstairs is the third-best way to go, and going upstairs is the fifth-best"), then set down our things in a copse of low-hanging branches. Lyra immediately separated from us and went wandering down the beach, pacing in circles, thinking intently. Soon she had covered about as much ground tromping around the beach as we'd covered on our hike. (If she'd had a Fitbit, she would outstep the rest of the family most days, but she'd lost her Fitbit in the airport less than twenty-four hours after we bought it for her.)

Harper, as was typical, stuck closer to us, peppering us with questions and commentary. What were those birds, look at those little squishy things at the tide line, did we feel how cold the water was?!, what was an orc actually and why did they look like that. I tried to relax into the questions,

We are taught that the ideal way to respond to whining is with exaggerated kindness: *I understand that you feel upset because this isn't going the way you wanted it to. That must be frustrating.* The resulting disparity between the emotion we feel and the expression we deliver seems emblematic of parenting, where so much of our energy goes toward battling our instincts in order to do that which is right. Needless to say, we fail at this quite often, and so our first response to whining is, not infrequently, "Stop whining," a phrase that has never, in the history of human parenting, stopped whining.

Whining is the sound of the devil's nails on hell's chalkboard.

It is the resolute unfairness of the universe that is, most often, the true subject of the whine. Not this vegetable or that homework assignment. That we live in a world in which all cannot be as we want it to be. Parents, for the most part, have grimly come to terms with this truism. Through hard experience, we have learned that asking will not make most things better. Viewed in this light, whining is an act of optimism. We think a child does not understand — but in fact, she does not *believe*, does not *yet* believe, that some unfairness cannot be remedied, and some injustices have no hope of redress.

having long ago given up the dream of quiet reflection. Quiet reflection in nature is for Thoreau, because he is childless and dead. This is simply how Harper experiences the world, and the best thing I can do is meet her there. I didn't know what bird that was, yes I saw those squishy things, no I would not feel how cold the water was, orcs were [ten-minute lecture on Tolkien's prewar Oxfordian classism]. Eventually Harper wandered away to poke with a stick at the squishy things; I'd been just boring enough. I enjoyed a few moments walking arm in arm with Alia.

The hike back was harder, hotter, uphill most of the way. The girls' lollygagging inspired Alia to tell a story about Lyra's toddlerhood: Toddler Lyra was so distractible that on the days we forgot the stroller, the two-block walk home from her New York daycare was an exercise in frustration, us forever urging her along despite her interest in pine cones, rocks, beer cans, and sitting down. One afternoon Alia, with nothing on her agenda, decided to simply let Lyra move at her own pace. There was no rush, she had nowhere to be, it was a beautiful day; why not let the kid direct the afternoon's walk? Ninety minutes later, only halfway up the hill, Alia said, "You win, Lyra." She picked her up and carried her, chortling and kicking, the rest of the way home.

The story was cute, one I hadn't thought about for a long time, and it also helped to occupy the girls' thoughts for a crucial uphill portion of the hike. We played Twenty Questions—the girls only selected characters from *The Lord of the Rings,* and we had to consciously ask obtuse questions in order not to guess them too quickly. Like, after two questions, it would be obvious that Harper was thinking of Legolas—that week she was always thinking of Legolas—but to stretch the game out we'd ask, "Does he have blond hair?" Meanwhile, we were not really paying attention to the *nature.* Whatever; we made it to the parking lot, where I told the children, "I'm really proud of you! You did a long hard walk and you were really good for some of it."

The trouble came in that parking lot, as it so often does. Just when success seems close at hand, as you unlock the car and toss everything in the trunk, your whole afternoon comes unraveled because someone asks if she can get on the internet. Lyra had just pronounced the day "fun," a judgment that did more for my self-esteem than any comment from an eleven-year-old should, then followed it up by asking if we could please bring her and her iPod to the library for the rest of the afternoon.

Jesus. Could not even unmatched natural splendor keep her from wanting to fuck around on the internet? I could see the whole argument spooling out in front of me, the way you see, for example, a curb coming up on your left that you can't steer away from quickly enough to avoid blowing two tires. I would respond too firmly, she would react badly, and soon she'd be upset and I'd be fuming. Together we would ruin our nice afternoon. I took a deep breath and said my first line.

"Lyra, we're not going to the library."

"But why not?"

"It's just not in the plans for today."

"So you've decided we're not going to have *any* recreational time on the internet today? You just *decided* that?"

"Yes, Lyra, that's what we decided. We have other things to do today."

"But I have something I need to do!"

"You can do it the next time we're online!"

"How can you just *decide* that?"

"Lyra, part of the whole point of coming here is to wean ourselves off our screens! *All* of us!"

"But *weaning* doesn't mean I go a whole *day* without being online!"

"What?"

"*Weaning* means you give me twenty or thirty minutes a day but not, like, hours."

"That's exactly what weaning *doesn't* mean! It means that we all get to a place where we're not upset if we can't get online."

"Of course I'm upset!" Her brow was furrowed, her eyes bright. "You seem to think you can just *decide* not to let me do this thing that's important to me!"

"I *can* decide that, Lyra." Speaking with fake, forced calm. "When you respond this badly to just having to wait a day or two, it makes me think maybe you should *never* be online."

"Shut up!" she yelled. We both paused in shock; this was the first time she'd ever said that to me in earnest, I think.

"Lyra, you may not use your iPod for any reason for the next two days," I forced out. "You may not speak to me that way."

"Fine!" She stormed into the car and slammed the door.

(I typed that recap the night it happened, when I was still burning white with self-assurance. Reading it back now, much later, it's easy to see how badly I handled the conversation, how I escalated it instead of finding a solution, how I brought a long-simmering resentment to the boil, how I—this is the most upsetting part—assumed the worst of Lyra. In my head, the request for the internet negated our hours spent together in nature; it was a bald admission that all she *really* cared about was her stupid iPod and the various message boards she was obsessed with. But to her, of course, she had spent hours doing something I wanted her to do, and she'd done it relatively uncomplainingly. Hours! Basically a *lifetime* hiking up and down hills and sitting on a beach. And then she politely asked to do something *she* wanted to do, and I went off the chain, and before either of us could stop the derailment, we were both furious at each other.)

In the back seat, Lyra folded her arms and stared out the window. Harper looked apprehensively from her sister to me, my knuckles white on the steering wheel as I concentrated on keeping to the left. Harper hated these fights and did her best to avoid them, preferring silent, frustrated tears to shouting. Alia backed me up that day, as we always back each other up in front of the kids, and that night, when Lyra tried to protest her way out of the punishment, Alia flatly refused to consider it. In private, she suggested, gently, that I try to find methods to deal with Lyra that didn't blow up whole afternoons. "I get it," she said. "It's really frustrating." But it was me who seemed, too often, I thought, eager to play bad cop.

Perversely, I was rewarded for my unnecessarily hard line when the following two days were among the nicest we'd had together on the trip. Knowing she simply wasn't allowed to get online seemed to unloose Lyra from worrying about *when* she would next get online, and so she played games, boogie-boarded, took walks with her sister, read books. She was more cheerful than usual, more willing to engage with us, happier with the world, it seemed.

The third morning she woke up and asked, "Can I go to the library and get on the internet?"

New Zealanders often point out that in their country, sheep outnumber people, but it's a misleading joke. After all, in America, chickens outnumber people; that's because there are far too many chickens trapped in a rapacious capitalistic system that reduces them to commodities. (That's also true of the people, in a way, of course.) But New Zealand has very few people and quite a few sheep, and the sheep enjoy much the same lifestyle the people do. New Zealand is dominated, geographically and culturally, by its farms. Even most of the city dwellers we met were just one generation removed from farming. "Most New Zealanders know where the money comes from," Bob Hancox, a professor studying New Zealand health and culture across generations, told me. "Farming. The dairy price is still headline news here every time it goes up or goes down." Contrast that with America, where so many urban and suburban residents have no particular memory of or tie to rural life—indeed, some feel that divide is at the heart of the current political schism.

Take Sarah, the stepmother of one of Harper's best friends in Wellington. Over dinner one night she told us about her farm childhood in Hawke's Bay on the North Island, about riding her own small pony out with the shepherds to move the cows from one field to another. "And when the lambs reach a certain age, you know, you cut off their tails," she said. "So I would pick up the lamb and hold it with its legs up, and they'd tie an elastic at the base of its tail and then—snip!" We looked on, aghast. "It was quite a point of pride to go home just splattered in blood from head to toe." She grinned and forked another bite of salad into her mouth.

Owing to New Zealand's isolation and its preponderance of small farms, the nation's food system is significantly different from America's.

While the country has not been immune to the obesity crisis faced by other Western industrialized nations—especially among its poorer residents—its food culture and agricultural system mean that for middle-class families, "There's no excuse for eating poorly; there's lots of good food," as our neighbor Gary put it. And that food is not just good but also close at hand; New Zealand was eating local before eating local became a goal for conscientious diners.

Whereas our Arlington grocery store utilized the global food market to ensure, for example, that you could buy mangoes in January, in New Zealand, it's so pricey to ship in produce from overseas that stores stock only a select few vegetables and fruits that are not grown domestically. (I saw bananas from Ecuador and outrageously expensive limes from Mexico.) Kiwis pay attention to their country's growing seasons; most anyone can tell you what's ripe right now and how they're likely to use it while cooking. We arrived in New Zealand at the peak of avocado season, when store bins overflowed with perfect ripe avos for less than a dollar each. Cafés in Wellington festooned every sandwich with avocado whether it needed it or not. Just a few months later, rock-hard avocados cost twice as much.

And meat? Forget about it. A New Zealander would no more eat a steak from elsewhere than drink an Australian sauvignon blanc. (Well, you'd drink it in a pinch, but if you must have an Aussie wine, go with a red.) As we traveled the North Island, we were surprised at how few cafés in small towns served veggie burgers or other vegetarian options. While the very good restaurants of Wellington were somewhat more likely to offer nonmeat entrées, New Zealand schoolchildren still got lessons about nutrition from a cartoon character named Iron Brian, who preached the importance of red meat. Where are all the vegetarians? Wasn't New Zealand supposed to be a country full of crunchy environmentalists?

Well, it is and it isn't; whereas Americans often express their foodchain consciousness by avoiding meat entirely, it's easy in New Zealand to express that same spirit while eating meat—indeed, *by* eating meat, much of which is local and humanely raised. (Not all, as a vegan friend pointed out. There's still some factory farming in New Zealand, although the Labour Party, which took control of the government six months after we left, has made noises about banning the practice nationwide.) Harper, our pescatarian kid, didn't become a carnivore while she was living here—luckily the fish and chips were very good—but she did respond with great equanimity to our week on a farm, where we watched the farmer and his shepherd weigh and mark lambs for slaughter, spray-painting a red X on the forehead of each of the shaggy animals that had hit its target weight. I thought she'd be aghast, but seeing the lambs happily grazing and sleeping and straight-up *gamboling* through broad sunny pastures seemed to take the edge off her horror at their eventual fate.

That connection to rural life is intimately tied to Kiwis' love of the outdoors. There's another strand, though, which seems equally important: The thoughtful animism at the center of Māori culture has spread into the consciousness of most New Zealanders, even Pākehā. While we were in New Zealand, the country's parliament passed the Te Awa Tupua Bill, the unique conclusion to Treaty of Waitangi–related litigation that originated in 1870. The bill recognizes the North Island's Whanganui River as a living being, an entity with the same legal rights as a person "from the mountains to the sea." This vision of a river's personhood stems from the longstanding beliefs of the local Māori iwi that the river itself is an ancestor, and it stands in stark opposition to, say, recent American case law determining corporate personhood.

"Look," Gary explained a few days after the bill passed as we drove along the harbor on the way to the Remutaka Forest Park, forty-five minutes outside Wellington. "I'm sure there are rednecks here and there who think, *Oh, that's so stupid,* but for most New Zealanders, anything that cleans the river up and treats it with respect—that's good with us." Gary was driving us to our first attempt at an extended tramp, a night in a bush hut a two-hour hike into the Orongorongo Valley. It was a training-wheels tramp, with Gary as the training wheels. He loaned us sleeping bags, booked the hut, and told us what to stuff into the enormous backpacks he had just sitting around his house. His joining us was a kindness, though (he assured us) not an extravagant one; "I really like tramping," Gary told me when I pressed him to make sure we weren't imposing. "My family's quite useless this weekend," he added, a touch glumly, "so I'm happy to take yours out." Tracey had a business trip and Trinity had a race and Grainger had a big soccer tournament. (It did not escape my notice that Gary went tramping with us rather than attending his children's sporting events.)

It was gray and cool when we set off, and soon a light mist filtered through the trees onto our rain jackets. By the end of the hike, as we prepared to descend from the ridge to the Orongorongo River, we looked out over a landscape clouded in rain sheeting north up the valley and obscuring the trees on the opposite ridge. We cinched up our jackets, flipped up our hoods, and elasticked waterproof tarps over our packs. By the time we squashed through the small bog that fronted our hut, mud sucking at our ankles, summer had fully transformed into late autumn. "Why do we have to *do* this?" Lyra wailed plaintively as a howling wind that seemed to have traveled straight north from Antarctica blew rain into our faces. Somehow a wasp stung me on my fucking foot.

The hut was chilly and utilitarian, although with its flushing toilet and gas burners, it was in fact the peak of luxury as far as Department of Conservation huts went. Gary and Harper took the hatchet out to the woodpile and split logs into kindling. "I'd help," I told Harper, "but my shoes are so wet." She rolled her eyes into little apostrophes like a *Peanuts* character.

After Gary had gotten a fire roaring in the squat woodstove (assisted, of course, by Harper), the hut warmed up, and our candles gave it a cozy glow. I cooked pasta for five, marveling that the bulky bags of noodles and jar of sauce and loaf of bread I'd hauled in would evaporate from my pack on tomorrow's return trip, transformed into energy. We played cards until bedtime, then explained to Lyra that there were no lights to turn on, so if she wanted to read in bed she'd need a flashlight. Gary's donated sleeping bags were so warm that we all shed our clothes in the middle of the night; our socks and hoodies littered the floor next to the platform where we'd burrowed into them.

The next morning was bright and sunny and I woke up determined to accomplish something. I managed to wrestle my sleeping bag into its compression sleeve, then loaded up the girls' packs, sneaking some of their stuff into mine to lessen their loads. They'd whined the previous day, but not nearly as much as you'd expect, given the weather—or maybe with my hood up over my ears, I couldn't hear them. Anyway, I didn't want to take any chances.

Gary recommended a different path to the river, one that avoided the bog, and I led us past another hut and down the graywacke scree to the floodplain. In the sun, the river, which had seemed leaden the day before, sparkled with personality like a living thing. The water glinted a gold-tooth smile as we waded across it, our still-damp shoes held in our hands.

The whining started immediately as we climbed the ridge. Alia and I distracted the girls as best we could with games of Ghost and Twenty Questions, sighing at how on a perfectly beautiful day the absence of distracting rain seemed, perversely, to encourage complaining.

The sun spangled through the trees, dappling the trail and the kids and the stream we crossed over and over again on sturdy wooden bridges. The sun dappled *everything*. The sun was a freakin' dappling machine. The wild profusion of ferns and palms and the still-damp ground made the forest look and feel like a tropical jungle, albeit one where the temperature was a perfect sixty-six degrees and there was no dengue fever. As I walked, I'd notice that the trail became more and more peaceful, but then I'd realize that was because I'd walked far ahead of my complaining kids. Then I would stop, and their voices would get louder and louder until finally they appeared.

Sometimes for a change of pace I would let them get ahead of me. About halfway down the track, I caught up with Gary and Harper, standing silently on a bridge and looking out over the trees. "What do you hear?" asked Gary, who has a lovely natural pedagogical bent.

"Water," Harper said.

"What else?"

"Bugs."

"Those are cicadas. What else?"

Harper squinted. "Nothing," she finally admitted, and Gary laughed. "Yes, nothing. It's perfectly quiet otherwise. But look at the way the sun shines on those trees. Beautiful, right?" They hiked off, leaving me dazzled and determined not to outsource my kids' appreciation of the natural world even to so kind a teacher as Gary.

A kilometer later I held out my hand to Lyra at a spot where the track hugged a hillside, the tangled woods scribbling down the hill below us. She gave me a dubious look but took my hand. "Lyra," I said. "Listen. What do you hear?"

"Water," she said.

"What else?"

"Cicadas."

"Yeah! And what else?"

"I don't know, Dad," she said, starting to squirm. I was reaching the limits of her tolerance for direct interaction.

"Nothing!" I said happily. "Nothing else! It's incredibly peaceful and quiet."

"Yeah, except for you," she pointed out, and walked away.

In our final weeks in New Zealand, we prepared for a true test of our outdoors-family-ship: a two-day, two-night tramp on a Great Walk, the Abel Tasman Coast Track on the South Island. As in Yellowstone, we wouldn't exactly be risking life and limb. We were sleeping, again, in DOC huts and had been well supplied by Gary with warm sleeping bags and a gas cooker. We wouldn't even be hauling around gigantic packs stuffed with those sleeping bags; I'd hired a tour company to pick up our packs each morning and deliver them by boat to our next location each afternoon.

Unlike in Yellowstone, in Abel Tasman Park I did not need to worry about bears. There are no bears in New Zealand; in fact, the largest predator of any kind in New Zealand is the possum. (It eats a lot of birds and garbage but does not eat trampers.) New Zealand is also free of poisonous snakes, and the last recorded fatal spider bite was in 1901. But what New Zealand, particularly the South Island, does have is the tiny pest that became the bane of our existence in our time here: the goddamn sandfly (*Goddammus sandflyus*).

Some versions of Māori legend tell a story of the demigod Tū Te Rakiwhānoa, who carved the deep valleys of the South Island's Fiordland. The land was so lovely, the story goes, that the people stood staring in wonder and as a result got no work done. Angered, the goddess of the underworld, Hine-nui-te-pō, created the sandfly to bite them and get them moving. I could believe that Hine-nui-te-pō truly was the goddess of the underworld: sandflies come straight from hell.

Here are the stages of a sandfly bite:

Day one: Stand still near a river or beach for any amount of time greater than four seconds. Feel a sharp pain in your ankle or calf or, god, the knuckle of your thumb. A tiny midge is biting you. Crap! Swat it away, preferably while doing a little dance! For the rest of the day the bite, as well as the other five bites you got, will itch like a mosquito bite.

Day two: Your bites itch a little more than mosquito bites. But whatever, no problem, you've had insect bites before, you can handle it.

Night two: *Holy shit, does that itch,* you think as you don't sleep.

Day three: Your bites are now angry red welts. They itch like hell.

Days four through seven: Still itchy, now angrier and redder, reminiscent of that zit you got on your nose just before homecoming.

Days eight through fourteen: They itch a bit less but still look terrible.

Day fifteen: More sandflies bite you.

On our various outdoor treks in New Zealand, we wore heavy-duty insect repellent with Deet. I pulled my socks to my knees, so I looked like an old-timey base-ball man. It didn't matter; the sandflies always found us. If at any point you read a description of wondrous natural beauty during our Abel Tasman journey, assume that a sandfly was biting me while I was viewing it.

Journal of the Smith-Kois Expedition
down the ABEL TASMAN COAST
of NEW ZEALAND
from the beach at AWAROA
to the beach at ANCHORAGE
(and points in between)

Being a chronicle of Birds, Children, Sand-Flys,
and Snacks

DAY 1. 30th March, the Year of Our Lord Two Thousand and Seventeen.
Weather fair and mild.

We party of four disembarked upon the beach at Awaroa, and members of the crew immediately called for Snacks. Espying an attractive island separated from the sandy shore by but a small channel of shallow water, we removed our shoes and waded to the island for luncheon. (PBJ, crackers, et cetera.) It was not to our credit as Explorers that we were quite surprised by the tides continuing on their clockwork course! "The tides!" we shouted, shaking our fists at Heaven, as but a quarter-hour later, the channel between us and shore had deepened significantly, such that we all became quite wet upon the return. Indeed we only just rescued the shoe of crew member L. as it began to float away. My spirits being undampened, however, I laughed at this inauspicious beginning to the journey. Both young crew members had to change clothes, and I myself was left with wet Underpants.

The hike to Bark Bay, where we would spend our first night, took four hours through dense forest, a mishmash of long pines, fat palms, and immense ferns, mostly absent the Mosquitoes of tropical climes but rich with avian life. L., whose mood had improved, was unexpectedly the first to recognize one of the multitudes of birds calling all round us like R2-D2s from the trees. She stopped in the middle of the track, pointed up, and said casually, "Oh, it's a fantail." We commended L. on her identification and admired the bird flitting from branch to branch, ruffling his brown-and-white tail feathers with the élan of a courtesan. What a spritely fellow he was! We soon noticed more fantails assembled around us, chirping their approval, each occasion we sat for Snacks. As fantails whickered overhead, we dined, at divers times, on Dried Fruit and Dried Beef, on Trail Mix, on Chocolate Chip

Cookies, on Apples, on Apricots, on Granola Bars, on Lolli-pops, and on Pineapple Lumps, a local delicacy that tastes like stale Starbursts coated in bad chocolate.

Snacks were important for the morale of our little party. I found, in fact, that it was not only the greenest of the crew members who became grumpy the farther we traveled from the previous Snack. Co-Captain A. herself looked forward to the next Snack with a passion one might call indecorous. (As it's important for the leader of an expedition to partake of the pastimes of his crew, I, too, ate Snacks.) After we cleaned up our wrappers and shouldered our packs, I enjoyed looking back to see the fantails descend upon the clearings where we had just sat, pecking stray crumbs from the ground.

The trail traversed a series of picturesque bays — Tonga Bay; Frenchman Bay; Sandfly Bay, which the crew refused to visit — and so along our course we often found ourselves climbing one valley's wall only to descend into the next. Though the temperature remained pleasant, the tramping was thirsty work, especially when we emerged from dark forest to bright ridgetops where we wended our way through scrub and sun. Within several hours we'd drained most of our four water flasks, despite A. making frequent reminders to the crew to *Sip! Don't glug!*

On the final descent into Bark Bay, the young crew members speculated, in their delirium, on the perfect vacation, the alternative they'd each choose over tramping four hours in the middle of nowhere. L. declared her ideal trip a Disney Cruise "where I don't have to do anything." H. concurred, though she suggested that in her ideal world, the Disney Cruise would be "even better, like each kid has her own room, and there's enough waterslides for everyone." A. and I smiled tolerantly, for what was the harm of such fancy, when the harsh wilderness might be the only life they'd ever know?

All in all the day was a success; from the young crew members we heard less Actual Whining than we did Ironic Whining, statements delivered in hopes of getting a rise out of the captains without actually being in earnest. ("Are we there yet?" seven consecutive times, for example.) When we arrived at the Bark Bay hut, we picked out four mattresses lined up in the loft; L. crawled onto one and slept for an hour, after which she and H. raced each other on the beach in the lovely blue-purple gloaming. I joined them for a jolly dash, at the end of which I had earned both the glory of crushing children in a footrace and a dozen sandfly bites.

Young H. took great pleasure in the preparation of the evening ramen—setting up the gas burner, lighting the match, fetching the water, &c. A life of exploration seems most appealing to her, if for no other reason than the pleni-tude of new tasks she can master and details to which she can attend. (Whence this helpful spirit? Perhaps her time spent at age four with the high priestess of the Montessori faith had more effect than I knew.) L., meanwhile, lay on a bench and read her Kindle. After dinner I sat with these two youngest crew members and said: "We hiked four hours and you guys did *great*. You were fun, and cooperative, and you barely whined at all. It was so fun to be with you both. I'm really proud of you." Perhaps not the iron fist of discipline with which some captains rule their subordinates, but I won't apol-ogize for hugging my crew!

D.K.

DAY 2. 31st March
Weather fair and warm.

Due to a misjudgment of the tides ("D—ed tides!"), we tramped two hours longer than I'd hoped today, for a total of five and a half hours. As Captain, I might have been expected to be better acquainted with the tide tables, a lapse I blame entirely on the lack of Cellular Data. Cookie supplies ran out by midafternoon. Also, late in the trek, legs weary, shoulders heavy, sandfly bites itching, I heard a bird chirp for like the fifty-fifth time and shouted, "Shut up, bird!" I relate this story with great shame. Though by and large the crew tramped bravely, I did hear mutinous whispers that this day "sucked big-time."

D.K.

DAY 3. 1st April
Weather cool and cloudy.

Triumph! The water taxi brought us back to civilization, where we ate Brunch.

It would be a stretch to say that everyone *liked* our trip along the Abel Tasman Coast Track. Lyra enjoyed that for hours, we weren't asking her to do things, although she didn't like that she had to walk really far. Harper enjoyed unpacking the sleeping bags and lighting the gas burner and cooking the dehydrated meals and packing the sleeping bags back up, but even her general enthusiasm was beaten down by hours of tramping each day. Alia and I found the trip beautiful and fulfilling and very difficult, including the weeks after, when everyone itched from scabies acquired from the mattresses in the huts. (Good news: New Zealand universal health care meant scabies cream was really cheap!) "I would do a tramp of one or even two hours," said Lyra as she tucked into a giant burger at brunch, "because after this, that would be, like, pffffft. It would maybe even be fun." She licked her fingers. "I'm absolutely never doing a five-hour hike again, though."

As we hiked we sang songs and told bad jokes and played as many games as we could think of. Lyra liked Ghost; Harper wanted to play Ghost, too, but she did not yet know how to spell so many words, which made it tough for her to compete. For a while Harper and I played imaginary gin, in which you just pretend you have a hand of cards and pretend to draw and discard and eventually Harper says, "Gin!" But for quite a while on the tramp, we hiked in silence broken only by occasional exhausted complaints or requests for snacks. In that tired silence we all found, perhaps, just a bit of meditative peace.

Because we were hiking on school days, most of the trampers we saw were tourists, Belgians, Germans, or Brits, mostly in pairs, young and old. But we did see the occasional Kiwi family, and on our trip into the Orongorongo, we'd seen tramping kids galore, plus a dozen adult hikers making their way down the trail with infants strapped to their fronts or toddlers bouncing along on their backs. One poor bastard had one of each, both of them squealing and waving their arms about; he looked like a stormtrooper being brought down by rowdy Ewoks. Seeing all these tramping tots had reinforced my sense that New Zealand kids start hiking early and are trained by repetition to enjoy the experience so that by the time a Kiwi kid is Lyra's age, she's learned to appreciate the outdoors *without whining*.

But in the run-up to Abel Tasman, I'd started to rethink that notion. At Alia's feminist book club several moms had asked her if she was bringing friends along for the girls. "I find that's the best way to keep them from driving me crazy through the tramp," one said. Another suggested developing a nature scavenger hunt to occupy children as they clomped through the woods, with strategically deployed lollies to distract them. And when we told friends that we were putting our giant packs on boats rather than hauling them around, no one shamed us. "We've done that!" said our friend Miranda. "No point giving kids something *else* to complain about."

So Kiwi kids *do* complain while tramping? They're not magical creatures who spend their childhoods appreciating nature? "Trinity's always enjoyed it," Tracey said of her daughter. "But Grainger's always complained, every step of the way."

"But you just make him do it anyway?" I asked—the kind of question that, even as the words are exiting your mouth, you're anticipating the other person's look of dismay.

Tracey looked dismayed. "Of course!"

Even adults confessed that their love affair with the outdoors wasn't completely uncomplicated. Miranda told us that her husband gamely put up with her passion for tramping even though his allergies left him miserable every second they spent in the bush. And then I read the Wellington writer Ashleigh Young's essay "On Any Walk," which perfectly describes the exasperation I often battled while hiking, but to which I thought Kiwis were immune:

> On any walk into dense bush, at some point we ask one another, "Why are we doing this?" We could be at home, we say, where there is hot water and a flushing toilet. The question ripples up and down the chain of walkers, and one or two people raise the serious possibility of turning back right now. Their voices are bright with certainty, seeming almost to hold apart the foliage we are struggling through, making our way easier for a moment...
>
> No one is enjoying the walk. Has anyone ever enjoyed the walk? Perhaps none of us ever enjoyed it, even early on when our legs were fresh. Maybe even back then we all secretly wished it were over. Even as we agree that the pieces of sky through the trees are very blue, as we admire the persistence of the tiny streams, the marvel of the koura scrambling through them, a thought hums between us: If we had turned back before, we would be home now.

Suddenly I got it. The difference between American families and Kiwi families wasn't that Kiwi families were somehow magically more attuned to nature than American ones. It was that Kiwi parents felt strongly enough about nature to endure everything that sucks about hiking and everything that sucks even worse about making kids do something they find boring. About what did I feel strongly enough to overcome my disinterest in making my kids do stuff they complained about, and not once but over and over, enough times to make it a habit?

I had taken my kids to classical music performances a couple of times, but not *repeatedly*. I had required them to sit through dinners with adults enough that they basically tolerated the experience of eating politely and not interrupting too often. (Well, we frequently let Lyra read at the table.) God, I didn't ask them to clean their rooms as often as Tracey and Gary made their kids go tramping out in the woods.

So it was great that our kids survived tramping two days through Abel Tasman with us. But if we really wanted to foster a lifetime in the natural world, we needed to do it again and again and again, and each time we'd need to put up with the complaining. That is to say, Lyra and Harper weren't the only ones who needed to learn to endure something unpleasant—Alia and I did too.

THE GOODBYE PARTY

When Olly and Sarah arrived, the first thing they did was head into the kitchen. I saw Olly's daughter Grace, who was in school with Harper, climb the steps to the back patio, pick her way through the adults, and cut through Fiona's yard to the tramp. I walked down to find Olly covering a plate with foil and Sarah pouring herself a glass of wine. "Made ourselves at home," Olly said with a grin. He was blond and tan, intimidatingly well built but with an affable, self-deprecating personality that made him easy to be with.

"No problem," I said. "What you got there?"

"Ribs," he said, pulling up a corner of the foil to reveal thick meaty bones crusted red and brown. "You should've seen what we brought *last* night, though."

"Last night?"

He plucked a red Solo cup from the stack by the sink, our un-Kiwi, un-green concession to our unwillingness to do dishes at this late date. "These take me back," he said, and he poured himself a cup of pinot noir. "Yeah, five o'clock last night, we were at your door ready for the party."

Sarah had her phone out and was scrolling through photos. "We roasted a beautiful leg of lamb," she said, showing me a snapshot that looked like it belonged in *Martha Stewart Living*.

"Very Kiwi," Olly agreed. "We got to the gate and we're like, 'Uhh, no one's at home.' Then I looked at my diary and—yip, they said Sunday."

"We ate the whole leg," Sarah said. "It was so good."

It's a testament to how comfortable we'd gotten with New Zealand generosity that I wasn't surprised to hear Olly and Sarah had made a leg of lamb *and then* a rack of ribs for our going-away party. They were, after all, the couple who had just shown up at our back door one sunny after-noon, hair still wet, holding three beautiful live paua—giant, delicious abalone—that Olly had prised off an undersea rock himself. (All I'd had to do was remove the pauas' digestive tracts, pound them with a frying pan to tenderize them, slice them paper-thin, marinate them for hours, and sear them.) Pretty much everyone had brought something lovely this evening: lamb sliders from Anna and Andy, shrimp cakes from Fiona and Regan, chocolate mousse from Eddie and Frankie, cardamom burfi from Jeet and Kate, wine from everyone. Alia had bought out the New World supermarket's good cheese and opened our final boxes of what we'd discovered to be the best crackers in the world, 180 Degrees Oat Crackers. (This message was not sponsored, but if a representative from 180 Degrees is reading this, I will take a crate.)

In the backyard, the friends we'd made all over Wellington drank in the final hour of sun beaming over the Tawatawa Reserve. Autumn was upon us here in early April, and as the sun sank below the ridgeline the warm air cooled quickly; Jeet and Eddie had never met before but worked together to build a fire in Bronwyn's backyard fireplace. It was the last nice day before the weather would turn definitively toward winter rainstorms and fog.

Harper came back from the tramp sniffling, with a bleeding elbow; Otto's brother was playing football with Grace's brother, she reported, and the ball hit her and she tripped over Ruba and fell down and cut her-self on the trampoline, and Eve had brought her back and could she have a *plaster,* please? "I didn't even know Otto was here," I said.

"The kids know the kids are here," she replied, "and the grown-ups know the grown-ups are here."

Two dozen sausages, smoking and spitting, lined up on the grill like regiments on a battlefield map. Anna and Kirsty drank wine with me as I cooked; whenever anyone asked if I needed help, I replied, "I've been training three months for this." All the kids reappeared as if summoned by sorcery and laid waste to the food; Fiona's son slipped through the back fence to bring more forks after we somehow ran out.

Now it was night. Richard fed log after log into the fire, which blazed brightly enough that the faces around the table glowed orange.

"Where are you going next?" our friends kept asking us, and Tracey kept interrupting to say, "It doesn't matter, it won't be as good as here." At eight o'clock, a band of guerrilla children crept through the shadows alongside the fence; at my call, Harper detached herself from the group and moved into the firelight.

"Where were you guys?" I asked as she climbed into my lap.

"We were at the tramp until the lady got mad at us," she replied.

Down the table, Fiona's eyes widened. "Oh no," she said. "Is it after seven? What did she say?"

"She just said that her daughter had an exam tomorrow so could we please be quieter," Harper reported. "That was the *first* time she came out. The *second* time she came out"—here Fiona's head sank into her arms—"she said we all definitely had to go because it was *too late*."

"Regan," Fiona said, head still covered, "can you please check to make sure no more kids are on the tramp?"

"The *third* time—"

"Who is this woman," Anna, who lived in a different neighborhood, asked, "who loves to yell at children?"

"She's my friend," Fiona replied glumly.

"She does not like it when kids have fun."

"She's overreacting," Tracey declared. "It's hardly late at all."

"How loud were you?" Alia asked Harper.

"We were *very loud*," Harper said happily.

"You can blame it on me," I said. *"Those fucking Americans."*

"Ah, that's a good idea." Fiona nodded. "I'll do that."

Perhaps all goodbye parties feel as though they encapsulate your entire experience in that place. Perhaps because you're already thinking about this part of your life as a segment, a discrete set of months or years, at the goodbye party you're primed to view the swirl of activity retrospectively, not only as a party but as the end to your narrative. But I saw, at the party, all the threads that had run through our time in New Zealand tangling together. The beautiful setting making the everyday feel special. The kids roaming the neighborhood, self-organized into packs of different ages, finding fun inside the house and out. (Even Lyra, who had at times withdrawn during get-togethers, gladly joined the crowd this evening.) The free-flowing social atmosphere, with adults meeting total strangers and finding things in common. One last bit of trampoline drama—it was all there.

Perhaps I felt that way because the party itself was a kind of product of the work of socializing we'd set out to do when we arrived in New Zealand. At one point Frankie came into the kitchen as I was pouring a drink and said, "You met a *lot* of people while you were here!" She was a poet, and while she seemed to enjoy social occasions, she was often a bit quiet in large groups—a mild introvert, perhaps, coping in a milieu in which mild extroversion is the norm. In her observation I heard a mix of wonder and skepticism; we *had* met a lot of people, and wasn't it kind of too many people?

"I mean, it was our job," I said. She laughed. "Everyone's great!" I hastened to add. "It wasn't, like, a hard job."

This was mostly true, although it was difficult at times. Alia and I treasure our friends but can find it wearing to *make* friends; for every coffee date where the quality of the conversation threw off sparks, there was a get-together where the kids just didn't play well together and the adults didn't have that much to say. And then there was the collateral damage of hurt feelings that came from being aggressive socializers— the last-minute cancellations, the families who seemed great on first meeting but who never reciprocated invitations.

Harper was a quick and easy friend-maker; by her third week of school, unfamiliar parents would greet her in town with a "Hi, Harper!" and she'd have to explain: "Oh, that's Bailey's mum," or whoever. Conversely, Lyra had no desire to invite over new acquaintances from school—indeed, even when an American family brought over their daughter, a girl exactly her age with all the same interests as her, Lyra had nothing to say—and this drove us to distraction. In some respects these first few months of our trip were a lesson in the futility of trying to make a kid become someone other than who she is. Lyra was the precise age at which inviting over someone whom she hasn't already known for a decade is more daunting than scaling Everest. She simply wasn't going to do it, and when I stopped bugging her about it all the time, we both got markedly more happy.

By nine thirty that night, most of the parents of small kids had left. Lyra had already crashed on her bed, fully dressed. Harper made her way around the remaining parents, collecting kisses on the cheek from adults who all seemed to have a story about going to a football game with her or seeing her scootering with friends down the Parade. Harper was really very good at her job.

After she picked her way down the dark stairs to go to bed, I produced the final goodbye present we'd received: a fat, perfectly rolled joint that had been pressed into my palm on a guest's way out. It was the perfect gift for a goodbye party, Tracey observed, both thoughtful and unpackable, so I'd have to use it right away. Richard shoved two more logs into the small inferno he'd maintained in the fireplace; the fire, the wine I'd drunk, the companionship all conspired to give the night a warmth that belied the autumn chill. I lit the joint and passed it around to our friends, some of whom took a puff, some of whom politely passed it on. Richard and Gary started reminiscing about a mountain-biking trip they'd taken years before. I leaned my chair back and looked up. Sparks twirled upward from the chimney, orange fireflies dancing against the upside-down stars of the southern sky.

Later that week Lyra said goodbye to her class; countering all my worries about Lyra not making friends, one girl gave her a little stuffed felt basket of French fries that she'd spent hours sewing and another chased her down to give her a final farewell hug. As she walked out of her classroom, she raised her arms like Nixon and shouted, *"The end!"* Harper's last day of school, needless to say, was a celebration of all things Harper; she basked in the attention, forgetting for an hour to be sad about our departure. Alia met Kirsty and Tracey and other Wellington ladies for jolly final teas. I shipped a whole suitcase of crap it turned out we didn't need back to the United States. I sold the Volvo to the only person I met in New Zealand who loved Donald Trump, a South African who'd just moved to town, for less than half what I'd paid for it, the final triumph of the Steves. We boarded the plane and headed to the next spot on the map.

Delft

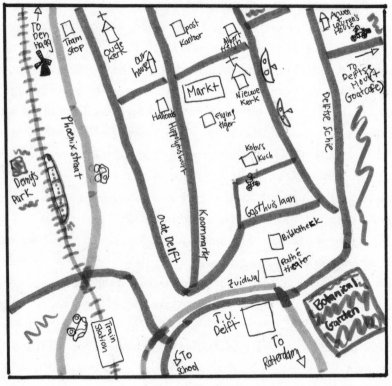

THE NETHERLANDS

April – July

PHANTOM DUCKS

In just a few days visiting Amsterdam, we'd been nearly run over about a thousand times by bicycles. Cyclists poured like water through every opening in the city's fabric, filling alleyways, weaving down sidewalks, overflowing the bike lanes. Addled by jet lag, we kept stepping into those cycle lanes and then, at the sound of sternly dinging bells, leaping out of them.

Now—after eyeing our four remaining gigantic suitcases, looking at the train schedule, and deciding to call an Uber—we were ensconced in Delft, the Dutch city we'd chosen to live in. We had a week to kill before the girls' school would start, so we explored the city. Step one: Get some bikes and menace some pedestrians ourselves. My goal was for that Uber ride from Amsterdam to Delft to be our final automobile trip for three months. Before we set out into the narrow streets of the old city center to find a bike shop, I looked myself in the face in the bathroom mirror and said, "You will *not* wreck a bike while test-riding it, nor will you overpay for these bikes by thousands of dollars."

Mission accomplished! By midafternoon we were the proud owners of two used adult bikes and two new-but-cheap kid bikes. In the Dutch style, they weren't mountain or racing bikes but city cruisers, meant to be ridden perfectly upright, your back straight as a marching soldier's. The tech at Halfords cycle shop had attached a brightly colored milk crate to the back of each bike so we could carry baguettes or whatever. We also had an agreement from the manager to buy back the bikes upon our departure in July. (I'd have been satisfied with a handshake, but he had drafted a three-sentence contract we both signed in duplicate.) We wheeled the bikes out into the brisk sunshine and stood on Wijnhaven along the dark green canal.

"Where are our helmets?" Harper asked.

"We didn't buy any," I replied. Everywhere we could see, cheerful Dutchmen and Dutchwomen whizzed around confidently, their blond heads exposed to the soft northern sun. "In the Netherlands, only tourists wear helmets."

"What?" Lyra asked. "What if we get in a crash?"

"We won't!" I said cheerfully. "Okay, now let's line up—oop!" For a Dutchman in a sleek blue suit riding a sleek blue bike had just swerved around me from the south. Another rider, approaching from the north, rang her bell to remind me that I was blocking traffic. "Everyone get on—yow!" Two more bikes veered around us; small traffic jams were developing on either side of our uncertain little group. "Okay!" I said. "Let's maybe walk our bikes to a less busy street." We wheeled our way across a bridge into the Markt square, where the primary obstacle was tour groups of Italians and Americans gathered around their guides.

Alia took out her phone, opened Google Maps, and pointed to a lake just east of the city. "I thought we could ride out here and see what we see," she said.

"Can we get a snack?" Harper asked.

"I am sure we will get a snack," I replied.

And so we set off riding, with varying levels of feigned confidence, down the brick streets of Delft. Three large canals traverse the old city from top to bottom, and we followed the westernmost one, the seven hundred-year-old Oude Delft, north past the Oude Kerk, its steeple leaning at a pitch greater than that of Pisa's tower. To our right was a wall of narrow three- and four-story buildings, each with a business on the ground floor and apartments above. I'd read that buildings in Holland were constructed so narrowly because in the Dutch Golden Age, property taxes were based on the width of one's frontage or the size of one's windows. I'd read so much about Dutch houses! Wasn't there something about gables? Dutch gables? I made a mental note to look that up. To our left was the canal, its still water festooned with lily pads and floating trash. There was no protective guardrail or fence, not even a curb, just a sharp cliff drop from the street to the water. I found the unbroken path from street to canal unnerving, as if, though I knew better than to ride my bike into the water, the ease of envisioning what such a ride would look like—how I would launch myself, Thelma-and-Louise-style, off the road, and land with a spectacular splash—could somehow incite me to do it. Alia led the way, with the girls in the middle and me covering our rear. "Try to stay to the right," I called ahead as faster bikes, laden with packages or children, passed us on our left.

Lyra, who had less bike-riding experience than the rest of us and who had previously stated that she found paying attention to her surroundings pointless, tended to weave a bit. When a hatchback zipped past us, mere inches from our bikes, she shouted in alarm. "That car almost hit me!" she protested. Then another car drove past, and she cried, "That one too!"

We turned east, onto a canal-less street, the uneven bricks making our wheels jostle and jump. Every few turns of the pedals, I'd ride over one single brick painted an elegant Delftware blue-and-white. This street was exactly two cars wide. A car drove toward us and eased by a wobbly Lyra. As we crossed the next canal on a high stone bridge, four boys zoomed past, each with a girlfriend perched sidesaddle atop his back wheel; last in the group, like a punch line, was a girl pedaling hard with a boyfriend sitting pertly atop hers.

We rode a white drawbridge over the Delftse Schie, the river that separates the old city from the eastern suburbs, then pedaled down tree-lined streets past apartments and houses whose design, after the gables (?) of the old city, was strikingly modern. After one misadventure crossing a busy street—Lyra was almost run down by a Vespa buzzing along the bike lane and was so angry she didn't notice an approaching car—we rode onto a canal-side path that bisected a marshy plain well stocked with waterfowl and clouds of gnats. To our south, tall pines marked the Delftse Hout, the small lake to which we were headed.

As we rode, Lyra and I conducted what I thought was a lighthearted conversation about the trials and tribulations of city riding. Too late I realized it was not lighthearted at all, and Lyra was very upset, her emotion compounded by how I'd been brushing it off. (This happened a lot, as my instinct to deflect conflict with humor plays poorly in the twelve-year-old-girl demographic.) It all came to a head with our bikes stopped on a footbridge, Harper and Alia well ahead of us. "I don't *want* to ride a bike in the street with cars driving past me!" she shouted.

"Lyra—"

"Don't say what you're going to say!" she cried, her eyes narrowing. "Don't tell me there's nothing to be scared of! I'm scared!"

"I wasn't going to say that," I lied.

"I don't feel safe riding in the street with cars everywhere," she said firmly. "I *don't. Feel. Safe.*" This construction seemed designed specifically to strike the conscientious modern parent with deep anxiety. *Wasn't making sure I felt safe,* I imagined her telling her therapist ten years from now, *really his only job, when you think about it?*

"It just takes practice to get comfortable," I said lamely.

Lyra looked me square in the eye. "Well, I'm not going to practice," she said. "I'm not going to do it. You can't make me do it." Then she rode ahead.

Doe maar gewoon—dan doe je al gek genoeg. Ask a Dutchman what makes him Dutch, and I promise you he'll quote this aphorism, which might as well appear on the national flag. It translates to "Act normal—that's strange enough." Sometimes it's shortened to the simple command *doe normaal.* Do normal!

Though the Dutch are not, truly, a monolith, a lot of Dutch regard their culture monolithically and talk about it that way. And the quality that defines Dutch people to Dutch people—at least, to the Dutch people who define themselves as Dutch people—is normalcy. How do you *doe normaal?* Be polite. Be on time. Be logical. Follow the rules, both written and unwritten. Accept that your needs come second to the needs of the community as a whole and compromise accordingly. Dutch society, it seemed to me as I read about it and talked to Dutch friends, was predicated on the notion of erasing distinctions between people. If everyone behaves the same, everyone is the same. Dutch self-effacement supposedly eliminates extravagant displays of wealth; it is considered improper to strive too obviously or demand too much. The famous Dutch tolerance is meant to eradicate discrimination; it is considered closed-minded to judge another based on race, religion, or sexuality.

I found it hard to believe that this could all be true. Surely the rich of the Netherlands are just as weird as rich people everywhere else, and surely the non-rich yearn to be rich. Surely Dutch "tolerance" is a canard, and minorities have it as bad there as everywhere else.

But even as I suspected that the Dutch were mostly paying lip service to these notions, I yearned to see how our family would fare in a place that shunned extravagance. Think how much better America would be if we gave even lip service to enforced equality! Americans' default assumption is that sharp societal inequalities are inescapable. Indeed, we middle- and upper-class parents exacerbate them, even as we feel oppressed by them, by insisting that our families secure every advantage in school, in life, in property. In Arlington, our street sees two to three teardowns a year— perfectly nice ranches, split-levels, or Colonials replaced by identically architecturally bland megahouses. These nine-bedrooms metastasize to the legally acceptable limits of the lot, leaving narrow landscaper-tended strips of lawn on all four sides. Just before we left town, builders put the finishing touches on a six-thousand-square-foot monster directly behind us that blocked the sunlight from our backyard. Though there was already a fence between our lot and theirs, the new residents—a young couple and their infant—built a second, taller fence next to it. The idea of living someplace where people would disapprove of such a display seemed quite appealing.

In the Netherlands, I read, families lived in modest-size houses and drove modest-priced cars (or rode bikes that are lovingly kept up for years), and none of them would ever be seen wearing, say, a fancy watch. A few weeks before we left the States, a coworker of Alia's who was married to a Dutchman told us it was that enforced medianness that had brought her husband to the United States. "It drove him crazy," she said. "He felt like no one could ever excel."

But the same cultural quirk that so annoyed that one Dutchman seemed like it could be our respite from a culture of relentless, exhausting excelling. I excelled at work and then I went home to my excellent house and family and saw other people building *more* excellent houses all around us, their Kumon-tutored and travel-baseballing offspring resetting the pace for all the other excellent kids. I remember a dinner with a mom we knew, an incredibly nice and engaged woman, who was upset to be told that her child was doing just as well as his classmates. "But I don't want him to be *average*," she said with despair.

In the Netherlands I hoped to find the sweet spot between "I don't want him to be *average*" and New Zealand's "You're a dog." Surely there must be one! A country devoted to rigorously enforced equality that also prides itself on its cultural and national accomplishments seemed just the place to find it. The Netherlands, Henry Henrysson's dream of a society, had, after all, the happiest children among twenty-one developed countries, according to a 2013 UNICEF analysis. Dutch children scored in the top ten of all six evaluative categories, from health and safety to education to their own evaluation of their happiness. (The United States scored twentieth out of twenty-one countries. We beat England!)

Perhaps Dutch kids were happy because everything was so *gezellig*. You've read all those articles on the internet about *hygge*, the Danish quality of coziness that has been bandied about both aspirationally and reproachfully? In books like *The Little Book of Hygge* and *How to Hygge*, authors hold up this homey, convivial comfort—woolen socks and gløgg with your family on a cold winter's night—as an impossible goal that type-A Americans might achieve if only they could *put down their phones*. Well, *gezellig* is, more or less, *hygge*, Dutch style.

I'd joined a Facebook group of Delft parents, and in the week before our arrival there'd been much discussion of two moms in Holland who had just written a book about Dutch parenting. Just down the street from Halfords was a bookstore featuring a tidy window display of *The Happiest Kids in the World*. And when we told moms and dads we met about why we'd landed in their town, explained the project and the book, they inevitably said: "Oh, there is a book on this subject! Have you read it?"

At this point, the parent would gesture toward her children and say, "These are the happiest kids in the world, you know."

I walked into Boekhandel Huyser, grabbed a copy off that display, and paid my nineteen euros—a small price for a shortcut to happiness. I studied the photos of the authors' families in the book's front material; they looked cheerful and approachable. For the next three months, I resolved, whatever Michele Hutchison and Rina Mae Acosta said to do, that's what we'd do.

Deep in the woods of the Delftse Hout, we pulled our bikes up to a rack under a towering oak tree and secured them with our brand-new locks. Lyra had reached the point in the afternoon in which her resentment at all we were forcing her to do led her to semi-intentionally do everything wrong. She made a big show of trying to shove her bike into a narrow space between two others, theatrically sighed when it didn't fit, struggled to push down the kickstand, then watched stone-faced as her bike toppled over into the soft grass and almost slid into a river. I recognized the tactic from my own passive-aggressive behavior when frustrated; she was parking her bike the way I navigated through automated customer-service prompts.

A small bar and café perched on the edge of the river. The air was still but for dragonflies zipping about like drones. One beer, one Diet Coke, two Fantas. The beer was the cheapest beverage—welcome to Europe.

Lyra's spirits improved after she chugged her Fanta. We played a few hands of cards and then I rented a boat—a pedal boat, of course—into which we all clambered, pushing off from the restaurant's pier. The sun was hours away from setting, but still, in April, quite low on the horizon, flickering through the spring-green trees onto the smooth surface of the river. We pedaled, our feet churning in a slow-motion version of the biking we'd just been doing. I recalled that when the girls were very young, they liked to sit face to face in the bathtub, soles of their feet pressed together, pedaling and chanting, "Bi-cy-cle, bi-cy-cle."

Churning up the river, we saw, tucked under a low branch, a nest made of a jumble of sticks, feathers, and chip bags. In it were a pair of waterfowl of a type we'd never seen before but that we would notice everywhere in Delft: fat little birds, ducklike, black as coal but for a white mask and bill that appeared stuck to each bird's head with Krazy Glue. One darted back and forth across the river, collecting twigs and then attaching them busily to the nest. The other protected the nest. "She's sitting on eggs!" Lyra announced.

"Let me see!" Harper demanded.

"Or it could be that *he's* sitting on eggs," Lyra amended. "Maybe they're a same-sex duck couple!" I refrained from asking where, then, the eggs had come from—after all, who knew? This was the Netherlands! Maybe they'd hired a surrogate! The girls oohed and aahed over the clutch of speckled eggs as the birds eyed us warily.

"What are those birds?" Harper asked. "Why do they have that mask?"

"I don't know," I began, then I had a great idea. I explained that they reminded me of the black-robed, white-masked character No-Face from Hayao Miyazaki's animated film *Spirited Away*. "So we can invent a new name for them, and then we can popularize that name everywhere, and eventually whatever stupid name they actually have* can be replaced by the name we invented: *no-face ducks!*"

"They look like the Phantom of the Opera," Alia replied. "They're phantom ducks."

"Ooh, phantom ducks!" Harper said.

"Phantom ducks!" Lyra cried.

"No offense, Daddy," said Harper, using a phrase she often employs just before saying something offensive, "but your name is bad and Mommy's is good."

"They have faces," Lyra pointed out.

Alia beamed; I fumed in a manner that was intended to appear jokey

---

*The actual name for this bird is the Eurasian coot, which, as expected, is stupid.

but was 10 percent real. How did I raise a couple of Philistines? *Spirited Away* is a way better touchstone than *The Phantom of the Opera*!

Yet I was happy to be having a fake argument as opposed to all the real arguments we'd had over the past few weeks with Lyra, who was officially sick of this trip. In fact, both of our kids were at a low point; where we saw the excitement of a new home, they saw only another place that wasn't their *real* home. While we were in New Zealand, I realized, they'd been able to tell themselves a story that, despite everything, maybe *that* was the trip. But now it was over, and they had had to leave the friends they'd made there, and instead of going home they were going to . . . *another* country, one where people didn't speak English with a funny accent but instead spoke a whole nother language. And we weren't even halfway done!

Harper's homesickness was, I think, as acute as Lyra's, but her personality helped her push past it more often. (When it hit her, though, it hit her hard, with full-on crying jags and wails of *I miss my friends.*) Lyra's homesickness manifested itself in a constant low simmer of rage that a couple of times per day boiled over, usually when we asked her to do anything with us. "Lyra, can you put down your book and come to see this church?" we'd ask, and but for a heavy, John Hughes–movie sigh, she'd ignore us. When we asked a second time, she'd snap.

My mom visited us early in our stay in the Netherlands, observed Lyra's reluctance to join in, and told me about taking me to Colonial Williamsburg when I was Lyra's age and how ungrateful I'd been. "So you can understand why Lyra's acting like this," she said.

"Well, Colonial Williamsburg was boring," I said defensively.

"Daniel," she said.

In our view, we hardly asked Lyra to do anything; we let her read or watch YouTube videos or draw or write nearly the entire day, and yet when we asked her to do *one thing,* she blew up. In her view, every moment of her life was her acceding to an absurd demand we'd made — going on this stupid trip. And now we were going to pile looking at some old *church* on top of that? It was too much.

So I was grateful to have peace for a moment, or actually a fake argument, which I found even more satisfying than peace. A fake argument suggested that our real arguments, painful and awful though they were, could make the difficult but not impossible shift into the realm of play.

"But this name is gonna be popularized the *world over*," I pleaded. "Do you really want these ducks to be named for a guy who lives in the sewer and can't even finish a mask?"

"Phantom duck is *perfect*," Lyra said.

"I'm not putting that in the book," I grumped. "I'm calling them no-face ducks in the book."

"When I edit the book," Lyra declared, "to cut out all the things about me you're not allowed to write, I'll change it."

"When you do what now?"

CHAPTER 4

A Revolting Attitude

Dutch people are objects of endless fascination for non-Dutch living in the Netherlands. There's even a popular English-language book on the subject, *The Undutchables,* which purports to explain the whole country. First published as a set of mimeographed leaflets in 1989, the book is now in its eighth printing and is, as one magazine called it, "a cult among English-speaking expatriates." *The Undutchables* is remarkably rude about the Dutch, whom the book calls "cloggies," making fun of their food, dress, children, personalities, and even their toilets. When I asked Dutch people about the book, they described it as quite funny and accurate.

To expats such as us, the rational and matter-of-fact Dutch are blank screens upon which we project our anxieties and fears about the way we conduct ourselves when in their country. Because the Dutch are famously forthright—Lyra once referred to something as stupid, and a passerby laughed and said, "She sounds quite Dutch!"—we often see those fears reflected back at us in the form of bluntly critical observations. Everything in their society seems, on the surface, to work so effortlessly that an expat who finds himself not fitting in agonizes over what it is about himself that doesn't slot smoothly into the systems he sees around him.

We spent our three months right in the middle of a tiny medieval city, which itself is right in the middle of a growing set of modern suburbs, which itself is right in the middle of one of the most densely populated megalopolises in the world. Start with the wide angle: The Randstad, an agglomeration of Dutch cities up and down the North Sea coast, an area smaller than Connecticut but encompassing Amsterdam, Den Haag, Rotterdam, and everything in between. Seven million people live in the Randstad, packed into those cities but also scattered in the small towns and agricultural spaces that still separate them. (In April, the rail line between Amsterdam and Delft was ablaze with tulips and other farmed flowers lined up in neat rows.) Randstadians take advantage of the extensive, reliable train system; the cycle paths and "bike superhighways"; and, yes, the congested roads between these cities. They often live in one place, work in another, and play in a third. Alia's high-school friend Shaun, for example, who emigrated to Holland over a decade ago, lives with his partner in Amsterdam's Jordaan neighborhood and travels every day to an architecture firm in Rotterdam.

Now zoom all the way in, to the old city, central Delft, halfway between Den Haag and Rotterdam. Built in the first half of the previous millennium, leveled by a gunpowder explosion in 1654, rebuilt over a hundred years, and now surrounded by blocky, late-twentieth-century suburbs. Paired near the Markt square are two dramatic medieval churches, the Oude Kerk, begun in the eleventh century, and the Nieue Kerk, "new" because it was begun in the fourteenth. (There's also a third magnificent church no one cares about because it was built—*yawn*—in the 1870s.) The streets mostly carry bikes and pedestrians; a car could, theoretically, battle its way toward the center, creeping through the narrow one-ways and swarms of foot-powered travelers, but it is by design not possible to drive all the way through, from one side of Delft to the other.

The old city we moved into served two constituencies. During the daylight hours the streets were packed with tourists on day trips from Amsterdam; they were most dense on market days, when stalls popped up alongside every canal, selling produce, flowers, and flea-market junk. On Thursdays the streets swarmed with meandering clots of tour groups that floated through the city's blood vessels until lodging firmly in front of some historic building and clogging all traffic behind them. At night, the old city was for students at the university just south of town; they smoked and drank in sidewalk cafés, then staggered home late, singing exuberantly.

Once we moved into our apartment, a slim three-story walk-up above a candy store, we realized who the old city is *not* for, really: families. It was convenient to make our way down our twisty steps to the street and be a two-minute walk from the grocery, a five-minute ride from the *bibliotheek,* with its surprisingly large selection of young-adult books in English. It was satisfying to look out our broad front windows and see the Nieue Kerk lit up against the night's clouds or to stand on the tiny back terrace and see the Oude Kerk peeking above the trees. (We couldn't see the third church, who cares.) But unlike in Island Bay, our neighbors weren't people with kids. They were single professionals, students, tourists, and young child-free couples without kids. Most families made their homes in those suburbs radiating out in every direction and then biked into the city for work, for play, or to catch a train elsewhere.

To the west, just on the other side of the high-speed train tracks that had been under construction for years, lay a cozy neighborhood of newer brick town houses and apartments. It wasn't what we thought of as typically Dutch—there were no canals or gables (??) to be seen—but it represented the kind of neighborhood in which most local kids actually lived. It was there that Harper met the first two of her Dutch friends, Demy and Eva, kicking a football against a graffitied wall in a little park. Harper shyly introduced herself to the girls and the three soon fell to playing, alternating kicking the ball around with Demy typing Dutch words into Google Translate on her phone to find their English equivalents. Demy was eleven, Eva nine; their apartments overlooked the park, and each day after school they were part of a gaggle of kids of all ages who played football, rode bikes, and goofed off in the tiny green space.

To the east, across the river, lived Ferdinand and Lindsay, who owned the Airbnb where we were staying. That's where we met Arwen and Lauren, their children. Because their mother was British, their English was fluent, and when we first stepped into their cozy kitchen, Harper's gaze flitted instantly to the counter, where a bowl was filled with a telltale goop.

"Is that *slime?*" Harper gasped.

"Yes," Arwen said. "It is slime." And Alia and I breathed a sigh of relief. They had slime.

As Harper and Arwen bonded over slime, Lindsay and Ferdinand introduced a collection of Dutch treats. Apple tart, ginger cake, cookies. Then Lauren, Arwen's older sister, held up a small box and asked, "Shall we have *hagelslag?*"

"Why do you have a box of sprinkles?" Lyra asked.

"Oh, this is *hagelslag,* the Dutch breakfast," Lindsay explained. "Everyone eats it." Arwen buttered a piece of bread and then poured an enormous pile of chocolate sprinkles on top of it. Lyra and Harper watched in awe.

Remember a few years ago when suddenly Greek yogurt became a thing, and the Greek yogurt section at your grocery store exploded, taking up shelf after shelf as ever more varieties of Greek yogurt hit the market? That's what *hagelslag*—sprinkles—were like at Albert Heijn,

Slime!

Slime, slime, slime, slime, slime. Fluffy slime, glossy slime, galaxy slime, pearl slime. Glitter slime, soft-serve slime, butter slime, floam. For the uninitiated, slime is a stretchy, goopy mixture of glue, boric acid, and food coloring that's easy to mix up and fun to play with. Fold it over and pop it like Silly Putty! Stretch it and knead it like pizza dough! Squash it through your fingers! Add other ingredients to it to see what happens!

By the summer of 2017 slime had become a viral fad, complete with celebrity aficionados (Salma Hayek's daughter!) and alarmist panic (will it burn my kid's hands?). And it was *everywhere.* Slime cemented Harper's and Arwen's fast friendship. ("You know those little pellets on the bottom of fishbowls? You put that in slime and it makes it crunchy.") In Wellington, Alia had walked into a Bunnings—the Kiwi version of Home Depot—looking for borax, an old-timey cleaning powder, and the saleslady had immediately asked, "Ah, making slime, are we?" They were out of borax. So was every Bunnings in town. They received a shipment the next week, fifteen cases.

our local supermarket. Lined up in neat cardboard boxes were regular chocolate *hagelslag,* dark chocolate *hagelslag,* milk chocolate *hagelslag,* white chocolate *hagelslag,* rainbow *hagelslag,* teeny-tiny *hagelslag* so small they resembled pencil shavings, and jumbo *hagelslag,* which looked like Tic Tacs.

And kids across the Netherlands eat this for breakfast, according to Arwen and Lauren and *The Happiest Kids in the World,* a book that gives a lot of credit for Dutch family happiness to the way families really value breakfast. Well, sure! If American kids were allowed to pour piles of chocolate sprinkles onto their breakfasts, I bet they'd be pretty jazzed about the most important meal of the day too.

It's worth noting that Dutch cuisine is pretty bad. It starts with the sprinkles—which aren't even that delicious—continues with lunch (usually an open-faced sandwich of meat and cheese on dark bread), and finishes with the traditional dinner of AVG—*aardappelen, vlees, groente,*

And in the United States, our parent friends were posting photos and videos of their children's slime successes and slime disasters on Facebook: tables spattered in candy-colored goo; couches distressingly stained ("vinegar gets it out"); grinning kids stretching their perfect slime like taffy. Sales of Elmer's Glue were going through the roof. Harper messaged her friends slime tips and tricks, new recipes, and new Instagram slime videos to watch.

For Harper slime had ascended from hobby to infatuation to full-on obsession. Like all the other slime-lovers in the world, by that summer she had stopped using borax in favor of contact lens solution, which includes tiny amounts of boric acid and is easier on your hands. (Someone could write a great business-school case study on the company that makes borax and the real roller coaster I imagine they rode for the first six months of 2017.) When Harper wasn't mixing slime or making her own slime videos (chattering happily as she kneaded and twisted, iPod propped up on the table), she was playing with slime, an expression of deep contentment on her face as the putty blopped and blooped.

or potatoes, meat, and vegetables, often in some kind of unappetizing stew-type deal. The Netherlands' position in the European Union meant we had access to beautiful produce, Belgian beer, French wine; these were great but not often indulged in during the week by the locals. We could also buy inexpensive French cheese, but Dutch people eat Dutch cheese, which is Gouda. There's *oude* Gouda, and there's *jonge* Gouda. It's as ubiquitous in Holland as it is boring. Though the Thursday market resembled a farmers' market, it struck me more like the produce stalls in New York's Chinatown, where sellers pile up the same world-grown produce as in grocery stores but charge a dollar less.

Holland *does* have good immigrant food! You can find spectacular Indonesian restaurants anywhere, and in fact, thanks to Holland's colonial misadventures, nasi goreng (Indonesian fried rice) occupies a similar place of pride in Dutch cuisine as chicken tikka masala occupies in England's. Doner kebabs taste exactly the same as everywhere else in Europe. The pizza is generally a three out of five on the Kois Foreign-Country

For a while, I'll admit, the slime drove me crazy. For a solid month in Wellington she couldn't quite get the recipe right, and the bathroom in Bronwyn's house betrayed evidence of various goopy misfires in the grout and tile. I found her constant requests for supplies and her monologues about the differences between types of slime maddening. But she was so delighted at the creation of each new batch, the simple chemical miracle of it. "I like mixing things," she liked to say as the ingredients slowly combined and then, abracadabra, transformed into something completely new. Was I really gonna resent my kid's joy, especially when it was found in something so hands-on and, in its weird, goopy way, creative? When I was nine, *my* version of slime was setting GI Joe guys on fire.

Soon enough she'd be done with slime. (Either that or she'd start making thousands of dollars a month selling slime on the internet, which would also be great.) But for now, slime was her passion. Slime, slime, slime, slime, slime.

Pizza Index, representing a solid understanding of the order in which ingredients go on a pizza but not much flavor. Desserts could be better. *Appeltaart* is tasty, especially with whipped cream, which the Dutch improbably call *slagroom*. There's always room for *slagroom!*

Despite all the potatoes and sprinkles, Oxfam has declared the Dutch diet the best in the world based on availability, affordability, quality, and relative rarity of obesity and diabetes. Dutch people like to credit the sneaky healthiness of their cuisine and all their bike riding; those of us who rode bikes around Holland for three months and did not lose any weight might also gently suggest there may be a genetic component.

In New Zealand we'd made friends with other families quickly, because in Island Bay we were surrounded by possible friends. (Also because a local radio station had let me give out my email address to the entire country.) Here in Holland, thanks to slime and *hagelslag,* we had friends east of town. Thanks to Harper programming Demy's WhatsApp number into my phone, we had friends west of town. But we had no friends *in* town. Luckily, school seemed like it would be a gold mine, friends-wise. Back when we were planning the trip, I'd spent hours emailing and telephoning educators all over the Netherlands, working my way up the chain of command, culminating in a triumphant call with an official in the ministry of education. He told me about a pilot program in bilingual education recently launched by a dozen or so schools across the country. One of them was in Delft. "Oh yes, it sounds quite perfect," the official said. "You will be there in the third year of the program. They conduct classes both in Dutch and English. They will enjoy the native English-speakers!"

Sign us up! I had a couple of friendly, if slightly bewildering, phone calls with Yvonne, the head of the school, who was very enthusiastic if slightly less fluent in English than I would expect from the principal of a bilingual school. "What a wonderful opportunity," she said, "to have American children in our school!" She explained to me that Lyra would be in group eight and Harper in group six and that while the school—located in a suburb just south of town—would be on inter-term vacation when we arrived in Delft, the final term of the school year would begin May 8. "But may I mark for the first day of their attendance as April the thirty? For that way we shall receive additional funds to the bilingual program, from the government."

"Sure," I said. "No problem. And half the classes are in English?"

"Oh yes!" she said. "Perhaps it is forty in English, sixty in Nederlandse."

The kids were uncertain about going to school in a non-English-speaking country. Harper, as always, overcame her uncertainty — "I'm learning Dutch," she told someone on our second day in town — but Lyra was more nervous. "I totally understand why you're nervous, but I really think it'll be okay!" I said. "It's a bilingual school. Yes, some of your classes will be in Dutch."

"I don't know if you noticed, Dad, but I don't speak Dutch."

"But all your classmates will be excited to practice their English! So even when things are happening in Dutch, you'll be able to keep up."

"Aren't there any English-language schools we could go to?"

"No," I lied. "Well," I backtracked almost immediately, "there are international schools and an American school in The Hague, but it would cost us like twenty thousand dollars to send you guys there for three months. And we want to experience actual Dutch life!"

"Experience," Lyra said with deep distaste. *"You're* not the one who has to go to school." In the end she provisionally agreed that maybe it could be okay, given that she had also been nervous about her school in Wellington and in the end that had been good. "But they spoke English there," she added.

"And te reo!" interjected Harper.

"Mostly English."

In general, Alia and I had not put that much emphasis on learning Dutch. First of all, it was extremely complicated, and people who spoke it sounded as if they were clearing their throats. Furthermore, it was hard for us to seriously push our children to learn Dutch, a language that they certainly wouldn't be able to learn in three months and that, in addition, is of basically no use outside the Netherlands. Both Alia and I had taken French through high school and so Alia was focusing her

Duolingo efforts on fellow Romance language Spanish in anticipation of the Costa Rica leg of our journey. (I was focusing on letting Alia translate for us in Costa Rica.) Anyway, 90 percent of Netherlanders spoke English! The only people we met who didn't speak at least *some* English were either kids or eighty-year-olds.

On the first day of school, after our kids poured sprinkles all over our kitchen, we all rode together past the train station, around the traffic circle, and to the school. It was tiny! A long bike rack housed maybe a hundred and fifty bikes; a cozy play yard nestled next to a neatly tended garden. It really seemed like a school for little kids that a bunch of big kids, including Lyra's classmates, also happened to attend.

Yvonne, a ruddy, cheerful woman with blond hair, ushered us into her office. Harper leaned forward eagerly; Lyra sat way back in her chair, a much quieter version of herself. Yvonne asked the girls what they liked to do at school. "I like reading and writing," Lyra said.

"Oh!" said Yvonne. "Do you notice that the school is located on I. B. Bakkerstraat? I. B. Bakker is a writer. All the street here is named for writers."

"Ooh," Lyra said politely. Harper leaned over to me and pointed at my notebook: "You should write that down," she whispered. I would later discover that Ina Boudier-Bakker was a popular early-twentieth-century domestic novelist who was best known for a book called *A Knock at the Door*. Anne Frank wrote in her diary that she couldn't tear herself away from the book, but a Dutch magazine supposedly published a very short review of *A Knock at the Door:* "Do not open!"

Yvonne explained that both girls would participate in programs with smaller children in the school's vegetable garden. Then she told Lyra that group eight, her class, put on a musical at the end of the year. "They have started rehearsals already, but I am certain a place can be made for you."

Alia and I rode home from school that morning feeling like we'd nailed it. "That school is so cute!" I said as we pedaled side by side. "Did you see the little garden in the back?"

"I loved the kid in the leather jacket," she replied. "Up on his mom's moped?"

"I think this is gonna be really good."

By the second day, though, our kids were both reporting that if their school was bilingual, they weren't seeing it. "Well, are some of your classes in English?" Alia asked Harper.

"English class is," she replied.

As far as we could figure it out, the pilot program, though officially undertaken by the whole school, seemed to be focused on group three, who'd inaugurated it in their first year, and the groups below. Had I somehow misunderstood Yvonne in our phone calls and emails? Thursday, Harper came home saying, "I didn't have a very good time at school today." When *Harper* says that, you *know* it's bad. On regular kid scale, that's the equivalent of "I was devoured by piranhas at school today." Lyra, meanwhile, was discouraged and annoyed, although we didn't understand how discouraged and annoyed until the day a few weeks later she flat-out refused to go to school. The only thing she liked was helping the group-one children in the garden, she said, but that was only once a week. Her teachers didn't make any effort to include her so she just read in class. "But I'm out of English-language books," she added. "Can we go to the library?"

We rode over one day after school to see if we could talk to Yvonne. As we pulled up, just before the afternoon bell, we saw her riding away on her bike; she gave us a cheery wave. "I must go home!" she called. When we finally got hold of her, she suggested a conference with Lyra's teachers, Meester Peter and Miss Daniëlle, who split time teaching group eight. Alia and I came in one day after school and met Peter and Daniëlle in the quiet, well-organized classroom, which looked out over the school garden. Lyra waited outside to be called in after we'd had our initial discussion.

Peter took the lead. "Lyra is very often arguing with the teachers about what we do in the classroom. It's not correct." He described a conflict he'd had with her recently in which he asked the class to do something and she refused to do it. At the end of the story he folded his hands. "So you can see a revolting attitude in her," he said. I started, then realized he meant "rebellious."

Daniëlle nodded. "It began on her first day," she said. "She argued with me for a very long time about what color of pen she was to use on an assignment. And the whole classroom was like, 'Whoa! On her first day!'"

"I guess it's not typical for kids to argue in class here?" Alia asked.

"Oh no," said Daniëlle.

"No, it is not done," said Peter. "She argues about many things. If we give her the opportunity to decide for herself, she is satisfied. But that is not the right way."

"It makes it difficult for her to make friends," said Daniëlle. "When the children see that, the classroom responds: Oh, we don't like a girl like that."

Alia and I exchanged panicked glances. This was, safe to say, much worse than we'd thought things were going, and we'd thought they were going pretty badly. "Does she have any friends?" I asked.

"She has one friend," said Daniëlle.

"Well, we certainly don't think she should argue with teachers," Alia said.

"I know she's been frustrated about not understanding Dutch," I said. "Do you think that if more of the class was conducted in English, she might be able to participate better?"

"But we cannot speak English just for the benefit of one student when the class is in Dutch," Peter said. "It's not possible."

We called Lyra into the room. She sat down at the end of the table and took us in—stern Peter, nervous Daniëlle, miserable parents. At that moment, it seemed, she made a decision: She would stand her ground. We told her that she couldn't argue with her teachers; she argued with us about whether she should be allowed to argue. To argue with your teachers disrespects both the teachers and the rest of the class, we said. She argued with that: "If something doesn't make sense or I could do it a better way, why do I have to do it their way?"

"It is good to argue about ideas or philosophies," Peter said. "But not to argue about what your teachers ask you to do in class."

Lyra crossed her arms. "I like arguing."

Daniëlle seemed near tears. All four adults at the table were completely baffled.

Peter spoke for quite some time, giving a few specific examples of moments when Lyra had not been respectful in class. On several occasions Lyra tried to respond, but he held up a hand. "No, I am still talking," he said. "When I am done, you may talk." When he finished, Lyra sat up straight and said, "First of all, you tell me that I talk too much, and then you talk to me for like eight minutes straight?"

I gasped. "Lyra!" Alia and I cried in unison. "You may not talk to an adult like that." Lyra's body language was breathtaking—arms folded, hunched in her seat, scowl as clear as an emoji's. I have never been as shocked by something my child did as I was by Lyra saying that. I felt ashamed at how disruptive and disrespectful my kid was being; I felt upset and worried at how miserable she clearly was at this school. But I also felt a kind of dawning admiration for her simply being her own pain-in-the-ass self, no compromises, no matter what.

At school in Arlington—and in Wellington—Lyra had not been a problem student. She got As and Bs. Her verbal flair and sardonicism made her an acquired taste for some teachers, for sure. But she also was eager to show her knowledge, interested in participating, and concerned with getting good grades. Most teachers she'd had up to now had seen the smart, eager kid behind the wise-ass and had connected with that kid, fostered her pride and pleasure at being smart. But here in the Netherlands, stripped of the ability to show how smart she was, she became the spanner in the works, the kid who basically broke an entire classroom.

Though the Dutch educational system achieves positive objective outcomes—the country ranked twelfth in a 2016 OECD survey of educational quality by nation, nine spots ahead of the United States—*achievement* is not the goal. The system is not particularly rigorous in any sense American parents will recognize; students in group eight have little homework, are often not given grades, and usually have no sense of how they compare to others in their class. Dutch education, Michele Hutchison writes in *The Happiest Kids in the World,* is not really about evaluating children and preparing them for university. "Education here has a different purpose. It is traditionally seen as the route to a child's well-being and their development as an individual." Their development, I hasten to add, into a very specific kind of individual: A Dutchman or Dutchwoman.

Hence the assessment categories that many Dutch school reports do use, as explained by Hutchison:

> There's General Behavior: The ideal child is independent, calm, modest, self-confident, spontaneous, and responsible. There is Care of the Environment, which takes into consideration whether their work is neat and their desk clean and tidy. Relationship with the Teacher is another category: The ideal pupil is helpful, curious, polite, attentive, and open to being corrected when wrong. Running parallel to this is Relationship with Other Children: Kids are encouraged to be cooperative, considerate towards others, resilient, and good at listening. Finally, the category Attitude to Work assesses the following attributes: standards, level of perseverance, concentration, ability to work independently, to listen during lessons, motivation and how quickly your child works.

With few exceptions, this is a remarkably thorough list of the attributes that Lyra does not possess. In the United States, she could be steered toward the kinds of classroom citizenship teachers found helpful by instructors who valued some of Lyra's positive qualities: her wit, her spunk, her quicksilver mind, her love of reading, her stellar writing ability. Those qualities were lost on Peter and Daniëlle, the academic ones because Lyra did not have the opportunity to show off her English skills, and the social ones because they did not conform particularly to the kind of student Dutch schools are designed to foster—the kind who will eventually become a Dutch person, who will spend life doing normal, because that's strange enough.

Dutch schools are dismissive of individual achievement and admirably concerned with fostering an environment in which every child is treated the same, as a part of one well-operating classroom. (It's the same impulse that informs the smoothing-over of class differences I so loved in the Netherlands, ensuring that the rich live in the same small houses and ride the same beat-up bikes as everyone else.) So rigorously is equity pursued that a Dutch school's version of a gifted program would give most American parents apoplexy. "Take a kid who's excellent in math but bad in spelling," explained Toine, a teacher at another Delft school. "The school will pull that kid out of math and put him in remedial spelling so he won't be too much better or worse than the other students. It's important to be average."

"Individualism isn't prized here," Hutchison said when I met her in Amsterdam. "It isn't even really condoned. The Dutch are fundamentally conformists." What happened, I asked, to people who didn't conform? How did the system handle them? "There's a Dutch mechanism to kind of sweep up loners and fit them into the crowd," she said, noting that often it was fellow students who did that work, scooping up unusual kids and incorporating them into the group. Ruut Veenhoven, a professor at Erasmus University in Rotterdam, was more blunt about how the Netherlands treats its oddballs once they reach adulthood. "If you don't function in that society, you are shunned by the neighbors, and if it's too bad, even by your parents. Either you get completely lost or you get support by state services. What typically happens is you look for a subculture where your qualities are prized. They do exist here." A grim future as an outcast punk for parallel-universe Dutch Lyra!

A child like Harper, who in addition to being smart loves fitting in with the crowd, can do pretty okay in a Dutch school. And indeed, Harper, after early bumps in the road, learned some Dutch, played on the playground, made friends, and tried to be helpful to her teachers. But a kid like Lyra who is doggedly, determinedly individualistic—indeed, whose quirky individualism has been fostered by her teachers and parents for years—is going to have a rough time. Lyra is never going to do normal. Her school was as unprepared for a kid like her as she was for a school like that.

She tried. We told her, very clearly, that she was simply not allowed to argue with teachers and established clear consequences if she did and clear rewards if we received word of good behavior. The next week we got an email from Meester Peter letting us know that she had not argued and was trying more. (He also noted that he and Daniëlle were translating more lessons into English, "where we thought it was necessary and useful," which, like, it is always necessary and useful, Meester Peter.) The next week Lyra got into it with a teacher who insisted she go outside for lunch on a cold day; Lyra, who for no apparent reason had worn shorts, did not want to and was sent to an empty classroom to do math worksheets all afternoon. By the end of the school year, while her classmates spent hours rehearsing the musical, Lyra mostly read and slept in class. Despite our entreaties, Lyra was not part of that musical; when we asked, Peter told us that Lyra had said she did not want to participate, so they did not make her. *You make her do everything else she didn't want to do, but you don't force her to do the one thing that might have helped her fit in your class?!* I did not say.

On the last day of school I met with Daniëlle one more time. "I really wanted to make her happy," she said sadly. "I wanted to create a bond, but I never succeeded. In these final days I think I came close." It's hard to write about our experience at our Dutch school because of all the ways we failed our kids, especially Lyra. Our impulse was to back up the teachers in every one of these difficult interactions, but now, looking back, I wish I had backed up my daughter. No, she should not have argued about every goddamn thing, but what if they had bent just a bit? What if Daniëlle's desire to connect with Lyra had pushed through her rigorous teaching philosophy and allowed her to focus a little longer on one lost, unhappy girl?

Daniëlle is part of a system that serves nearly all its students incredibly well, although at the expense, it seems, of those few who can't adapt. I'm not surprised she wasn't interested in upending that system for a child who was staying for only three months. I know that it wouldn't have been reasonable to do so. I guess what I wanted to see from Peter and Daniëlle was a willingness to be unreasonable, just once, in the service of my kid. That's a very un-Dutch thing to say.

When I think of those terrible months of us making our kid go to a school she hated, I feel glum not only about how her teachers handled her but about how I handled my child's unhappiness. Why didn't we just bail her out? Let her skip? Take her side, even once?

But though her bad behavior fills me with a hot parenting shame—even as I write this, a year later!—I also feel just the tiniest amount of pride in my obstinate American kid. "You can see a revolting attitude in her," Meester Peter said in that awful meeting, sitting in the classroom where Lyra never really felt at home. Thinking of that now, it reminds me of the musical *Matilda,* which we've all listened to so many times. In the second act, the students of Crunchem Hall rise up in rebellion. The song they sing is called "Revolting Children," and in it the kids declare themselves "revolting children, living in revolting times."

I under-researched and made mistakes and didn't prepare the school for my kids or my kids for the school. Lyra's teachers, for reasons as sensible as they were disappointing, didn't make things any better. But the result was that, primarily due to the fuckups of various adults, Lyra found herself living in revolting times. Of course, of *course,* she was revolting.

"This is the problem with Holland," Lyra said authoritatively. "Kids in Holland have independence with their bodies but not about what they think about things."

With this statement, delivered through a mouthful of *hagelslag* one morning, Lyra perfectly encapsulated something I was struggling to understand about the Dutch attitude toward parenting. We heard over and over, from parents we met and from *The Happiest Kids in the World*—which by now Lyra, desperate for books in English, had read twice—that the Dutch prize freedom and independence in their children.

Dutch parents certainly take a different attitude toward risk and injury than American parents do. Kerryanne, an American-raised teacher and artist with a Dutch husband, pointed out that Dutch parents assume kids will get hurt while playing and are very careful to moderate their response to injury, even with little children. "When kids fall down, parents don't run to them," she said. "They walk, unless there's blood." Even when parents accompany their children to the park, they're much less attached than is typical in an American playground, where a parent is often engaged one on one with his child in the sandbox or pushing a swing or whatever. Kerryanne, who's raising her sons in the Netherlands, remembered a trip to visit her parents in Massachusetts: "I was at a playground and the boys were playing, and I had a book. And I saw a group of parents and kids all together, the parents on top of the kids, and they were sort of talking to each other and looking at me and it dawned on me: Oh, I'm not right up on my sons, that's why I'm getting the stink eye."

It's not that Dutch parents "aren't aware of the risks," Hutchison writes in *Happiest Kids*. "They are just as aware as Anglo parents, they simply approach risk in a saner fashion." Dutch parents teach skills that are meant to help kids avoid the worst—swimming lessons, for example, start early in a country with a lot of canals and very few railings. And where New Zealand uses a publicly funded accident-insurance scheme to avoid personal-injury lawsuits, in the Netherlands it's traditional for citizens to insure themselves to the gills. Indeed, the Dutch are so well covered by personal liability insurance that a few years ago the government issued a report warning that millions of Dutch consumers were significantly *over*insured, often owning two or three policies where they only needed one.

"The Dutch believe that children need to be let out to run each day," Hutchison writes. Kids are expected to play outside, no matter the weather—there is no such thing as bad weather, only bad clothes, goes the Dutch commonplace—and are given free rein of their neighborhoods in a way that reminded us of New Zealand. Kids run wild, playing football, shouting and riding bikes from the time school lets out until precisely 6:00 p.m., when every single kid goes inside to eat dinner.

Our kids were rarely outside making trouble, despite our urging. We lived in the central city, where there weren't really any other kids. Harper had some success using my phone to WhatsApp Demy and Eva and visiting their neighborhood, and she sometimes got up to shenanigans with her friends Arwen and Nora, but she found it a struggle to engage with new kids her age, who often were just learning English as she was just learning Dutch. Lyra had no school friends and straight up didn't like playing outside, and it required prolonged battles just to get her to take her Kindle out to a bench on our street to read in the sunshine instead of in her room. "What does it matter where I read?" she demanded.

"We want you to get fresh air and be out from under our feet for a while!" Alia said.

"You're not going to make me Dutch." Eventually she showed us, by leaving her Kindle in a park somewhere.

Yet for all the wild, unfettered freedom kids had in the Netherlands, it was true that, for example, every single child knew to come home at six sharp. "Kids want to have the freedom," said Toine, a teacher and parent, "but they want to know where the freedom ends. It's independence, but within strict limits." Dutch kids *could* be offered freedom and independence because their culture, from birth, indoctrinated them in the principles and rules of "normal" Dutch behavior. Dutch families eat dinner at six. Dutch children play outside even in bad weather. Dutch teens don't rebel, I heard again and again, because by the time they were teenagers, they were well on their way to becoming well-behaved Dutch adults. I began to interpret this Dutch mania for "independence" as a kind of narrow cycling path: You have absolute freedom to ride anywhere you like...within that path. It would never have dawned on anyone to stray from the path.

Ruut Veenhoven, who studies Dutch national happiness, agreed when I posed this as a kind of unsolvable conundrum. "We ask children to be independent—but they cannot be so independent that they refuse to go to school," he said. "They cannot be so independent that they make it difficult for other students or the teacher. You're an outsider, so you see this more clearly perhaps than we can. We praise independence, but we establish strict unspoken limits." Even parents, in their adherence to the spoken and unspoken rules and deference to authority, thought of themselves as independent but acted as conformists. You know how parents might, every once in a while, take their children out of school on a Thursday for a four-day weekend trip? When we did that, Arwen's father, Ferdinand, was shocked. "Well, it is a school day," he said, "so the children should be in school." It turns out that Netherlands law severely restricts the reasons children may legally miss school. Expats are even warned that truancy officers patrol Schiphol airport, handing out hundred-euro fines to parents whose children don't have permission to be absent.

Is this what I wanted for my children? For me? In *Happiest Kids,* Hutchison poses some useful questions about Dutch happiness: "If you are a conformist, does that make you more content? Or is it that if you are a happy person, you don't feel the need to challenge the norms?" In his studies of national happiness, Veenhoven defines *happiness* as "how satisfied you are with your life as a whole." Being satisfied with a limited set of emotional and cultural options stands in direct conflict with the American model of viewing our possibilities as limitless. But given that American possibilities *aren't* truly limitless but constrained by any number of systemic and structural inequities, the American view also contributes to unhappiness, to us feeling forever dissatisfied, because we aren't fulfilling our enormous potential. Even those with every advantage in America are damaged by the country's supposed limitless horizons; in certain sectors of American society, including my own, individualism—applied by parents to their privileged kids—curdles into exceptionalism. And for all the gripes I have with Dutch culture, I find their rejection of exceptionalism valuable and admirable. (Except when it was my exceptional kid getting rejected.)

We never quite solved this problem. It might be unsolvable for American parents staying in the Netherlands for a short time; it may solve itself for parents who move here long-term and raise their kids in this environment from the get-go. Like many European countries, Holland is big on assimilation; while they're not taking one-year-olds out of their homes for mandatory assimilation classes, as the Danes recently announced they plan to do with immigrants in mostly Muslim neighborhoods, there have long been Dutch-language requirements involved in becoming a permanent resident of the Netherlands. And just as the social codes of childhood push children toward the middle, so does Dutch culture overall push new arrivals into the mainstream.

So if we'd raised our children in the Netherlands all along, it was easy to imagine that they would have become "Dutch," behaved like Dutch children, and we would behave like Dutch parents. How long would it take? Three years? Ten years? Who knows! Imagining a Dutch Harper was easy: She took to Holland, after some early hiccups, like a phantom duck to water, a happy conformist who, by the time we left, was tossing around Dutch vocab and had explored every corner of the city. I found it both fascinating and slightly disturbing to think of a Dutch Lyra, a child so transformed by her upbringing as to become essentially unrecognizable compared with the remarkable, difficult child she is now—or a child who never transformed and therefore found life a struggle.

And a Dutch me? I couldn't even imagine it. To say so certainly didn't feel like a judgment on the Netherlands. It felt, instead, like a judgment on me.

CHAPTER 5

Fietsen

We just wanted to see a windmill. Delft has one windmill remaining of the fifteen that once lined its city walls, and it was pretty close to our apartment, so in our first week in Delft we rode over. The low clouds hugged the Oude Kerk; the streets were quiet this weekday morning. The windmill, right next to the tram stop to Den Haag, was closed, but it was picturesque. We took pictures.

It was on the way back that we ran into trouble. Heading into town down a narrow street, the girls rode side by side, as if phalanxed for protection. Ahead, a young man cruised toward us, riding hands-free. "Lyra, Harper, single file," I called, but the guy was moving pretty fast and they didn't move quite fast enough, and, with an action-movie set of maneuvers, the guy took evasive action to swerve around them both before veering wildly into an adjacent alleyway with an exclamation that, even in another language, could easily be identified as a curse.

"Lyra! Harper!" I called immediately. "Stop, please!" They pulled over, looking shaken. "You've got to pay closer attention," I lectured. "You really almost crashed with that guy!" This wasn't the first near miss, and each one reminded me of my shaky New Zealand driving. At least there I'd known the rules of the road; it was just that they were all backward. Here in the Netherlands I kept finding myself unable to navigate complicated traffic situations in the old city, the ever-multiplying vectors—bikes, cars, mopeds, pedestrians, all moving in different directions at different speeds—overtaxing my processing power.

Outside of town, where the streets were wider and more clearly marked with bike lanes, we were starting to do fine. We used the directional hand signals I'd discarded as uncool back in third grade; we obeyed lights and nervously accepted the right-of-way when it appeared to be ours. There, cycling was more like driving, with lanes and clear rules that almost everyone followed.

But in town, chaos reigned—yet the chaos was smoothly navigated by Dutch riders. Our lack of instinct gummed up the works. How did Dutch people know what to do on two wheels?

Alia and I weren't novice bikers. I still remembered, with pride, the snowy February day a friend and her mom were driving down Franklin Street in Chapel Hill and the mom said, "Who are those two idiot children riding their bicycles on a day like this?" and our friend said, "Oh, it's Dan and Alia!" I'd even taken a weeklong cycle tour of Provence with my dad, torturing my undercarriage on a hard racing-bike seat as we clattered across cobblestones and vineyards. (My first accessory purchase in Delft was one of those big, squishy, ass-size seats.)

Riding regularly in our suburb in Virginia was tougher. The streets around our house were busy with fast-moving traffic. Though some Arlington roads featured bike lanes, they were frequently cut off by parked cars, delivery trucks, or piles of junk set out for collection. And whenever bike paths were forced to intersect traffic, traffic always won. After two near misses at an infamous intersection near the Key Bridge—the kind of hair-raising near misses that feature screeching tires and passersby shaking their heads—I gave up riding to work. I didn't trust that my helmet was enough to protect me in a face-off with a driver who, fresh off the freeway, didn't happen to look the right way as he turned.

For that was the real issue with cycling in Arlington and, in fact, in most cities in the United States. Optimistic municipalities might have painted lines on the street or paved a few bike paths, but that infrastructure broke down in the places where it encountered automobiles. Cars came first, and the drivers of those cars rarely thought to look for bikes. Drivers parked and then swung their front doors wide; they made right turns without looking behind them; they pulled out of parking lots and cut across bike lanes at speed. They ruled the road, and who could blame them? The network was built to maximize their speed and efficiency, and anything that might slow them down was a glitch in the system.

To cyclists used to being second-class citizens in America, watching the way bikes navigate the Netherlands is revelatory. It's not just that the train stations all house massive underground bicycle garages with thousands of *fietsen* locked up on tiered racks as far as the eye can see. It's not just that every street has a handsome bike lane, paved in dark red and separated from traffic and parked cars. It's that on Dutch streets, bikes come first. *Fietsers* take priority in design, in traffic flow, in right-of-way. Traffic circles are laid out so that cyclists traveling around them need never stop for cars. Busy streets have not only designated cycle crossings but, often, over- or underpasses so cyclists never have to slow down.

Most important, drivers look out for cyclists, cede the right-of-way, and are rarely surprised by them. Why? Because those drivers are cyclists themselves. The Netherlands has more bikes than people—22.5 million bicycles and 18 million people as of 2017—which means that nearly everyone bikes. The young? Dutch kids are in child seats from birth, on balance bikes by two, cycling unaided by four. The old? Battery-assisted bikes, which make cycling much easier for those getting on in years, now account for 30 percent of the Dutch bicycle market by volume.

And the person next to you on the roadway in the Renault Clio? She's driving today only because she has a meeting way out of town, or she has to bring furniture home from the store, or she broke her arm. On many other days she would be riding next to you, helmetless, unprotected from cars except by custom, respect, and the forethought that comes from being able to think like a cyclist. In the Netherlands, drivers don't turn right without checking their blind spots. Drivers don't park in bike lanes, not even just for a minute to drop something off.

Consider the danger, familiar to every American cyclist, of getting doored—crashing or swerving because some driver opened his car door right in your path. In a recent study, 22 percent of Boston bike crashes involving cars in a single year were dooring incidents; anyone who cycles in a town or city has had a near miss with a door. That just doesn't happen in Holland. In part that's because many bike lanes are placed to the *right* of parking lanes, next to the sidewalk, with plenty of buffer space between the bicycles and the cars. But even on streets where bikes must travel on the driver's side of parked cars, cyclists don't get doored because drivers check behind them, often habitually reaching to open their doors with their right hand to force themselves to twist and look over their shoulder.

All this means that cycling is not only convenient and fast in the Netherlands but incredibly safe. Even though no one wears a helmet in the Netherlands, it's far safer to cycle there than in the United States, where OECD data shows forty-nine cyclists killed per billion kilometers ridden. In the Netherlands, that number is eight. "The risk per kilometer is lowest in the Netherlands compared to other countries," confirmed Wim Bot of the Fietsersbond, the Dutch cyclists' union.

Parents ride with infants strapped in BabyBjörns to their chests; bigger kids travel in child seats, on parent/child tandem bikes, or in the ubiquitous *bakfiets*—the Dutch cargo bike, which can fit two or three kids plus groceries in its wooden container. Preschools employ bike buses, which allow one teacher to transport eight kids, lined up in rows, watching the world go by. We saw Delft residents riding with dogs trotting alongside their bikes, pulling roller suitcases behind them, and balancing hi-fi speakers with one hand. Friends sit sidesaddle on the back wheel or stand on front-wheel pegs. "What's typical of Dutch cycling is people like to cycle beside each other," Bot said. "That's what we did when we were high-school kids, going to school with a friend talking about which teachers you detest." Indeed, as Hutchison writes in *The Happiest Kids in the World,* "One of the most romantic things you see the Dutch do (and there aren't many romantic things they do) is to cycle holding hands."

An Utrecht University study calculated that the Dutch love of cycling saves the country twenty-three billion dollars (thanks to lowered health costs, decreased pollution, and productivity increases) and sixty-five hundred premature deaths per year. And this all happens without inconveniencing drivers! Cars get freeways all to themselves; they can travel long distances easily and are well directed by careful Dutch road design. Dutch drivers, all of whom are cyclists themselves, prize their role in an orderly, safe system. Put an American driver on a road behind a couple of bikes and he'll steam at these two-wheeled chumps blocking his way. Put Dutch drivers on roads teeming with fourteen million cyclists and you'll get... the country that's number one for driver satisfaction in the world, according to a 2017 poll conducted by the traffic app Waze.

So the benefits of living in a cycling-mad country were obvious, and early returns were good. Despite Lyra's initial resistance, she grew to enjoy the ritual of the bike ride, and once we got out into the country and started pedaling lazily down bucolic pathways, her complaining was minimal. (I asked her if she preferred biking to driving, and she said, "No, obviously, because I can't read on a bike. But it's not *bad*.") Harper loved having her own bike and lock—she alone had insisted on one opened with a key, which she kept inside a little purse—and she had already set herself to learning her way around town, which included memorizing all the absurd street names. (We lived at Hippolytusbuurt 15, for example.) Alia and I were absolutely in love with not having a car; we didn't have to worry about parking, and we felt virtuous even when we were going out for, like, cake.

We still had work to do, though, getting comfortable riding around old Delft. Take, for instance, the intersection right by our flat. Two parallel streets ran on either side of the canal, intersected by a bridge that carried on in either direction. So it looked like this:

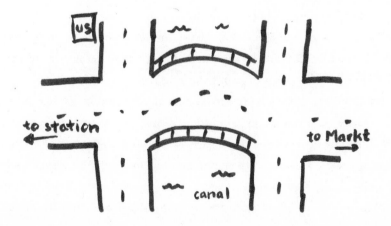

The north–south canal roads were busy because they provided a through route from the bottom of town to the top; the crossroad was busy because it was an easy path between the center of town and the train station. Busy with cyclists and pedestrians, not cars, but still—that was a lot of directions for people to come from and a lot of different speeds for people to be traveling at. Plus artists usually had paintings for sale on the bridge, and crowds were often lined up for herring at the fish market on the northeast corner. And that's not even to mention market Thursdays and Saturdays, when the entire intersection was clogged with old ladies selling knockoff Delftware and books in languages Lyra couldn't read. And every once in a while a car *would* creep down one street or the other, adding yet another variable into this quatraffic equation.

All this meant that the daily act of crossing the intersection, making a turn, coasting to a stop in front of our flat, dismounting, and locking the bikes up (or bringing them inside) was fraught, given how many cyclists and walkers were on our tails and approaching from the opposite direction. Yet Dutch cyclists (and pedestrians and the occasional driver) navigated it perfectly. "From a young age in the Netherlands we're trained to take note of others," said Angela van der Kloof, a cycling expert and project leader with the Delft transit consultancy Mobycon. "Not by a teacher but by the way we do things. I think we are very much used to physical negotiation." Dutch people live in small houses, walk on crowded streets, and jostle against one another as a matter of course. When cars sidled past them on an old city street, they were unbothered, whereas I held my breath.

While we were cycling, our uncertainty often made us indecisive or tentative, which did no one any good. The lowlight came one afternoon when Lyra mounted her bike in front of our flat, wobbled, swerved, and collided with an elderly Dutchman on an elderly bicycle. They both toppled slowly onto the bricks. Lyra looked outraged at first, then terrified when she saw how old the other party was, woolen scarf and all. All four of us apologized over and over; the gentleman helped Lyra up, brushed himself off, and rode away.

The advice of *The Happiest Kids in the World* was for parents to let children make these mistakes—to view these moments as learning experiences for them, not as chances to leap in and solve the problem. No one was riding fast enough to be seriously injured, the theory went, so crashes and near misses would do more to teach kids how to handle themselves than parents lecturing them about it. "If children cannot gain real-life experience, they will never be able to face the difficulties of the traffic on their own," according to Hutchison and Acosta. "The same can be said about general 'street wisdom'; the advice is to let your children deal with potentially dangerous situations, then they will learn how to assess risks and avoid trouble when they are out and about."

After Lyra's misadventure with the gentleman in the scarf, she looked quickly at me, clearly anticipating my reprimand. I paused, swallowed the reprimand, said, "You all right?"—and then asked her to take the lead on our trip to the library. And she did, without complaint.

As the weeks went by, our kids did indeed get better on the roads of Delft. So did I. The key, I learned, was to ride like a Dutchman. I couldn't be tall and blond, but I could bike as if I were; I could ride tall in the saddle with the self-possession of a guy with sharp, visible cheekbones. Dutch *fietsers* ride like they belong on the road. Because they *do* belong on the road—the road is built for them. Once I picked a lane and owned it, made strong directional choices at intersections, and stopped riding in fear, I fit into the flow of Dutch traffic much better. Making eye contact with other riders and pedestrians, each of us using the other's feedback to negotiate those individual interactions, solved nearly every encounter that might have previously paralyzed me.

"In North America, if you want to bike, it's like playing tennis," said van der Kloof. "You need a racquet, a ball, the right clothing, and a tennis court. Talking about biking, you need a bike, you need the right gear, and you need a bike lane. It's about claiming my space: I have the right to be here." But, she continued, because she's Dutch, she "had never thought about being in public space in that sense. Of course I have the right to be here. I don't need to claim it! Maybe here in the Netherlands we think of it as our space."

By mid-May, halfway through our stay, we were all feeling much more comfortable. We had found an ease and even happiness in cycling around Delft and its surrounding countryside, an ease that I, at least, felt in few other aspects of Dutch life. We'd even ridden with some visiting American friends ten kilometers to Den Haag, where we were completely blown away by the children's section of the Gemeentemuseum, which depended on tablets and geotagging and some very complicated interactive electronics, none of which—unlike at a children's museum in any other country—was broken. (Children's museums in the Netherlands are amazing. The MENO science museum in Amsterdam features a once-an-hour demonstration of an insanely complicated Rube Goldberg–type machine that seems to work perfectly every single time.)

The kids were riding to school by themselves, three kilometers each way. This time they spent together every day made me wonder even

Lyra:

Biking in Delft was totally awesome. The terrain was perfect for biking. There were no hills whatsoever, so I could bike for ages without getting tired. I felt really independent riding alone.

The way bikes are normalized here is super interesting and fun to see. In America, riding a bike to school or to work might be seen as weird by your coworkers or classmates. But in the Netherlands, it isn't strange at all! In fact, it's normal, and weird to drive a car instead!

Bike paths are really well maintained, and they're large and spacious instead of cramped and tiny like they are in America. People ride recklessly, sometimes without hands or not paying attention to their surroundings, because cars are extremely attentive of citizens.

I didn't like it at first, actually. I thought I was bound to get lost, which was fair, as the roads all look really similar. It took me a long time to feel comfortable riding with cars around me, mainly because I'm not a big bike rider, and in Virginia the cars don't give a flying burger about you when you're on a bike. But it didn't take me long to realize that car drivers in the Netherlands are extremely conscious of you. There's no way you'll get hit unless you're a total idiot, which hopefully I'm not.

more: What was their relationship like, these two girls? Much of it was conducted out of my view. In some ways it seemed like a traditional older/younger pairing: Harper looked up to Lyra and wanted to play with her; Lyra mostly disdained her younger sister but occasionally dispensed indulgences. But in other ways, their dynamic was interestingly reversed. Harper was the first to memorize the route to school, so for a while Lyra depended on her to lead the way. Due to inattention and exasperation, Lyra never really figured out how to use the key in the front door. So that became Harper's job when they got home each day.

"Lyra, how are you going to live on your own someday if you don't want to learn how to cook or clean or anything?" we asked once, and Lyra suggested that as a grown-up she'd just live with Harper, who knew how to do all that stuff. This became a running gag in the family, Lyra musing on their life together in a New York City apartment. At these moments Harper blushed with pride. I admit that this idea of them living together as grown women filled me with joy even as I understood that it was a child's vision of adult life.

Most of the time Lyra seemed amused and unbothered by her status as the one who didn't know how to do stuff. But Harper sometimes took her authority a little too far, responding to Lyra's moments of absent-mindedness with a sitcom-y "That's so Lyra" vibe that clearly hurt her sister's feelings. Lyra would snap at her, Harper would get upset, and the order of nature was restored. I'd heard so many stories from women I knew who fought with their sisters as children and now were fiercely devoted to each other, and all I hoped for Lyra and Harper was that they'd find their way there. It was hard those times when they didn't like each other as much as I liked them both. Of course they didn't! They were not each other's dad. But I still found it painful to watch.

The girls' ride to school took them out of the old city, past the train station, and through the most magnificent traffic circle I'd ever seen, a gigantic roundabout at the Delflandplein that with great ease mixed bicycles, cars, express buses, and the tram to Den Haag. What's most remarkable about it is that bikes have the right-of-way over cars for the entire circle. At no point in this major intersection do bikes ever have to stop for cars; instead, those painted triangles on the pavement make every car stop and wait patiently for the stream of bikes to pass. Despite thousands of cars and bikes coming through every day, there were zero crashes reported in the Delflandplein roundabout between 2014 and 2017.

Every time I rode through this intersection, I tried to imagine a version of it in the United States. Not only couldn't I imagine Arlington building such a thing, I couldn't imagine Arlington drivers obeying the rules. In America, each time bikers reach any kind of intersection, we have to slow down to see if that driver turning left has seen us or if that car that's approaching will stop. Even when we do have the legal right-of-way—on a bike path or when others have a yield sign—we bikers often acknowledge a car's stopping with a little half wave, which my time in the Netherlands made me view as maddeningly obsequious. *Thank you for obeying the law and not killing me,* American bikers are saying. Dutch cyclists don't do that. They assume, correctly, that drivers will see them and obey the law. It's a subtle distinction that encapsulates the status difference between bikers in Holland and bikers in America.

It seemed unlikely that America could ever change; we couldn't replicate what I assumed was a century and a half of cycling history in the Netherlands. But in fact, Holland, like the United States, had at one point found itself overwhelmed by cars—but its citizens transformed their society in a generation in a way I found fascinating and inspiring.

Because the Netherlands is flat, biking was an integral mode of travel for the first half of the twentieth century. (As chronicled in Pete Jordan's *In the City of Bikes,* Dutch resistance to the Nazis often revolved around bikes; Amsterdammers defied traffic rules, puckishly avoided bike confiscation, and even ran the printing presses that produced resistance newspapers on electricity provided by stationary bikes.) But in the 1950s and 1960s, cars ascended in status in the Netherlands, as they did in industrialized nations around the world. Cycling infrastructure was overtaken by roads, and neighborhoods in Amsterdam were razed to make room for highways.

With cars came carnage. In 1971 alone, thirty-three hundred people—including more than four hundred children—were killed on Dutch roads. A burgeoning protest movement seized on these figures and on the traffic choking Dutch cities as a worthy cause. "The seventies was quite a special time over here," said van der Kloof. "It was the time of the second feminist wave. It was the time of a lot of student activism, and central power was moving down and out to the local governments." A number of organizations, from the nascent cyclists' union to Stop de Kindermoord ("Stop the Child Murder"), began agitating to take the country's streets back from automobiles. In one memorable protest, sixty *bakfiets* converged on Amsterdam's city center at rush hour. The protesters, part of an organization called the Troublesome Amsterdammer, pedaled slowly to hinder drivers as much as possible.

While most of the activist organizations were led by young men, Stop the Child Murder was the project of mothers, many of whom wished to use cycles in their daily life but felt that traffic did not allow them to do so. "Women's mobility and men's mobility typically are different," explained van der Kloof. "Women have shorter trips, multiple trips, oftentimes accompanied by children. Typically men have longer trips, but fewer. Well, these shorter trips, trip-chaining with children, in the Dutch context, can be done on the bike. That's why I think especially women were so interested in this. It was really serving their mobility needs." And Stop the Child Murder had a profound effect on the debate, as local municipalities began experimenting with restricting cars on certain days or in certain areas. The energy crisis offered further justification for emphasizing cycling over driving.

The Netherlands, like New Zealand, is a small enough country that it can make sharp turns on policy and culture. Dutch cities began scrapping plans for extending or expanding automobile access. In Delft, for example, according to Bot, a major bridge into town from the south was meant to be the first step in a multilane road carved through the old city all the way to the central Markt square. "Just in time," said Bot, "those plans were abandoned," and only the bridge remains.

Delft, as it happens, was the first city in the Netherlands to benefit from the confluence of protest and policy in the 1970s. A local planner, Joost Vahl, was experimenting with calming residential street design, specifically a curvy, shared-use, speed-restricted street called a *woonerf* ("home zone"). As Delft became one of the first Dutch cities to incorporate cycle lanes into all its development—particularly in neighborhoods outside the old city, like Voorhof, where Lyra and Harper went to school—those same speed restrictions became a crucial part of Dutch neighborhood design. As Bot explained, studies demonstrate that thirty kilometers per hour is the maximum speed a car can be traveling for a cyclist or pedestrian to be likely to survive a collision. Therefore, he said, "thirty kilometers is the maximum speed in every living area in the Netherlands." That consistent speed means that "it's safe to have shared space between users of different forms of mobility."

These days, Dutch transportation policy and local planning both try to maximize bicycle use while making that use as safe as possible—usually quite successfully, because, as van der Kloof noted, "Here the policymakers ride bikes! That makes a difference." Dutch traffic design strives to create what Bot calls "forgiving infrastructure"—infrastructure that allows users to make mistakes without those mistakes creating crashes, and allows users to crash without killing each other.

"It's a huge asset for families that you are being able to cycle to any destination in a safe way," Bot said. For parents with young children, "it's a much more friendly way of moving than moving in a car." As Elizabeth, an American blogger raising three kids in Delft, explained, having your kids with you on bikes is so much more pleasant than yelling at them from the driver's seat. "The world moves by you and your child together, as opposed to when you're driving and your child is a passenger," she said. "Our kids fight in the car all the time, whereas we hardly ever have fights on the bike."

And once kids can ride by themselves, cycling helps create the kind of independence that Dutch parents prize. "Children from quite a young age are able to discover their world, meet friends, and go to places," explained Bot. "Compare that to a situation where they're stuck in their homes waiting for parents to drive them by car. It develops nice and self-assertive kids." Simply put, a child who can ride around town by herself is a child who's effectively quadrupled her unassisted play radius. Harper's best friend in Delft, Arwen, lived just across the Delftse Schie, about a mile away—just far enough that in Arlington, we'd end up driving her to a playdate rather than telling her to walk. In Delft she made that ride by herself a million times.

Cycling was also helping the kids become admirably tough. Even in spring, Holland has plenty of cool, rainy, windy days—not Wellington-like weather, but gross enough to justify the (affectionate?) nickname the Dutch have for their own country: "Chilly Old Frog-Land." The first rainy morning, the girls wanted to know how they were going to get to school, and their faces sagged when we held out their raincoats. It wasn't as if we were punishing them or anything; we didn't have a car! There was no other choice! When they begged us to ride *with* them, Alia asked, "Why would we do that? We don't want to get wet."

"But we don't either!" the girls protested.

"Oh well!" Alia said brightly.

"If there isn't a choice and it's just something you do, they simply get on and do it," Hutchison writes in *The Happiest Children in the World*. She credits her children's having to ride to school in the rain with developing their resilience. It was remarkably satisfying to see our children's outlooks changed by their new way of living, as they bent themselves to meet the place we were. Sometimes you just have to do stuff even though you don't love it. (Lyra's response when I made this point: "I already know that! I had to go on this trip, didn't I?")

Even if we weren't able to get Lyra out on her own as much as we would have liked, we all still found the Dutch cycling lifestyle basically delightful. We made a habit of riding each weekend out to a farm and café past the Delftse Hout for lunch, lemonade, and beer. It was a pleasant ride through a quiet wood and along a country lane, made all the more pleasant by the baby goats Lyra and Harper were allowed to play with at the café while we waited for our food. We rode fifteen kilometers to Rotterdam, my phone strapped to the handlebars displaying directions. Harper even convinced me to let her ride sidesaddle on the back of my bike like all Dutch kids do; she screamed in delight the whole trip. To competently ride a bike around a Dutch town is to feel completely assimilated into the higher-level life of the city and the country, part of a smoothly operating machine, one that offers pleasure, safety, and satisfaction to each one of its cogs. We never felt more Dutch than when we were *fietsers*.

CHAPTER 6

The Poldermodel

Holland is underwater. Much of the country is actually below sea level, protected by dunes, dams, and levees. In fact, a sixth of the land in the Netherlands is *polder,* land reclaimed from the sea decades or centuries ago, drained and protected by elaborate systems of dikes and sluices built and maintained over hundreds of years. Look at a map of Holland as it existed five hundred years ago and you'll see a country with its insides scooped out; much of the land south of Amsterdam was then covered by seawater, including the Zuiderzee, which is dry land today but was then an enormous inlet connected to the North Sea by a narrow channel. Between 1927 and 1959, the Zuiderzee was drained and diked off, adding over six hundred square miles of land to the Netherlands, and nowadays the coast stretches in a straight line from the north all the way down to the Hook of Holland near the Belgian border.

Only as doggedly competent a people as the Dutch could have pulled off such a feat. But to them, it seemed completely rational. There was land just under the water! They could practically see it! Why shouldn't they spend thirty years uncovering and protecting it? I like to imagine early-century farmers saying with a shrug, "It is possible," the refrain I heard from Dutchmen and Dutchwomen to describe tasks ranging in difficulty from pouring a lemonade to completely retooling the national transportation system. Neither task, after all, was *not* possible.

The legacy of those *polders* goes beyond the acres of farmland that sit on them. The story of the *polders* and the centuries of cooperation it's taken to maintain them inflects the self-image of the Dutch as serenely rational seekers of comity and compromise. And so has risen the Dutch *poldermodel,* a philosophy of governance, of corporate decision-making, and of family life that prioritizes flat hierarchies and consensus building.

After all, a complicated network of levees and locks can't be sustained without buy-in from every citizen, from the wealthiest landowner to the poorest farmer. And decisions about the *polders* made from on high, without input from all, run the risk of ignoring the wisdom of the men and women who maintain and repair the dikes, each of which is crucial to the survival of the entire system. So *polder* planning was done deliberately and deliberatively, with long stretches of discussion and debate and with no decision made without full consensus.

That philosophy, of cooperation despite differences, governs many group interactions in the Netherlands, from businesses to family life. "The *poldermodel* is still very important for organizations here," said Bouke, a manager at a Dutch music-video channel. "Project managers at my company, that's how they begin projects: You gather everyone together, you discuss the project, the situation. You invite suggestions and concerns, and that ensures you get buy-in from everyone."

Dutch companies typically deliberate every large decision across large swaths of the organization, often discarding or amending the wishes of management in favor of building consensus among all the members of the team. Plans take forever to make, and once made, they take forever to alter. *Being nimble,* a buzzy catchphrase in America, is not prized in Dutch business. "It certainly means that organizations here can be sluggish," Bouke allowed. "But it's also quite unlikely you'll make a truly bad decision. You might not make the best one, but you won't make the worst one either."

Being satisfied with a decision even though all parties involved agree that it isn't the best one feels like a bananas way to work to me, but it is very, very Dutch, befitting a nation that as a whole prizes competence over excellence and collaboration over authority. The country doesn't have a strong tradition of entrepreneurship, at least not in the lone-wolf-in-a-garage way we tend to think of the concept. ("I've never met worse salespeople than the Dutch," an American who runs a robot-ics start-up in Delft told me.) Some organizations seeking to compete more aggressively will hold long, inefficient meetings about efficiency. "I've sat in meetings in which everyone at the company is trying to agree whether to abandon the *poldermodel*," Bouke said, laughing, "but you can't get everyone to agree!"

In family life, the *poldermodel* has been adopted enthusiastically by Dutch parents. Whenever I asked Dutch mamas or papas what made family life unique in the Netherlands, they instantly, universally answered with variations on *compromise*.

What does this mean in practical terms? It means that, as one Dutch mom explained, "Everything is negotiable." All family rules and deci-sions are up for debate and discussion. "Even kids are asked their opin-ions," said Olga Mecking, a Polish writer raising three children in Den Haag. "Their wishes are always taken into account." In *The Happiest Kids in the World,* Rina Mae Acosta tells a story of putting her three-year-old to bed and undertaking a negotiation about each individual aspect of the process—"back-and-forth haggling" about "brushing his teeth, how many books to read, what pyjamas to wear, when to turn off the light, and when to finally close his eyes." It sounded, frankly, like a nightmare. I don't *want* to debate every single step of bedtime! I want my kids to go to bed! Yet, as at the Hoogheemraadschap van Delfland, the eight-hundred-year-old regional water board whose headquarters were just a block away from our flat, no Dutch family makes a final decision until everyone has bought in.

It did not escape my notice that the debate and compromise encour-aged within the family is the same debate and compromise that is simply not done in the classroom. Why this disparity? Lyra suffered from arriv-ing in her classroom at the end of the year, when the school's and the class's daily rituals had already been discussed, agreed to, and followed for months. After all, the expected result of a well-*poldered* group is that everyone will obey the decisions the group members have hashed out. Once policies are set inside a company, employees follow them, even if they don't love them; once rules are set at a school, children follow them without complaint. Dutch people love rules in part because they had a say in creating them. Lyra had no say in, and no love for, the rules.

Our family was starting from zero; we had no procedures in place for being a Dutch household. So if Alia and I were serious about trying to parent in the Dutch style, it seemed we had to at least try to *polder*. Acosta admits that the process can be "exhausting" and sometimes "infuriating" and praises her Dutch husband for his patience. She makes note of the rules of the road for negotiation: parents must explain their position clearly; children must come up with their own reasoned arguments, not just protest and interrupt. Alia and I agreed that, for the month of June, we would make a concerted effort to incorporate the *poldermodel* into our family.

On the first day of June, I called the girls together for an after-school family meeting. ("Harper? Present. Lyra?" "Ugh.") Alia was out for the afternoon, but I'd gotten her approval to serve as her proxy. We were in the living room on the bottom floor of our house. Outside our window, Thursday-market tourists crowded the street, browsing through Delftware tiles and broken toys. Harper sat attentively on the ottoman; Lyra sprawled inattentively on a couch. "Okay," I said. "In our first weeks here, I haven't really been a very good Dutch parent. So for the month of June I'm going to try to be the Dutchiest parent I can be."

Lyra groaned good-naturedly. "Does that mean we have to go places?" she asked.

"No, that's not where I'm going with this," I said. I held up *The Happiest Kids in the World*. "Dutch families value discussion and compromise. It's important in Dutch families for kids to have a say in rules and in plans." Lyra sat up straight with a canny *I'm listening, I'm listening* look. "So," I said, "I'm going to try to"—here I took a deep breath—"encourage more debate and negotiation between us."

"I LOVE IT!" Lyra said. Harper looked alarmed.

"And I'm going to try and compromise more instead of always insisting that we do things my way."

"I love compromise," Lyra declared, then added after a moment of thought, "when you compromise with me."

"You also have to compromise!"

"Okaaay, jeez."

So, I said, let's start with screen time, the subject about which we most often clashed. Alia and I had held firm to a one-hour-per-weekday screen limit, which applied to anything done on a computer but *not* to reading books on the Kindle. (TV was not an issue. Neither of our kids ever watched TV. We *wished* they'd watch TV, a medium we understood and could easily monitor.) "So explain to me," I said, "why you think you should get more screen time."

"Well," Lyra said, puffing up like a prosecutor on *Law and Order,* "I think that *reading* on the computer should not count as part of my screen time. Like, why should there be a difference between reading fanfiction on a computer and reading a book on my Kindle?" For a long while, I'd resisted Lyra's equating fanfiction with real books, despite her case that "books are just basically fanfiction but, like, authorized." But I'd been trying to relax about that on the grounds that even if *I* didn't love fanfiction, there was no reason to pooh-pooh something essentially harmless and for which Lyra held great passion.

"Okay," I said. "I can agree that we should allow some extra screen time for reading. But it can't be unlimited. How much time do you think you should have each day for online reading?"

"Well," said Lyra, "I would *like* to have two extra hours, so I'll compromise with *one*."

I laughed. "Okay," I said. "I also want to make sure you go outside as well, so if you are using all those hours to read, you also need to find things to do outside."

In some ways I appreciated Lyra's forthrightness. I've never been a good negotiator; when I got hired for my first job in publishing, my boss told me the pay could be "fourteen or fifteen dollars an hour," and I'd replied, shrewdly, "Let's say *fourteen.*" However, it seemed like trouble to have my daughter negotiating so aggressively with a guy who negotiated so poorly.

"By allowing our three-year-old child to negotiate," Acosta writes, "we're teaching him how to set his own boundaries. When Julius questions our authority, he's simply trying to exert ownership of his own life." Over the next few weeks, I tried to encourage our kids to exert ownership over *their* own lives. Where I would once have shut down bartering or bickering with a "No" or a "Because I said so," now I attempted to view such moves as the first steps in painful but healthy negotiations that could yield results more likely to be satisfactory to everyone.

Guess what? It sucked. "Everyone in the family, including the youngest, has a say," Acosta writes about her family's successful *polder*ing. But it turns out that I'm not interested in everyone in the family having a say! As a parent, I'm a natural autocrat, and I found it *torturous* to open simple, commonsense parental diktats to debate.

My mood darkened as every conversation about what to eat for dinner or whether we should go out on a beautiful day or whether eight days was too long to go without a shower turned into grueling trench warfare. My mood darkened further as I thought about what this distaste for incorporating my children's desires into my parental decisions said about me. It turns out I'm *not* really a chill, nurturing, cool dad! It turns out that I *don't* have any interest in fostering independent thinking and a skepticism of authority. At least not when the authority is me!

Alia, too, got sick of the endless negotiation. When she was a kid, she *loved* arguing as much, her mom says, as Lyra does now. In fact, Alia jokingly blames her decision to go to law school on all the adults who told little Alia, "You should be a lawyer!" As an adult, she *hates* arguing, finds it a waste of time; indeed, her least favorite thing about being a lawyer is the constant antagonistic debate, the way every interaction is forced into an oppositional dialectic. Making our house into a courtroom was not the kind of work/life balance she was looking for.

And following the *poldermodel* started to make me feel like a union-busting boss trying to weaken my employees' bargaining position. I found myself behaving like management, making disingenuous initial offers that didn't reflect my true wishes in anticipation of the haggling to come. I don't actually care if my kids make their beds every day! But I became a guy who *told* them to make their beds every day in the hopes of getting them to pick up their rooms at all.

Where was the *gezellig?* Our flat was not the cozy, delightful home of Dutch lore, although it seemed very conducive to homey family life: a lovely three-story flat with attractive gables (???) set above an honest-to-God candy shop. Each high-ceilinged room was lit by broad windows and connected to the other levels by a traditional *trap,* the steep spiral stairway that offers a space exactly one-third the size of an adult foot on which to step.

Dutch parents are *very* into the home as the crucible of togetherness; families set aside several nights per week as home nights, when everyone just spends the evening together. Most Dutch parents' work schedules allow them the sacrosanct *mamadag* or *papadag,* the regular day spent at home. (Between all the *polder*ing, the hard five o'clock quitting time in every office, and the weekly *papadag,* the Dutch had an admirable knack for not working very much or, they would say, working very efficiently.)

Alia and I were doing our best to work on a Dutch schedule. Each morning after we sent the kids off to school, where Harper would learn a little Dutch and Lyra would sleep, we would find our working spots. I wrote and edited in the living room, overlooking the canal, except when I actually needed faster internet than we could steal from Kinki Kappers, the barbershop next door, at which point I'd cross the canal to my favorite café or ride to the *bibliotheek,* the beautiful local library with its airy working space and three-euro Coke Lights. Alia vetted stories and locked down our Kansas housing but also used *mamadagen* to ride to Den Haag or the countryside, exploring the Randstad. We both closed our computers around five, then walked or rode to the market for our daily shopping trip.

But we didn't feel like we were living in a Dutch home. Between negotiation sessions, debates about whether a kid had been looking at a screen for an hour or merely fifty-five minutes, and my tiresome angst about my failure to be even a tiny bit Dutch, Hippolytusbuurt 15 was a pretty tense, uncozy place. In desperation I paged through *The Happiest Kids in the World* and reread a section in which Hutchison attends an inspirational seminar given by a Dutch parenting expert, Catharina Haverkamp. The seminar's name? Keeping Things *Gezellig* in the Home. I emailed Catharina Haverkamp and begged her to meet me for tea.

"I am in the book?" she asked in an Amsterdam café a few days later. I pointed out her name in my copy of *Happiest Kids*. "I am in the book!" she said. "More people have been calling me, it is true." Haverkamp is very tall and striking, with bright white hair; she's also an actress, and Dutch TV viewers remember her as the housekeeper in a nineties sitcom called *My Daughter and I*.

"It's a challenge to start talking to children and be more of a democracy," she acknowledged. "Parents find it difficult, because they are afraid to lose the authority. They're afraid they have to do what children want."

"Exactly!" I said. "How do you parent according to the *poldermodel* without having to do everything the children want?"

"Ah!" She held up a hand. "But that is not correct. It is not about whose way is best. It is about solving the problems together. Instead of 'I solve it for you'—'No, let's talk. What are your ideas to solve this problem?'"

I understood the goal of working together, I really did. But what did you do when the way a child wanted to solve the problem was wrong? When, for example, it would make the problem worse? "Let children make faults!" she said. "Don't panic. You can all learn from how the children's suggestions go."

I shook my head. "I think the problem is that I can't let go of that authority," I said. "I know that we'll end up doing things that are not the way we want our family to run." I brought up an example several parents had mentioned to me, that when Dutch families go on vacation, they split up the planning for the trip, and the kids plan as many days as the adults. "If we do that with our kids, we'll just end up sitting in our hotel those days doing nothing! That's not the way I want to spend my vacation."

"Yet it is their vacation as well," she pointed out. "And they often

don't want to spend it the way you do. You must give up this require-
ment to be the boss, to be strong. We are not equal to each other, but we
are worth the same. *Niet gelijk, maar wel gelijkwaardig.*"

"I'm sorry?"

"Write that down," she said, then spelled the phrase for me. "We are
not on the same level"—here she actually put her hands in the air at two
different levels, to signify a tall adult and a small child. "But the *value* of
the child and the value of the parent is"—she moved her hands together—
"the same."

I chewed on that for a while, along with some apple cake *met slagroom.*
"How do you define *gezellig?*" I finally asked.

She sipped her tea with the studied movements of someone considering a difficult question in a play. "I would say," she said, "when everybody in the family has the feeling of *belonging.* Here we don't say, 'You're
great,' 'you're the best,' 'you're my princess.' We say, 'You are okay.' 'You
are good who you are. You are good enough.'" She put down her tea and
spread her arms wide; she seemed to take up our table and the tables to
either side of us. "The most important to the human being," she said, "is
the feeling of belonging. When you have a person who has a good feeling of belonging, he will make good choices, live like a fish in the water.
It's his natural environment. You have that feeling of belonging from
knowing *I am good enough.* Good enough, that's for us very important
thing."

Well, there, elegantly delivered, was my midpoint between "I don't
want him to be *average*" and "You're a dog." Haverkamp suggested that I
listen to myself, really listen to myself, and never use a tone with my
children that I would not use with another adult. And open myself up,
she said, to the idea that truly respecting the kids' opinions and ideas
would mean, often, making family decisions I didn't agree with.

I returned home discouraged but determined. Surely I could find it
in my heart to speak more respectfully to my kids, right? Over the next
few days I focused on engaging them in negotiation within parameters.
That is, Lyra knew there was a rule that she had to spend a certain

amount of time outside each day, but I let her be entirely in charge of how that time was spent rather than strong-arming her into activities with us. One Saturday, I was rewarded with what seemed like our children's most Dutch experience yet: They rode together to meet Arwen at a movie (*Despicable Me 3,* in a rare non-dubbed-in-Dutch screening). Afterward, Harper went out to play with Arwen and Lyra rode home by herself. While they were gone I celebrated by drinking two beers in an outdoor café and then toppling over while trying to mount my bike, to general applause. (In the end, I walked home.)

My conversation with Catharina Haverkamp had crystallized the answer to one question I'd been wrestling with. If, as she suggested, to feel *gezellig* is to feel as though you belong, we were a long way from *gezellig.* We just didn't yet belong in the Netherlands. For instance, we still had hardly any Dutch friends.

It's not that Dutch people were *un*friendly, exactly. It's that they weren't *friendly.* Or at least, not friendly in the way I was used to, in the way that we tried to be or that the friends we made in New Zealand were. Dutch families did not tend to invite us to do things. When we met Dutch people at school or at dance class or in the DelftMama Facebook group and told them about our trip and the book, they expressed polite interest and ignored my weighted hints that perhaps we could get together sometime. When we invited *them* to do things, they accepted, joined us for what seemed to be a perfectly nice time, and then never spoke to us again. I can't count the number of pleasant afternoons I spent in cafés with Dutch moms and dads having wide-ranging conversations about politics, Dutch family life, and...well, I guess those were the only things we ever really talked about. Those afternoons ended with a handshake and a comment from me that we must do this again sometime — a request that I delivered quite matter-of-factly in April and then with deeper anxiety over the months we were there. By June, my coffee partners must have been able to smell the desperation coming off me. "Of course," they would reply, and we would not do that again sometime.

In the Netherlands, our family didn't experience the stereotypical

European hostility toward Americans that we'd feared the current administration might engender. If anything, we got the impression that Europeans sympathized with our plight; many Dutch neighbors in those coffees and playdates referred to their own nation's flirtation with a clownishly repugnant right-winger, Geert Wilders, who just a few months before had lost his bid to become prime minister. So it didn't seem to be anti-Americanism that steered locals away from us. I suspected that the Dutch didn't believe I had anything useful to say. Look at it from their perspective—as far as they were concerned, their society worked like clockwork. It made perfect sense that I would want to learn from them. But what on earth did they have to learn from me?

Although it's mostly backed up by the evidence of Dutch society, the Dutch certainty that they've figured it all out extends to some truly comical places. One Dutch dad told me about the paella spice mix sold at Albert Heijn, how delicious it was. "But when Dutch people go on vacation to Barcelona," he continued, "they will load their car with all the Dutch food, including the paella mix. And if they order paella at a restaurant, if it's not the way it tasted from the box at the grocery, they say, 'This is not *real* paella.'" Absurd, yes, but in my case, this wasn't about paella. This was about parenting, which statistics and a popular book showed that they did better than anyone else. What were they meant to learn from an American dad who was so at sea, he was traveling around the world to become a halfway-decent parent? And why put oneself out there for someone who was going to leave in a month anyway?

So we weren't making friends with that many Dutch people. But we *were* making friends with expats. The Polish mom who wrote freelance essays; the Brit with a Dutch husband; the fun-loving American professors in Amsterdam. Not only did we make friends with them, we made friends in a way that seemed familiar and comfortable: an encounter would lead to a conversation that would lead to recommendations of other expats we should meet; friendly introductions were made over email within minutes. A Spanish mom meets us for *appeltaart* and introduces us to a garrulous American she runs into on the square; the

American tells us about a travel blogger and her air force husband, and they become some of our best friends in town. Every time we saw a person in that chain around Delft, we stopped for a nice long chat. Meanwhile, I was convinced that the *Dutch* people we'd met were steering clear of Hippolytusbuurt just to avoid us.

Our interactions with expats felt different from our *borrels* and coffees and after-school playdates with Dutch people. They were easy. We talked not just politely but *personally;* we drank wine and laughed; we watched Eurovision. The conversation didn't flag, and our kids played together easily. They were free of the pressure, I think, that Alia and I put on our interactions with the Dutch, and so, despite my antipathy for traveling only in expat circles, we soon found that our favorite social engagements were with other expats.

One sunny Sunday in Amsterdam, we rode the canals with Sarah, a university professor who'd grown up in Kansas but who'd moved to Holland with her American husband three years ago. She told us how they depended on friends for babysitting and playdates; the very boat we were riding on, a tiny skiff with sunbathing cushions set out on the cabin roof and constant sloshing belowdecks, was co-owned with a woman they'd met in their neighborhood. "We've really made a lot of friends here," Sarah told me. They were preparing for a move to Scotland. "We'll miss it a lot."

"How did you *make* Dutch friends?" I asked.

"*Dutch* friends?" Sarah laughed. "We haven't made a single goddamn Dutch friend," she said. "We know our neighbors, and we like them. But all our *friends* are expats." It's not that they didn't try, she maintained; like me, she came to the Netherlands determined not to be subsumed in expat culture, and she'd set out to find and connect with locals. But that didn't really happen.

"They don't need us!" she said as another boatful of smiling Dutchmen drinking Jupilers putted past. "They have their own friends and they've had them for years; they don't see the need to add more."

"Right," I said. " 'Why would I make friends with these Americans? That's not rational.' "

"You make expat friends because they're the ones who are looking for friends, like you."

One day, as we were parking our bikes in the enormous cycle garage at the Rotterdam train station, Alia said, "I think if we were here longer, we would definitely make friends." I'd been grousing about how none of the locals ever emailed me back; she, unsurprisingly, was more forgiving of the Hollanders I was dumping on.

"And if we learned Dutch," I said.

"We would definitely need to learn Dutch."

Dutch people have a curious relationship with the English speakers in their midst. They are happy to speak English with them, often to a point that makes it hard for committed expats to learn Dutch, according to Dr. Allison Edwards, a researcher in linguistics at Leiden University. "They immediately switch to English the moment they hear the slightest accent," she said. "It's a very, very, very common gripe here among people who are trying to learn Dutch." Indeed, the Dutch unwillingness to speak Dutch with foreigners can feel, to some longtime visitors, less like politeness and more like standoffishness. English-language blogs about the Netherlands abound with stories of expats' struggles to make friends with Dutch neighbors and coworkers, narratives that often revolve around language.

For if you're not speaking Dutch with a Dutch person—because they switch to English or, in our case, because we didn't know any Dutch—it can be hard to forge a relationship. Dutch is the language of social connection and friendship. It's the language Dutch people speak to one another at parties, although they'll turn when a non–Dutch speaker arrives and offer a quick English translation. Michele Hutchison, who works as a translator, has noticed that the English interpretations she hears in social gatherings often don't quite reflect what was actually shared from friend to friend.

"I *am* friends with some Dutchwomen," said Lindsay, Arwen's mom (and our Airbnb's owner), who came to the Netherlands from London fourteen years ago. "It took learning Dutch. And it took quite a long time. Ten years or so." *Ten years!* I was beginning to think of Holland as the world's most perfect society—if and only if you've already been here for a decade. It certainly seemed wondrous from the outside: a society with humane working conditions where kids are welcome everywhere, where everyone bicycles, where feminist men committed to equal parenting abound, where companies are just as happy with two half-time employees as one full-time worker, where the government pays for a postpartum nurse to come to your house, where teenagers are polite, where families with sick kids get hardship stipends in the mail.

The country's distaste for ostentatious displays of wealth—on a tour of Den Haag, Lindsay's Dutch husband, Ferdinand, pointed out the royal palace, which was obscured on all sides by the houses around it, and noted, "Modesty is built into the design!"—engendered progressive policies designed to redistribute that wealth. These policies could be as noticeable as high income-tax rates or as subtle as zoning decisions. Several people pointed out to me that one of the best schools in Delft was purposely built next to a public housing project, an effort to ensure access to quality education for all.

However, the more we talked to people, the more we saw inconsistencies in Holland's self-image. Take the country's famed tolerance for minorities. I heard several white Hollanders boast at how their progressive society had essentially eliminated racism in cultural life. Yet even after the 2017 elections that rebuked Geert Wilders, anti-immigrant rhetoric remains part of Dutch politics; for instance, in 2018, the burqa ban Wilders had pursued for a decade was passed in the Dutch Senate. And Dr. Edwards noted that the same Dutch people who will happily speak English to an American expat have different views on assimilation depending on who's meant to be assimilating. *"Immigrants,"* she said—a word that in this case meant people from Africa or the Middle East— "are almost immediately expected to learn Dutch and integrate." Meanwhile, those taken to be well-educated, white Westerners—people brought to the Netherlands by Shell or Phillips, for example—are not looked down on if they don't immediately learn Dutch. After all, they aren't *immigrants;* they're *expats.*

It's clear that tolerance is not the same thing as true acceptance. Noted Kerryanne, the American mom whose two sons were adopted from Vietnam, "Racism here is funny. They pride themselves on not having outward violence of the type you see in the U.S. But just tolerating someone is not the same as welcoming them into society. Who wants to just be tolerated?"

On a number of fronts—immigration, race, disability—the Dutch don't always see that treating all people as if they're the same ignores the ways people are different, often to frustrating or damaging effect. Many white Hollanders assume their nation has good intentions, which can make them blind to racism, even when it's blatantly apparent to an outside observer. We weren't in the Netherlands for Christmas, which was just as well; I wasn't sure what would be more difficult, explaining Santa's blackface helper Zwarte Piet to the kids or explaining why all their white classmates thought Zwarte Piet was great.

And even the famed Dutch tamping-down of personal ambition, which, I was told, forbade competitiveness, overwork, and ostentatious displays of wealth, had its limits. Jack, an American who was running a start-up in Delft, laughed when I asked him about the lack of pressure to achieve personal success in Dutch society. "Oh, they're still totally competing, but about personal satisfaction," he said. "Like: How much did *you* relax on your vacation?" And Dutch people had no problem *being* rich, Jack declared. They just knew they weren't supposed to talk about it.

Nevertheless, I'd never lived someplace where so many things about parenting simply *worked,* from work/life balance to the computer displays at children's museums. It seemed to me that if you could just stick out the ten years it took to learn Dutch and shed your cultural characteristics (American individualism, a Muslim hijab, whatever), make friends, and transform your family into the cozy, deliberative limited liability corporation that is a Dutch household, you'd be set for life.

In our final week, I made one last attempt to transform the Smith-Koises into the Smedt-Koosen. What we needed was an expert to step in and tell us what we could do better—or, at least, do more Dutchly. Luckily, I knew just such an expert: Michele Hutchison, the coauthor of *The Happiest Kids in the World.* I'd already interviewed her. Now I wrote to her with an odd but simple proposal: Let us hire you as a consultant. Observe, advise, and teach us.

Michele was game. I assumed she envisioned the possibility, as I would have, of developing some kind of cottage personal-Dutch-coaching industry, allowing her to spread the tenets of her book to needy families worldwide. (If she does start such a business, I highly recommend letting her train her keen eye on your family for an afternoon.) *It'll definitely be weird,* I'd written to Michele, *but it'll probably be fun!*

On our family's final Saturday in Delft, Michele and her ten-year-old daughter, Ina, rode the train south from Amsterdam and walked through the mess of the market to our house. Michele is a slight, soft-spoken British woman with short blond hair. She appeared at our front door with Ina in tow, a bright blue cast on Ina's wrist, thanks to a football collision a few weeks before. Ina had brought some crafts and some Dutch pancake mix, which she thought American kids might enjoy making on a cloudy weekend day.

"How do you girls feel about the *poldermodel?*" Michele asked Lyra and Harper.

"I like it," Lyra said. "I like arguing about things, and I like that my mom and dad compromise sometimes."

"I like it *okaaaayy,*" Harper said. "Sometimes the *polder* goes on too long." The other day, Harper had stuck her fingers in her ears while Lyra and I were debating some stupid-ass shit and yelled, "You're always arguing!"

"And what about you?" Michele asked me.

"I just don't know," I said. "I think that maybe it's best for big decisions."

"Like year-round trips," Alia said.

"Right." I nodded. "I think this trip would be going much better overall if we had included the girls in our planning—let them have a say in where we went and what we did."

"Why didn't you?" Michele, Lyra, and Harper all asked at once.

"I don't know." I groaned. "I didn't want to raise their hopes only to, like, dash them if it didn't work out. But that wasn't a good enough reason. This was something our whole family was doing together. I should have let the whole family have a say in the decision."

"That's good," Michele said. "That shows respect for your kids' feelings and views. What about today? What should we do today?"

"I'd really like to go to the market," I said. "See if anyone wants to buy anything and see what Ina is allowed to do with money."

"I have my own Maestro," Ina said, pulling a debit card from her bag.

"I want that!" Harper announced immediately.

"I bet you do," I said. "Where does the money come from?" I asked Michele. Our kids got a weekly allowance, their age in dollars divided in the manner we'd read about in a book by *New York Times* writer Ron Lieber: one-third for spending, one-third for saving, one-third for charity. The allowance was not tied to chores, on the grounds that we wanted them to do chores because they were part of a household, not because they got paid for them. The only stumble in that philosophy was that we hadn't really managed to assign them any chores yet.

"We placed some in the account," Michele explained. "She really has a lot of friends she likes to buy birthday presents. So we took the number of friends and multiplied it by ten, because here you don't spend more than ten euros on a present."

"Really," Alia said, clearly thinking of the twenty-five-euro stuffed lion Harper had cajoled us into buying for her friend Nora's birthday party.

"No, it's just not done. It's an unspoken rule. That way you make sure no one is financially prevented from participating."

"Well, at least we won't see Nora's family again after that party," Alia whispered to me. I thought, not for the first time, how much easier our months in Holland would've been if more rules were less unspoken.

Lyra was not that interested in going to the market. "Can't you just try it?" I asked.

"I don't like trying," she declared.

"That shows admirable self-awareness," I replied. I checked my fervent desire to tell her that this was what we were doing and she needed to join us *or else* and instead suggested a compromise. "Is there something you'd like to do that we could all do after the market?" I asked.

Lyra grinned, recognizing a kind of game we were playing for the strangers' benefit. "I think you know what I want," she said. "More screen time!" As Lyra had in a sense broken her classroom, so she had found a way to single-handedly cause the collapse of the centuries-old *polder-model,* which, it seems to me, cannot work when its participants' desires are weighted unequally. (If one farmer didn't mind floods, everyone's *polders* would be in real trouble.) There were nearly unlimited things we wanted from Lyra, but there were only two things Lyra ever wanted: (1) more screen time, and (2) never to have to do anything. Given how those were the exact things we most opposed, we found the tools we could employ to compromise with her somewhat limited. (Notice that I was still thinking of these interactions in terms of compromise, not consensus.)

We finally bribed Lyra into joining us by promising to make a first stop at the candy store downstairs, where, after quizzing Michele ("Dutch kids can buy *anything* with their money?"), she purchased a gigantic candy bar. Michele pointed out that Ina would be more likely to buy something small, as Dutch kids believe in moderation. "Just because one Dutch kid is that way doesn't mean *all* Dutch kids are that way," Lyra said. Michele and I shared a silent look of alarm at Lyra's attempt to invalidate the entire marketing hook of both our books.

The Markt was packed, the usual tents filling up the square. There were tents selling tulips, tents selling sausages, tents failing to sell clogs, because clogs are not actually comfortable. Plus there was a tent simply packed with mops of various sizes and lengths, including the window-washing mop with an extendable stick that towered over the tent, waving lazily in the breeze. (Dutch people are *very* tidy, yet another way I am not Dutch.) The air felt at all times like it was about to rain, but it never quite rained. Harper and Ina wanted to stop and look at everything; Lyra didn't want to stop and look at anything...until we reached a stand that stocked simple dresses printed with cats. Lyra froze and then said, uncertainly, "Can I try that on?"

It fit. It was so cute! We offered to split the cost with her; given our shock and delight at her expressing interest in any article of clothing that wasn't a promotional T-shirt I got for free, we would absolutely have paid for the whole thing, but it seemed appropriate, under the circumstances, to go Dutch.

Meanwhile Harper seemed utterly flabbergasted at the notion that Lyra had purchased something and she hadn't. She looked around, plucked a twenty-euro wallet off a table, and declared, "I want to buy this." Alia tried to gently dissuade her. Then she tried to firmly dissuade her. "What would you do?" I asked Michele.

"What's wrong with your other wallet?" Michele asked Harper as Harper opened that wallet to pull out money with which to buy a new wallet.

"Nothing, I love it," Harper said. "But I also want this one."

"It's her money," Michele said.

"It's my money," Harper said.

"It's your money," I said.

"I know it's her money," Alia whispered to me as Harper bought the wallet, "but it's so dumb."

"*Definitely* dumb," I agreed.

Harper carried the new wallet over to us. "This will be my wallet for traveling around the world," she said, holding it up, "and then when we get back to America, the other wallet will be my wallet until I go to college."

"That's quite thrifty," I said, "if you're really never going to buy another wallet until college."

"Right," Harper said.

I thought again of Michele's insistence that Dutch children are left to make their own mistakes. What nagged at me about this interaction was that, while *I* knew buying the other wallet was a mistake, Harper herself did not know or care that it was a mistake. Here she was, making a totally avoidable error, which *should* have made her as annoyed as I was, but instead, she was walking around with two wallets, blithely oblivious, perfectly *happy,* as if—oh.

Alia:

I understood why Dan was sometimes down on the Netherlands. Most notably, school was really rough on Lyra, and we had a hard time making meaningful connections with Dutch people. (It was super fun to meet expats, but that seemed like not the point of the trip.) I recognize that winters there, with their cold and short days, probably sucked.

If we were trying to *actually* live in the Netherlands long term, these things would have presented serious problems. But in the short term, I kind of loved the place! I never stopped being charmed by the narrow streets, the canals, the central squares, and the fact that it was full of seventeenth-century buildings instead of McMansions. I adored the biking, even biking in the rain. (I didn't even mind biking home from Ikea carrying a giant backpack full of plates.) I liked walking to the bakery and the cheese shop and the Thursday/Saturday markets, and I liked buying (and drinking!) cheap French wine. I loved not having to drive my kids anywhere, both because I personally didn't have to spend hours in the car and because it really created independence in them. They were forced to learn how to get places and then navigate those places without adult supervision. And it freed me up to pursue more of my own interests, like the time that I biked by myself to Mauritshuis in Den Haag to see Vermeer's *Girl with a Pearl Earring*, since no one else in the family was interested in seeing it. (This was stupid of them. We lived in Vermeer's hometown. Of *course* you should go see *Girl with a Pearl Earring*.)

Beyond these specific benefits of Delft, I liked living in Europe, with its near-infinite travel possibilities and its efficient, thorough, and affordable transportation systems. We didn't jet off (train off?) to Paris or Berlin or Milan every weekend, but we did take the train to Vienna and fly to London on seventy-five euro tickets. The fact that we could even consider doing so gave Europe a kind of fizzy energy that I haven't felt in other places. Like many Americans my age, I grew up studying the history and cultures and languages and literature of Western Europe. Having all of that so near me was very intoxicating.

As the trip reached its midpoint, I had mixed feelings about being away. On one hand, I personally had loved exploring our new temporary homes in Wellington and Delft, especially given that I was on a substantially reduced work schedule. And there were a lot of things about it that I think the girls enjoyed too. On the other hand, I often felt frustrated that the girls were not always as game as I wanted them to be. One goal of this trip had been to make them more worldly, but they were not as eager to explore new places or meet new people as I was. I had trouble getting them to care about the shops of Cuba Street or the palace where William of Orange was shot or whatever. They were not, in my view, making the most of this very cool and unusual opportunity they were given—at times, they even seemed to resent it. I knew that it was totally normal for nine- and twelve-year-olds not to be interested in the same things that I was, but didn't they know that plenty of people would give their left arms to do something like this? Weirdly, when I pointed this out, they didn't seem impressed.

I also worried that I wasn't learning enough about how to improve our family life when we returned, which was supposed to be the whole mission of the trip. Yes, I learned that biking for transportation (rather than exclusively for exercise) is great. But I couldn't exactly transport the Netherlands' flat geography and cycling infrastructure to Arlington. Sure, I learned that the work/life balance fostered by the culture and public policy of the Netherlands and New Zealand was great for families. But I couldn't magically convert the employer-based American health-insurance system into a single-payer system or remove the barriers in the United States that prevented people from better balancing their lives or just up and leaving their jobs to try something new. I felt like I hadn't learned all that many actually transferable ways to improve our lives. What would we have to show for ourselves when the trip was done? This was for sure a concern of mine. But, happily for me, that was mostly Dan's problem.

THE DANCE RECITAL

In our final weeks in Delft, we settled into a kind of groove. Harper had made friends and was busily learning Dutch at school. Lyra was being totally ignored at school and rode home each afternoon well read and well rested. Our days were punctuated with endless up-and-down-stairs-ing, which combined with the biking led to some sharply defined calves. I wrote each day at Postkantoor, the café across the street, the Platonic ideal of an outdoor working space: good Wi-Fi, beautiful garden, seats in the shade always available, cheap beer, and snacks. One afternoon at Poskantoor the air was suddenly filled with fluttering flies, buzzing aimlessly everywhere. Diners shooed them away from their faces, only to burst into laughter as they realized, Oh, they're fucking. They're pairs of flies fucking, flapping about incompetently, landing in my salad and forcing me to pick them out. An hour later the bacchanal was over and they'd all disappeared.

We continued to love biking around town. A bicycle is stolen every five minutes in the Netherlands, but ours weren't, although one market day the old men selling crappy Dutch knickknacks, annoyed that our locked bikes were in the way of their stalls, flipped them upside down over the bike rack so that they dangled above the canal like crooks being intimidated by Batman. Sometimes you rode past a bicycle that had been fished out of the canal leaning against a streetlight, brown with muck and stringy with lily pads. As spring turned to summer and the waterfowl tended their nests, baby birds appeared everywhere, geese and herons and baby phantom ducks, who are an ashy gray and lack the white masks. Birds everywhere started getting very territorial, leading to a splendid afternoon's comedy as a swan family guarding its cygnets stood watch over a popular bike path near the Delftse Hout. Anytime a person rode by, the enormous cob flapped his wings, extended his neck, and hissed like the devil. It took Harper half an hour to work up the courage to ride past him, and when she finally did, she scream-laughed hysterically the whole way.

A few days before we were to leave, Harper's weeks of hip-hop dance classes culminated in an evening performance at the community center near the train station. As a parent of a kid who says *yes* to everything, I've been to a *lot* of children's dance performances. I've watched Harper twirl to the Dance of the Sugarplum Fairy and jam to Justin Bieber's "Boyfriend." I once saw her perform a choreographed number to "Call Me Maybe," the inventive, representational choreography of which—handphone, point-at-self, emoji-like shruggie—will never not run through my mind when I hear that song. These performances have happened in elementary-school gyms and ballet studios and preschools and auditoria. But what they all had in common, I didn't realize until Harper's performance in Delft, was that Harper had not shared the stage with grown adults in leotards also giving *their* dance-class recitals.

The community center was packed. We could barely get in the door. "This is a *lot* of people for a dance recital for a bunch of ten-year-olds," Alia said. Lyra (there under protest), Alia, and I snagged seats near the top of the audience bank, then watched as other attendees were forced to sit on the steps or stand on the balconies surrounding the stage. We were handed programs listing eight separate dance numbers.

"Did Harper learn eight dances?" I whispered.

"I think it's other classes run by the same studio," Alia speculated.

The show opened with some kind of long, complicated comedy act featuring the studio's dance teachers in hobo costumes telling what seemed to be jokes about Delft. Even though they spoke in a completely impenetrable language, the rhythm of the two-hander stand-up routine was perfectly identifiable:

Hobo 1: Dutch Dutch Dutch, Oude Kerk Dutch Dutch. Dutch
    Dutch Dutch *Duuuutch* Dutch Dutch Trump Dutch!
Hobo 2: Dutch Dutch Dutch?
Hobo 1: Dutch Dutch Dutch Dutch Dutch!

Whatever it was they were saying, they had clearly written and rehearsed the bits carefully, because they *killed*. Lyra turned to me and said, through helpless laughter, "Why is this funny?" Those teachers, in a bunch of different costumes, did vaudeville-y entr'actes between all the dance performances.

Harper's group came out early, ten nine-year-olds dressed in matching tied-off shirts and jean shorts. They assembled onstage, each one in the ready position with her head down and her hands at her sides. Harper broke the moment for a second and waved to us. Then the music started, a really bad Dutch pop song, and the group launched into an immaculately choreographed dance number. The only thing more elaborate than the performance itself was Harper's makeup, which she'd applied before the show; allowed, just this once, to wear foundation, eyeliner, and lipstick, she'd caked it on.

After Harper's number, a sexy Spaniard, maybe sixty years old, came onstage and introduced the next act in what I can only guess was alluringly Spanish-accented Dutch. The next group, it turned out, was an adult flamenco class. They were followed by a gaggle of toddler ballerinas. After that came a dozen teenage girls of all sizes and shapes performing jazz dance to the Weeknd. What on earth was this? Granted, I was no longer a qualified expert on the subject, but it seemed to me that these girls were actual, legit Cool Teens. Yet they had all signed up for a local studio's jazz dance class! What was happening?

Near the end, twelve adults dressed all in black performed—I kid you not—an ambitious contemporary dance piece, somewhat sensuous, with a hint of melancholy at its core. All the kid dancers watched from the balcony. It appeared that the piece ended with the death of the company in some kind of cataclysm? Not entirely clear.

Lyra said, "That was...great?" I couldn't help but agree. For a moment I was overcome with love for this weird little country and for my children who struggled to find their places in it, both the one who could and the one who, like her father, could not. I still found the Dutch mysterious and frustrating, and I hoped that the next leg of our trip would deliver less angst and argument and more, well, *gezellig*. But any country square enough to encourage its citizens to pursue their goofy-ass love of dance, civic-minded enough to build them a state-of-the-art community center to perform it in, and sane enough to give them the kind of balanced lives that made spending time on such a thing possible—that country had a lot going for it.

Then the hobos came out again and started singing, and *then* the song they were singing turned out to be a final dance piece with *all the dancers from every recital onstage,* a hundred of them or more, three-year-olds in tutus and middle-aged men in black jeans and the sexy Spaniard and the Cool Teens. And in the middle of all of them, Harper, doing normal with all her Dutch friends. She had the biggest smile on her face.

Sámara

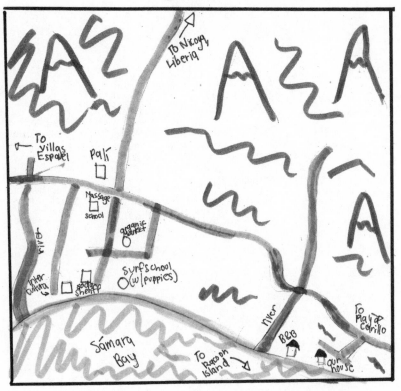

COSTA RICA

July – September

TIDES

At lunch on the beach in Sámara town, Lyra counted the mosquito bites on her legs. "Forty-seven," she announced proudly. After Lyra left the table to wander around the sand, Alia looked worried. "There's really a lot," she said. "What if one of those bites is the one with dengue fever?" I didn't know how to respond to that. *What good does it do to even ask that question?* I wanted to, but did not, say.

It was our third day in Sámara and I'd been not saying things a lot. That was preferable to saying things, because I was irritable and annoyed with everything, and frequently, upon hearing my own tone to my wife or children, I would inwardly wince and wonder how it was that I, a reasonable and nice person, would say something like that. It felt like the Wednesday of our journey. We'd been away from home for seven months and yet so much more lay ahead, and instead of being excited—even here, in paradise—we were all grumbling and snapping at one another. Especially me.

This steaming-hot morning, we'd left our Airbnb and taken the half-hour walk along the beach into town, where we'd eaten a pastry at one bakery, checked out a few bike-rental places, eaten another pastry at another bakery, and then, exhausted, sat down to lunch. I'd sold our bikes back to the Halfords in Delft a week before and now all I could think of when I saw the wide, flat low-tide sand along the Pacific was how good it would feel to ride across it.

In town, Alia had struck a deal with a guy named Gerald who maybe owned a surfboard-rental place on the beach. ("I don't own it. My friend owns it. I live in Switzerland; I'm just back home for a few months.") Gerald maybe had some bikes ("Myself, I don't have bikes; my friend has bikes") and had told Alia to come back after lunch. A litter of roly-poly puppies tumbled over the sand while we waited for Gerald's friend to bring the bikes, and Lyra and Harper tumbled around with them. Soon they were holding an average of 2.5 puppies each and introducing them to us, possibly with their actual names or possibly with names they made up for them. "This is Toby, this is Cosmo, there's Bambi, Isla, and Carly." The puppies' mother, Luna, panted in the shade. Their father, unnamed as far as anyone knew, was begging tourists for food a ways down the beach. Both Luna and her mate were similarly boring brown mutts, yet they had somehow produced the most miraculous collection of variegated pups: one black and brown like a Doberman, one the color of hot cocoa mix, one a dead ringer for Breyers Cookies and Cream, one like a golden retriever, one fluffy and panting in the heat.

Gerald's friend arrived with four perfectly serviceable beach bikes whose seats were all cranked up to their highest possible levels. "I think she's Dutch," Harper whispered. "I can tell because she's tall and blond." In fact Saane *was* Dutch, which *I* could tell because when I asked if we could rent the bikes for a week she replied, "Yes, it is possible." Gerald went off in search of a tool to adjust the seats on the bikes, and Alia and I sat down again to wait. I wanted to enjoy the moment, sitting with my wife on a beautiful beach while my children played with adorable puppies, but I couldn't stop myself from feeling annoyed that it had been more than half an hour since we'd arrived at the place where we were to rent bikes and none of us yet had a rideable bike.

The kids played with the puppies. A coconut palm shaded us from the broiling sun. Without warning, a very large, very heavy coconut *whump*ed into the sand next to me, giving me a fucking heart attack. "You have to be careful of those," Saane said cheerfully.

Gerald returned with a multitool and I cranked the kids' seats down. They struggled to pedal through the soft sand at the top of the beach. "Go down toward the water," I advised. "The sand will be harder there."

"The water's coming up," Harper noted. Indeed, with the tide coming in, the surf line was much closer now than it had been at lunch. "It sure is," I said. After some more loosening and pushing and tightening, I got Alia's and my seats to their proper levels and hopped on my bike to try it out. "Let's get going!" I called, but then Alia waved me back to the rental spot.

"My seat's still high," she said. "Can you lower it a little more?" Exasperated, I dropped my bike to the sand, loosened her seat, pushed it down more, tightened it again, handed her the bike. "Here."

We started riding down the beach, and the water really was getting pretty high. It dawned on me, as a wave washed right up over my bike's wheels, that my entire conception of how the tide might affect the beach was pretty misguided. To the extent that I had thought about it at all, I had assumed, well, they wouldn't put the beach so low that at high tide you couldn't still walk along it. But of course, there is no *they. They* didn't put the beach anywhere. The beach was where the beach was, and the Pacific Ocean was in all the places it was, and right now, one place the Pacific Ocean was was almost completely covering the beach.

We dismounted and walk-pushed the bikes through deep, wet sand and tangles of driftwood. The ocean kept washing over our feet. One surprise wave soaked my pants to the belt. It was fantastically hot. I forged ahead as quickly as I could. I just wanted to get back to the house. "C'mon, guys, we can do it!" I called.

"I hate this," Lyra shouted from far behind me.

"Why did we do this?" Harper asked.

"Girls," I snapped, "that's not helpful."

Alia caught up to me as I stopped to rest. We hadn't said a word to each other in quite some time. I began trudging forward again and she joined me, both of us staring straight ahead. Finally she said, in a low, even voice, "When I asked you to help me with the seat, and you *rolled your eyes* at me, that made me feel terrible." It was like a fever breaking. I knew instantly that I was being a gigantic asshole, that I had been cruel to her for no reason. "You're absolutely right," I said. "I'm so sorry. I'm really, really sorry I spoke to you that way."

"Thank you," she said tightly.

"I'm sorry, I'm sorry, I'm sorry," I repeated. I knew it was unfair to want her to absolve me but I wanted her to so much. "I'm sorry."

"I know." She nodded. "Okay."

"Everything is going bad."

"It's okay if it's going bad sometimes," she replied.

We pushed through sand and sticks for another five minutes before I let my bike topple over with a groan. Harper and Lyra caught up a few moments later.

Harper pointed inland and said, "Can we just ride on the road?"

Why hadn't we just ridden on the road? There was a dirt road running parallel to the shore that we could see from where we stood. We rode on the road. It was so much easier. The road meandered between houses and shacks and a tiny grocery store. The only problem was the river.

About thirty meters before our house on the beach lay the mouth of a wide, shallow river. Inland, the highway crossed it on a rickety one-lane bridge. This road we were biking on, however, sort of trailed off into a dune just short of the river, so once again we walked our bikes through sand to see whether there was somewhere we could cross it. "At low tide you can walk right over it," I said hopefully. At the moment, however, the river no longer drained to the bay in a sandy latticework of cool water but instead had become one with the sea, waves pushing and breaking across the river's basketball-court-size mouth. We watched a woman holding a backpack over her head make her way across to our side, fighting through water up to her armpits.

"Oh my gosh," Harper said. "If it's that high on her, think how high it would be on me!"

"Ugh," Lyra ughed.

"I hate this too," I said. "I'm sorry I yelled at you guys. I told Mom I was sorry for being really mean to her. This sucks."

Lyra shook her fist at the sky. *"Tides!"* she shouted.

I laughed really hard. "It's true," I said. "You would think by now we would have learned."

"Once again tides have *foiled* us."

And so we backtracked, rode to the highway, dodged cars on the one-lane bridge, climbed a steep hill on our beach bikes with their fat underinflated tires, and made our way through our neighborhood to our house. After we got home, we ate a lot of snacks. I didn't stop yelling at my children about stupid stuff, but I toned it down a little.

Later that night Alia was making dinner and I asked Harper if she wanted to ride out on the beach with me. "Sure!" she said, hopping up from the table.

"You've got ten minutes!" Alia called from the kitchen.

We wheeled our bikes through the gate, through the garden, past a horse snorting softly in the dusk. It was cool, finally. It was low tide, finally. We rode south, toward the end of the beach at the bay's final curve. When we turned our bikes around, the sight before us made Harper say, "Oh!" The sun had set. The flat bay and the wet sand were bright mirrors to the sky, so that all before our eyes glowed with pink and orange fire. A bright and powerful happiness filled me the way your lungs fill with air when you take a deep, deep breath.

Harper and I rode, our tires making quiet *shhhhhps* across the sand. Behind us, our tracks were perfect parallel lines. "This is so beautiful," I said. "I wish I'd brought my phone so I could take a picture."

"Pictures never look as good as real life," she said confidently.

"We'll just have to remember it, then," I said. "Will you remember it with me?"

"Yes," she replied, with great seriousness. "For my whole life."

Alia called us in to dinner. We could hear her across the sand.

CHAPTER 7

Every Day

The first thing I see when I wake up is mosquitoes.

This morning I open my eyes and there are three of them, just inches away, three perfect biting machines perched on the outside of the mosquito net. I sleep on my side, and they've been drawn by my radiant heat and the carbon dioxide of my breath. Now they wait patiently for the source of all that alluring CO_2 to expose himself.

It's about seven a.m. and the sun is already bright through the shutters. Outside I can hear chirring insects, the crows of roosters, and—underlying it all, as it will be every moment here in Sámara, Guanacaste, Costa Rica—the white noise of surf. There is always the noise of surf, every day, and this day will be like all those days, each and every day possessed of a placid sameness that is both the appeal of this place and also its own ordeal.

It's not hot yet, but you can tell from the absolute stillness that it's going to be. That stillness is the norm here. Even when it storms, there's rarely a breeze in Sámara. I've been trying to match it with a stillness of my own, but within moments of waking I reach out under the mosquito net and snatch my phone before anything can land on me, and soon I'm scrolling through the emails that have already come in from the East Coast, two hours ahead of us. The fan whirs above; we have not turned it off since our first evening in the house.

On Twitter, a British writer I like has made note of an Old English term, the spirit of which I ruefully recognize: *úht-cearu,* meaning "early-morning care," the worries that accumulate when you awaken in the wee hours. Such *úht-cearu* have been a regular feature of my life as long as

I've been working—the slow pileup of concern, the to-do list I'm composing even as I half doze in the dawn. Each morning such worries are the beginning of a day in which I feverishly try to pack the hours between sleep with work, fun, and family time (which is, of course, fun *plus* work). According to U.S. Bureau of Labor Statistics data, the American worker is about 80 percent more productive today than she was fifty years ago, though wages—adjusted for inflation—remain flat. In my work and personal lives, I strive to be as productive as possible, churning out words on the page with the same ruthless efficiency with which I churn out meaningful personal interactions with my friends and children. (A funny line on the office group chat! A quick hug with Harper! What's next?) Like the American worker, I'm wondering: Am I seeing a return for all this efficiency? Is this satisfying? Is this making me happy? I love being dependable, and valued by my boss; I love that I find daily ways to connect with the people I value. But it feels unhealthy, as if I treat a moment of tenderness with my family as just another widget off the line. One purpose of coming to Costa Rica is for me to try, as hard as I can (LOL), to dial down the urgency with which I conduct my everyday affairs. If the goal of Wellington, in hindsight, was to become more adventurous, and the goal of Delft was to become more orderly, then the goal of Sámara is to become a bit less efficient, in work and in life. To *relax* a little.

Costa Ricans have a term for relaxing a little: *pura vida*. It's the mantra of a Costa Rican vacation, the legend on the T-shirt you bring home, the conspicuous addition to the email signature of the guy from Chicago who just surfed in Guanacaste for a week. It's *hello, goodbye,* an all-purpose phrase that expresses the general concept of taking life easy—with an added dash, in an ecotourism-dependent economy, of green. (The nation's president recently announced an initiative to make Costa Rica the first country in the world to eliminate all single-use plastic—straws, shopping bags, bottled water—by 2021.) In both its warmth and ubiquity it's the *aloha* of Costa Rica, and, as with *aloha* among Hawaiians, I've been surprised to find that most locals take this ready-made marketing slogan quite seriously and subscribe to its tenets religiously.

Yes, all tourist-facing entrepreneurs—guides, surf instructors, restaurant owners—seize every opportunity to *pura vida* a gringo, but also: *"Pura vida,"* parents say, babies on hips, when I visit their houses; *"Pura vida,"* tatted-up dudes on the street intone to each other as they fist-bump. Kelvin, a teacher at the Intercultura language school who translates for me as I interview Sámara residents, told me, "Instead of crying when you are born, baby Ticos say, '*Pura vida.*'" The only dissenter to the concept of *pura vida* I met was a tough older woman, a host for foreigners studying at the Intercultura, who told me that when she was young she visited Honduras and the Hondurans made fun of Costa Ricans "because even when things are not good we say, '*Pura vida, pura vida,*' like stupid people." Kelvin laughed as he translated her message, then said ruefully, "That's true, we do that."

Alia stirs, takes out the earplugs we both wear to sleep (protecting me from the various jungle noises; protecting Alia from my snoring), and starts scrolling through her phone too. "What horrible thing happened while we were asleep?" she asks, a not-a-joke remaining from our stint in New Zealand, where by the time we woke up, two or three insane stories would already have broken in America. "Nothing too big," I reply, then I read from Twitter a headline of U.S. government insanity that, once upon a time, would have been front-page news for a week.

I dress quickly—the same pants I wear every day, a tolerably clean shirt—in order to give the mosquitoes less time to home in on this big white flesh target. The little crab who lives in our bathroom sink is out of his drain today; when we first moved in, he would skitter around the porcelain whenever we turned on the water, urged on, I imagine, by us shrieking, "Oh God!" Now we're all used to one another; he doesn't bother moving, and in return, I do my best not to spit toothpaste on him.

In the kitchen, as expected, Lyra is sitting on a stool at the wooden bar table, headphones on, typing away on a laptop. She wakes up early every morning, waits until exactly 6:00—the time we told her is the earliest she's allowed to leave her bed—and then immediately gets on a computer until someone tells her to get off. Her official screen-time limit is two hours a day, doubled from our limits in Delft due to a lack of anything else for her to do here, but if one day Alia and I slept till noon, she would absolutely be on a screen for six straight hours. Today, though, we don't get in our usual *polder* about closing her computer and getting ready for Spanish because she has something she wants to tell me about.

"Remember those big blue birds?" she asks. "Like on the porch?" A few days ago, an enormous white-throated blue bird, like Fawkes the Phoenix if he were a blue jay, had perched on the back of our porch chair, squawking and gabbling and, at one point, stealing a piece of toast from a plate. "There were two of them this morning who just flew in and sat on the table."

"Were you right here?" I ask.

"Yeah. They didn't care." As I use the broom to sweep feathers from the floor, I ask Lyra to get off the laptop so I can add a new entry to a list I've been keeping. A sour look, two "I'm almost done"'s, and an exasperated stomp later, I open up a Google Doc:

COMPLETE LIST OF ANIMALS THAT HAVE MADE THEIR WAY INTO OUR KITCHEN IN COSTA RICA

- Mosquitoes
- Large red crabs I slapshot out of the kitchen with the broom
- A tiny frog
- Geckos galore that live near the light bulb and, when a moth lands on the wall, silently converge and eat it
- A stray cat
- A stray dog
- Two or three tiny hermit crabs per night
- Big fat flies, electric blue, that hover in front of your face like Snitches
- A beautiful purple-and-blue butterfly with the same wingspan as a mass-market paperback
- A fuzzy caterpillar that looked *exactly* like a dapper mustache wiggling its way across the tile
- A disgruntled bullfrog

- Whatever it is that ate half a papaya off the counter while we were asleep, hopefully we'll never know
- Innumerable wasps, some of whom, it turns out, built a nest by the microwave
- The smell of skunk for seven consecutive nights but not, thank God, an actual skunk

I add:

- Two giant blue birds who flew in over the security gate and spent a morning sitting on our kitchen table

This list is, of course, in addition to the 1,000,000,000,000,000,000,000 tiny ants who are our constant companions in the kitchen. Whereas at home in Virginia, the sighting of a single ant necessitated a drop-everything hunt for where it came from, a determination as to whether there were more, and a cleaning-and-Raid campaign to ensure the leak was sealed, here in Costa Rica we have simply made peace with the notion that there will always be ants. Ants are eternal and endless. The edges of the kitchen shelves are a high-speed anterstate highway, rivers of ants flowing to and fro, as efficient and unimpeded as bicycles in Amsterdam, swarming any morsel that drops on the counter within minutes. All we can do is seal our food tight and ignore them; indeed, I've come to admire their advanced civilization, and to appreciate the way their relentlessness has converted Alia, for the first time in her life, into an advocate for secure food storage, instantly eliminating a top-ten source of conflict in our marriage.

I unlock the security gate and slide it open. Like many houses in Sámara, ours flows freely from indoor space to outdoor; there are no screens on any windows, and while the bedrooms are enclosed by four walls, the kitchen is open to the outdoors on two sides. (Hence the animal visitors.) When we're asleep or away from the house, we unfold the eight-foot-tall iron gates covering those two open sides and padlock them shut. The yard is also enclosed by an electric fence with locked gates at the driveway and to the beach. Rental houses can be targets for thieves in Costa Rica, though the country, despite a few high-profile crimes, is generally quite safe for attentive tourists.

The house's only communal space is outside—a broad, roofed porch with a few resort-style loungers and an enormous table carved from the trunk of a reddish-brown pochote tree. That table is where we eat, where we read, where we play game after game of cards, where we apply insect repellent, where we stare out to the sea just yards away. The tide is going out now, the ocean flat. The palm fronds framing the view are motionless, as green as a crayon. Four wild horses graze on the grassy expanse between the porch and the beach; as I watch, a roan the exact color of our table wanders too close to a dapple gray, who whinnies and gives him a halfhearted kick. Alongside the porch a carpet of white flowers has bloomed in the morning sun—"*buenos días* flowers," our Airbnb owners called them. By 11:00 a.m. they'll close again, but right now they're busy with tiny black bees. A big old iguana crawls through them, neatly lops a flower off its stem, and chews contentedly.

The grand wooden porch table is, as usual, covered with papers and books and bottles of insect repellent. Whenever anyone's about to visit us from the States, we ship them twelve-packs of insect repellent from Amazon and make them haul them here in their suitcases. Not for us the Off! for Families they sell for five thousand *colones*—about ten bucks— in the local grocery store, the active ingredient of which is some kind of natural citronella or something. Daddy needs the hard stuff that goes on like pine tar and is 40 percent Deet. If I can't feel it rewriting my genetic code, you can keep it.

Now I spread repellent over all my exposed skin and spray my shirt. The cuffs of my pants are perma-stained with lotion, and I'm certain all my clothes will need to be thrown in the trash when we return to America. "Alia!" I call suddenly. She's at the bathroom sink. "I've got the blue arm!" Over the past month we've each, once every few days, discovered mysterious blue streaks on our upper arms and hands. Given that we're always sweaty and sticky, it's not a surprise that something is smearing paint or pigment on us, but we've yet to identify what on earth it could be. "What have you been doing?" she says once she spits. "What did you touch?"

I think back. "I don't know!" I say. "My toothbrush? The gate? The fridge?"

She raises her eyebrows. "It's a mystery," she says. "I just hope we solve it."

"That's good," I say. "It'll lend some suspense to the book."

"Ha, yeah," she says. "Like a murder mystery, but dumb."

The girls and Alia have Spanish class at eight, so for the next forty-five minutes our morning is a more humid version of a morning at home. The children eat smoothies made with nearly black bananas rather than bowls of Honey Nut Cheerios, but we must still continuously usher them through task after task. Each time we remind Lyra to do a thing she is not doing, she gives an exasperated groan and says, "I'm doing it!" yet is not, in fact, doing it. She is not collecting her Spanish folder, she is not brushing her hair, she is above all not putting down her iPod. She's also not putting on shoes, but given that she's now on day twenty-six of a no-shoe streak she's pursuing with Ripkenesque determination, we don't bother asking about that.

At eight, more or less, I join everyone in the car, exit the car to open the gate, get back in the car, back through the gate, get out of the car to lock the gate, get back in the car, and drive. They'll be late, but everyone is late in Costa Rica. The girls argue about who gets to choose the song we play in the car first because the Intercultura is exactly three songs away, so whoever chooses the first song also gets to choose the third one. The old iPhone where I store all my music has been malfunctioning badly—sometimes you have to bend it, hard, against your knee to get the screen even to turn on—and on days when we can't get it to work, Alia and I sing the jingle from a circa-1998 Washington, DC, shoe-store ad: "My city, your city, I said Shoe Ci-taaayyy." It's to avoid this fate that Lyra starts bending the phone before we even get in the car. Their arguing seems particularly pointless, given that they've both just discovered M.I.A. so all drives are soundtracked by M.I.A. medleys. Lyra wins the argument and chooses "Paper Planes." "I was gonna pick that too!" Harper marvels.

We rumble and clunk over the rocky dirt road out of our neighborhood. After our first week, we returned those bikes to Saane, unconvinced we would ride enough on the winding, hilly coastal highway to make them worth it. I walk into town if I can get going before it's too hot, but mostly we drive the long-term rental car we've gotten from the National office in town. I do not love driving in Costa Rica, though I don't fear it the way I feared it in New Zealand; it's just slow and unpleasant, and our car has smelled like rancid cheese since a half gallon of milk leaked in the trunk a month ago. We pass a mixture of bland but well-tended weekend rentals, mostly used by Ticos from Liberia or San José, and family homes that look ramshackle from the outside but inside are tidy and friendly. By now I know every rock and rut in this road, know to take a wide left around the mud puddle by the ancient refrigerator and wait for the chickens to trot, unhurried, out of my way.

The coast road is freshly repaved, a clean river of smooth blacktop winding its way north through the hamlet of Torito, then down toward Sámara proper. We wait our turn to cross the narrow bridge over the same unnamed river that blocked our way as it entered the sea that day on our bikes. We're mostly driving through what looks to my eye like a rain forest—it's a forest, and it rains all the time—but that is in fact technically a Costa Rican dry forest, because Guanacaste is the driest part of the country. (Real rain forests get even more rain, have even more animals, and are completely impenetrable instead of nearly impenetrable.) The road is fronted by tiny, in-home businesses marked with hand-painted signs: *Pescateria, Lavanderia, Ceviche Here, Kayaks for Rent*. Sámara is free of large resorts and hotels, so most of the business is homespun. Hearing Harper and Lyra make gunshot noises and sing "We pack and deliver like UPS trucks" as we drive past Ticos waiting patiently at bus stops, fanning themselves in the morning heat, just adds another flavor to the imperialist stew of our entire Central American adventure.

Our stay here has brought home just how much this book I'm writing feels like it's from a different era, a time in which I would take quite an uncomplicated view of an American family coming to Central America to live a purer, simpler life. In a time of heightened understanding of privilege and exploitation—a year in which the magazine *Granta* can publish an essay called "Is Travel Writing Dead?"—my family's adventures feel both more difficult and more charged.

I do my best to interact with locals and interview them for the book, but there's no doubt that of all our four 2017 hometowns, this is the place where we can't even attempt to replicate the life of the locals, because we arrived from a level of privilege that disallows that possibility. The life we're exploring here is not truly Tico life; it's the life of the faux refugee, the gringo bailing on the rat race and looking to Costa Rica to cure the ills of American society. The expat community in Costa Rica is growing by the year as families and retirees are lured by political stability and *pura vida;* they inject money into the economy while also stretching the small towns where they settle in unfamiliar and sometimes unhappy ways. For the most part, it's that community we've joined here in Sámara; we're in no position to pretend to be Tico for three months, but I've learned to admire the expats even as I recognize the presumption of their—our—life choices.

Intercultura is a funky two-story building on the beach with a big front garden and an outdoor pavilion for get-togethers. (The other day, on that pavilion, Harper and I took an after-school merengue class that left us both drenched in sweat and bad at merengue.) Alia, ambitious in her Spanish-learning goals, took lessons in Arlington before we left, has been Duolingo-ing on the road, and signed up for half-day classes at Intercultura as soon as we arrived. Lyra and Harper have taken Spanish in school in Arlington for years, though we've been dismayed at just how little they've retained. I've used the excuse of work to shirk Spanish classes; in truth, like Lyra, I often shy away from activities I find frustrating. Trying to get my head around verb conjugation at forty-two is way too daunting.

"Well," says Lyra as we step into the school, "I bet all my friends are in math right now." The girls protest sometimes about us making them take Spanish while we're here, but this week—as their friends in Virginia glumly text them about the return to school—they've grudgingly conceded that a few hours of Spanish on the beach is preferable to the full September of fifth and seventh grades they're missing. (Tico kids have been attending school some of the time we've been here, but we declared this part of the trip "summer vacation." The girls will start school again when we land in Kansas on October 1.) On Tuesday, amid the adorable Facebook photos of neighbors' kids sporting backpacks and pained smiles, I posted a shot of Harper and Lyra chilling in one of Intercultura's hammocks. (They have five, lined up in a row like they're running some kind of siesta factory.) We've tried to avoid oversharing on social media, hoping not to become those people who post only gorgeous sunsets and hoover up hate-Likes, but every once in a while the anticipated responses are too delicious to resist. It's the same feeling I have when I log on to a videoconference from here, knowing how the palm trees and hibiscus blossoms in the background will read to my colleagues. Yesterday during a meeting about push notifications, my coworker Josh took one look at me and immediately flipped me double birds; it was very satisfying.

In the Intercultura office I wave to Kelvin, who's tapping away on a computer and chatting with a coworker. After the girls head off to class, I walk over and say, *"Hola, amigo."* He switches easily to English and says hi. Everyone at Intercultura knows me as the guy who's *very* interested in Costa Rican culture yet knows no Spanish.

"Do we have *futbol* tonight?" I ask. Kelvin organizes a student soccer game on Wednesday nights at an amazing turf field carved out of the jungle, brightly lit and surrounded on all sides by netting to keep balls from flying off into the dark. It's owned by a gentleman who charges a thousand *colones* for an hour's play and who likes to sit on the sideline, blowing a whistle whenever there's an egregious foul.

"No, man, I don't think so," he says glumly. "There are no students anymore." September and October are the quietest months around here; rainfall peaks, tourism is way down, and many businesses close as their owners go on vacation. Kelvin, tall and handsome with short dreads, a tight beard, and Elvis Costello glasses, looks in his faded surfwear straight out of a Silver Lake magazine shoot. I get the impression he enjoys going out at night with young Intercultura students, most of whom come from Switzerland or Germany. *"Pura vida,"* he says as I leave.

Just those few moments I spent in the air-conditioned office really highlight how hot it's gotten outside since we left home. For instance, my glasses instantly fog over. It feels like the inside of a rice cooker out here. One of the many dogs I now think of as Sámara regulars trots by; he's the one who's the spitting image of our dearly departed Dora, except 20 percent bigger. His owner calls for him from the beach: "Nacho!" The beach is mostly empty this early but for a single jogger, Nacho's owner, and the surf instructors desultorily hauling out boards for the customers that probably won't come. Playa Sámara, about two kilometers long in full, traces the parenthetical arc of the bay. Here in the part of the beach that fronts the town proper, tall coconut palms shade the upper reaches of the sand, where a path meanders through restaurant seating areas and jumbles of driftwood. The edge of the water is a football field away. I've never before seen a beach where low tide means an extra several minutes' walk just to get to the ocean.

To a degree I didn't anticipate before we arrived in Sámara, our daily life revolves around the Pacific Ocean. You smell the ocean. The weather is dictated by the ocean. Family activities are centered on the ocean. I stop by the surf school Harper's dedicated herself to, La Isla. There Gerald greets me with a handshake and a *"Pura vida."* "Can Harper surf this afternoon?" I ask. After a couple of lessons and a lot of practice, Harper has declared herself to be completely capable of catching her own waves. I'm pretty sure that she still gets a lot of help from the instructors who go out with her to wrestle the big board through the surf, pick out a wave, and turn her around as it approaches; Harper's position is that she *enjoys* surfing with other people but doesn't *need* them. Anyway, sometimes when Gerald doesn't have another lesson scheduled he'll go out with her for an hour and we pay him ten thousand *colones,* which is like twenty bucks. "Sure, my friend," he says. "No problem. Tell her to find me here after class." It seems possible she'll be his only customer all day.

I text Alia to let her know about Harper's surf date, then walk up the town's main street to the post office, a single room next to the tiny police station. The door is closed but a handwritten sign is propped up in the window: *Abierto.* Inside it's dark; a rattling old window unit struggles to keep up with the heat. In halting Spanglish I ask if there's any *cartas* for Smith or Kois; the mailman shuffles through a pile of letters and small packages and hands me two postcards for the girls from my dad—he's a postcard-writing machine—and a book from a friend in New Zealand for me.

I think of him as a mailman, though for us that's not true—he doesn't deliver mail to us. In Costa Rica, your mail is delivered once the mailman gets to know you, but the process is made more complicated because no one in Costa Rica has an address. Or, rather, people have addresses, but a typical address is "fifty meters north of the gas station, then two hundred meters west." Houses have no numbers, and, "as in the song of U2," writes the *Costa Rica Times,* "the streets have no name."

Residents who get a lot of mail can pay for boxes here at the *correos,* or they can just stop by every once in a while to see if something's waiting. Most people take as a given that mail will be misplaced, and one package found me only because it wound up, through some mysterious mechanism no one could explain, on a table at Intercultura. Although, hey! I got it! The system worked!

This means that getting anything important delivered to you in Costa Rica is pretty iffy. My company, insanely, tried to FedEx fancy computer equipment to me; three weeks later the office manager was still making daily calls to the cell phone of a random warehouse supervisor in El Salvador, who wasn't letting the package through for reasons of his own. (Eventually my company gave up and issued a return order; the box arrived back in Washington, DC, seven weeks after they shipped it.) After Alia's phone died, she had her new phone shipped to some American friends who were about to visit us; they packed it in their suitcases along with all our insect repellent. Shipping *to* the United States or elsewhere is equally challenging; most Ticos simply find a friend who's traveling abroad and ask him to mail their package from his destination. The girls mailed a flurry of postcards to friends and family from Sámara early in September; they would arrive, many with the stamps torn off, the following March.

All this nonsense—really? No *addresses?* Be serious—is obviously a pain, but it has the beneficial side effect of keeping Amazon and other online retailers at bay. Despite a rate of internet connectivity of 88 percent—that's double the average in Central America—only 12 percent of Costa Ricans shop online, according to a 2016 survey. (Amazon does employ over five thousand people in San José; it's the fifth-largest private employer in the country. Those Ticos work as cloud-computing developers, fraud specialists, and customer-care agents for Amazon Mexico and Amazon Brazil, part of a fast-growing corporate-services sector that takes advantage of Costa Rica's well-educated populace and low business costs.)

In Sámara, you do your shopping in the shops. If you need something the Sámara shops don't carry, you drive forty-five minutes to the Nicoya shops. If they don't have it in Nicoya, you drive another hour to the Walmart in Liberia. (Our one trip to Walmart yielded the most frightening receipt I've ever seen, for 251,630 *colones*.) To the extent that there is nonlocal shopping in Costa Rica, it often nonetheless incorporates—and distributes money to—local facilitators. Ridley in Sámara can pick up French cheese or an Xbox for you on one of his semiweekly San José shopping trips. (There's a 20 percent markup.) If you live in San José and want to order something expensive from Amazon or Apple, several companies offer secure mailboxes, including a new package service provided by the national post office. (There's a fee.) The result is that local retail is alive and well in Costa Rica; every town is packed with locally owned small shops, from independent *supers* (markets) that dot even the littlest villages to surf shops crowding each other out in Tamarindo to Sámara's own stationery store, where Harper buys glue for slime.

The lack of addresses also means it's really tough to give directions, at least in the way Americans have become accustomed to—that is, dropping a pin in Google Maps and texting its location. Our Airbnb host WhatsApped us a Waze link; that nevertheless got us only to the correct neighborhood, around which we then drove aimlessly in the middle of a pounding rainstorm until we saw our host waving at us from the driveway. Our friends Canuche and Mercy had a hell of a time getting their new Sámara hotel recognized by Google; the company would send Canuche location-confirming postcards with time-sensitive codes, which the mailman wouldn't deliver for weeks. Finally, months after they opened, Villas Espavel finally appeared on Google Maps.

The Story of Mercy and Canuche

Canuche and Mercy came to Sámara in 2015 with severance from Canuche's job at a Seattle construction company and a plan to stay for a few months. "We had no 'what are we gonna do tomorrow' jobs," Canuche tells me. They stayed with their two kids, then six and four, in a grungy apartment by the river. Soon Canuche was making the case for staying for a couple of years, appealing to his and Mercy's long-agreed-upon desire to parent abroad at some point in their lives, both to raise citizens of the world and to encourage a second language "while their brains were still spongy and flexible."

The decision wasn't an easy one, especially because they both contracted dengue fever right around the time they were discussing it. Canuche, in love with the ocean and the eco-conscious spirit of Costa Rica, was "the cheerleader." To a guy who'd worked in construction for years, the lot across the street looked "juicy": flat, near the river, set back in the jungle but close to town. It was owned by a Belgian woman who'd come to Sámara on her own eighteen years before, had run a three-villa hotel, and who, it turned out, was ready to sell and retire.

That clinched it. Mercy felt they would never have a better chance; their Spanish was good, they had the money, their kids weren't in high school. But most important, Mercy says, was that she "always wanted to be running something *together*. For him to take all that energy he was putting into the business and put it into *our* thing." So they bought the lot and the villas, hired a contractor, and spent six months building their own house and renovating the three units into five. When we came to Costa Rica and met the family, Villas Espavel had been open for nine months.

"It's so fun to be sharing work goals and family goals," Canuche says, and he's a guy of boundless enthusiasm for the hotel, for Costa Rica, and for their family's adventure. Mercy seems more measured, more of a realist; when she mentions the economic slump Sámara is currently enduring, with tourism down compared to previous years, Canuche quickly declares, "Well, it's cyclical. It'll come back." They spend their days troubleshooting problems at the hotel, driving to Liberia to stock up on supplies, standing in line outside the house of the woman who runs the local water board to pay the bill. ("Our goal, generally, is to engage with the local bureaucracy as little as possible, but, you know, some things you can't avoid," Canuche says. "Like you have water.") They take classes and watch telenovelas to hone their Spanish; Mercy feels comfortable enough with the language that she recently ran a parent meeting in Spanish at their children's private school.

Most of their friends are expats, though Mercy smiles wryly as she tells me that. "Expats are easy to make friends with because they're so *game*. They're already the people who are here trying something crazy, so if you're like, 'Wanna meet at the beach at three?' no one's gonna say no." But Mercy wants to befriend Ticos, too, not to be "the American who only makes friends with other Americans." "Just the other night we had our first dinner party with a family that was born and raised here!" she says. "It felt like a big deal to us. We only sort of understood each other, but it was really great."

It's easy, I think, to scoff at Americans like Mercy and Canuche. They landed in a rustic, rural beach town and immediately built a boutique hospitality property. (It's beautiful, for the record.) But I'm disinclined to scoff at those who seek paradise in their own specific ways, as long as the trail they leave behind themselves is a bountiful one. Mercy and Canuche's longing to become part of the community here in Sámara makes Sámara better—they spend money on local labor and craftsmen, pitch in at a school that serves not just expat kids but Ticos as well, work hard for long hours to learn Spanish, and put themselves out there to connect to the town and surrounding area. I'm moved by their yearning, because, I'm sure, I recognize in it my own—and the ways I'm falling short of seizing this opportunity.

"This is a two-year adventure," Mercy says, and I glance at Canuche, who determinedly looks out to sea and doesn't reply. Mercy often pokes fun at the gulf between her beliefs about how long they might stay in Sámara and his tongue-biting on the subject. "I say stuff like, 'When we go home to Seattle...'" She laughs. "You'll notice he never says that." For now, though, they seem energized by the adventure they're on, and their kids romp with dogs, paddleboard, learn to surf, claim they don't know Spanish and then have long conversations with their Tico class-mates. Maybe they'll go home in a year. Or maybe, as Mercy jokes, "After we put in eighteen years, *we'll* find the next schmuck to sell the property to."

From the post office I walk down the rocky, pitted beach road, past the elementary school and the sarong stalls. There's a dad on a sputtering motorcycle weaving around the puddles, a kid who looks like a first-grader sitting in front of him on the seat, his face invisible under an oversize helmet. There's our friend Adam, riding by on his bike; I wave. There's the burly asshole who spends his days wearing an orange vest and guiding tourists into parking spaces on the street, then demanding protection money; I scowl. He's sitting on a bucket, glumly awaiting the tourists who, in the rainy season, likely won't come.

Sámara Organics is the anchor for a quiet, shade-protected shopping plaza pitched mostly to gringos; in addition to the organic market, there's a falafel shop, a coal-fired-oven pizza place (a five on the Kois Foreign-Country Pizza Index!), and the delicious homemade ice cream shop that's now tragically closed for the season. There's also a pint-size "microbar" with twenty beers on tap—the only place in town that sells anything other than Imperial and Pilsen, the Miller and Bud of Costa Rica. Organics, run by Angelina, an American expat with a son around Harper's age, stocks a mix of produce from nearby small farms and, like, a *lot* of essential oils. I buy a couple of shallots—this is the place in Sámara to get shallots—for a recipe we're hoping to make when Adam and his family come over for lunch this weekend.

Shallots and mail safely packed away in my tote bag, I wave goodbye to Angelina and head back to the beach. I cut through the beachfront bar Lo Que Hay, my favorite place to work and drink micheladas, but it too is closed for the month, the kitchen locked up and the chairs stacked on the sand. So I'm headed to Intercultura, where there's Wi-Fi and shade. At low tide in the sun, a thin layer of hot seawater covers the sand for yards in every direction. For long stretches of the beach, you cross tiny estuaries, tide pools slowly draining back into the sea, in which the flowing water creates beautiful sand braids of dark and light—the black volcanic sand of which the island's beaches were originally made twisting around the newer, whiter coral sand, ground out of the geologically young reefs growing in the bay. I find it mesmerizing to trace their shape and watch them change from day to day.

I spend the rest of the morning camped out under a canopy at Intercultura, writing and calling in to meetings. Telecommuting from Costa Rica isn't that different from telecommuting from anywhere else. I sweat more. The internet's worse, which tends to make me, perversely, more productive. The power goes out a lot. There are other issues too; twice while I've been on videoconference calls, my coworkers have demanded to know what caused the surprised face I'd just made. (Once it was a whale breaching out in the bay; the other time it was a woman riding past, entirely nude for some reason, on a horse.) But at a company where for years I've communicated with my coworkers through email, instant-messaging, and videoconference, doing so from another country in a compatible time zone isn't that much of a change.

Every ninety minutes the girls are released into the courtyard for a break, where they both delight me and annoy me, as is often the case. Alia shakes her head and asks, sotto voce, if I'm worried at all about what Lyra's doing on her iPod, which she pulled out as soon as she left class. Meanwhile, Harper has some questions for me about what I'm writing, who I'm talking to, what's that on the computer screen, what am I listening to, if I'm supposed to be writing why am I looking at Twitter, et cetera.

On one break, they ignore me and run over to Nuria, who sells empanadas and banana bread by the school. Nuria waves to me as the kids point back at the Intercultura courtyard. She lives just over the bridge in a cozy house with her husband—a gardener—and her twin daughters, thirteen-year-old students at Secondaria Sámara. As happened with many of the Tico parents I've talked to, I was struck by the similarities between her and my concerns about screen time—"Oh yes," she told me, with Kelvin translating, "when they need to study, they only want to be on the phone." But she also discussed dreams and fears for her children's future that stand in stark contrast to the dreams and fears I'm used to hearing from friends in Arlington and expat friends here. When Nuria thinks about her kids' future, she doesn't say she just wants them to be happy, or to maintain their innocence as long as possible, or to make the world a better place. Nuria wants one daughter to become a lawyer and one to become a veterinarian. She doesn't fear that they'll lack empathy or that their jobs will not be a match for their skills. She fears that they'll be caught up in the drug trade that travels up the coast from Colombia and across the Caribbean from Jamaica; the murder rate in Costa Rica, though the lowest in Central America, is double the United States' and growing, and three-quarters of those murders are tied to drug trafficking. Hearing things like this over and over from Tico parents has been a reminder that *our* hopes and dreams for our children— at least the ones we feel comfortable saying out loud—take stability and safety as a given. Nuria and other Tico parents don't necessarily begin there.

"How was class?" I ask as they all file out into the courtyard at noon. Lyra gives me a vague "It was good," then settles into a hammock with her Kindle. Harper considers the question with a bit more care. "I wish there were other kids this week," she says. "Sometimes it's fun to only have Lyra with me, but sometimes it's annoying."

"It's always annoying!" Lyra, who it turns out was listening after all, calls from her hammock.

Harper grins, then feigns outrage in a way that reminds me she treasures any interaction with her older sister, even if many of those interactions are borderline abusive. "Annoying for *me!*" she says hopefully, but Lyra's reading again and doesn't respond.

The rainy season has made Spanish classes a solitary affair. Alia is essentially getting private lessons at a discount rate; the other American kids who made Lyra's and Harper's Spanish classes especially fun in previous weeks are long gone. A highlight was the two boys who informed Harper that their dad was an actor from Hollywood; some Googling helped me determine he'd had a four-episode arc on *Justified*. I immediately followed him on Twitter in hopes he'd want to make friends. No dice.

"Harper, Gerald can go surfing with you after lunch," I say, and Harper brightens the way she always does when an activity, any activity, is mentioned. Meanwhile, Lyra groans. "Does that mean we have to go to the *beach*?"

"Yeah, Lyra," I say, rankled, and even though I know I should let it go, I am as usual incapable of letting it go. "I understand that you want to go home. But—"

"But you're gonna make me stay here anyway because I'm just a kid, and what you want is more important than what I want," she says. This is delivered so sarcastically while also being such an accurate description of my actual beliefs that my entire argument-processing system briefly shorts out.

Maybe, I think, I can make this a little more transactional. "While Harper is surfing, is there somewhere else in town you'd like to go with me?"

"Where would I want to go?" She sighs and turns back to her book. Alia gives me a beseeching look: *It is not necessary,* she is saying, *to fight about this.* In fact Lyra and I are both too hot to really work up a head of steam. She's right; a town with no library and no bookstore is a town that offers no place Lyra is interested in visiting. She doesn't like to shop, is not hugely interested in the local culture, and only grudgingly agrees to explore with us. Given the choice, she would always simply rather go home.

Of course, in many ways Costa Rica is the place we've gone on this trip that's *most* attuned to Lyra and her desires, in the sense that it's the country that has asked the least from her. She's had a couple of weeks of Spanish class, and occasionally we do something modestly outdoorsy, but mostly we spend our days closely approximating Lyra's idea of a perfect life: sitting around, listening to music, playing cards, staring at screens. If we could somehow ship her gigantic secondhand-book collection from the storage space to here, her life would be perfect. She does have that Kindle, on which she can borrow library books. At this point, actually, she has two Kindles: her new Kindle, which she had to buy with her own money when she lost her first one in Delft; and her original Kindle, which a kind Dutchwoman bought for five euros in the Delft Goodwill and then mailed to Alia's mom after tracking me down on Twitter. She's usually maxed out on her e-book loans from the Arlington library, and occasionally she picks up the odd e-book from the Wellington and Delft libraries as well. But she's flat-out running out of things to read.

And so, many, many times each day, we'll see her staring at her iPod or clicking away on a laptop; sometimes we ask her to find something else to do, but in truth we're all pretty exhausted from months together, day after day with just us and the mosquitoes, all biting one another. And Lyra's probably getting more exercise than I am. She's taken over the tile path around the side and back of the house, making it her personal pacing track, where she walks and thinks for half an hour at a stretch. Sometimes she heads down to the beach, where she'll walk and think some more, ankle-deep in the warm water. If she hadn't lost her Fitbit, I expect she'd hit twenty thousand steps on the regular.

Lunch is about thirty meters down the beach, at Soda Sheriff. A *soda* is a specific kind of Costa Rican restaurant, affordable and tasty, serving a familiar menu of *casados* (mix plates) and *arroz con*s. Every town has a couple of *soda*s, usually named for the owner or for some proximate landmark. Soda Sheriff is next to the police station. The instant we sit down, Lyra asks, "Do we have cards?"

Thank God for cards. One problem with spending time with your children, Alia and I have discovered in this year of spending time with our children, is that a lot of the stuff you can do with children is just awful. Kids' board games are bad. Pretending to be pirates or whatever is bad. Crafts are bad. Playing sports with kids is bad until about age thirteen, when the opposing trajectories of your athletic abilities and your child's athletic abilities intersect, and then it's good for like a week, and then they reliably crush you and it's bad again.

In February, in a cabin deep in the New Zealand bush, Gary taught our children cabbages and kings, a game in which you deal out all the cards and everyone competes to get rid of his or her hand. The winner, the king, has an advantage in the subsequent round, as she steals the best cards of the loser, the cabbage.

"Wait a minute," I'd said as our kids fanned their cards out in the candlelight. "Isn't this game the same as asshole?" The girls giggled. "Well, yeah, mate," said Gary reasonably, "but when you teach it to kids, you call it cabbages and kings."

So, yes, cabbages and kings is just that drinking game you played back when all you had in your fleabag apartment was a deck of cards and

The Complete Rules of Cabbages and Kings

Players: three to six.

The goal is to get rid of all the cards in your hand.

Deal out all the cards, including two jokers. In the **first game,** whoever has the two of clubs leads.

Play continues clockwise around the table with each player playing a card **higher** than the previous card played. (Suit does not matter.) If you cannot play a higher card (or do not wish to play), you may pass; once you have passed in a round, you cannot rejoin until a new round begins with a new lead. Eventually someone will play a high card that everyone else passes on; that person gets to lead the following round.

EXAMPLE: Alia plays a 2. Dan plays a 4. Lyra plays an 8. Harper plays a 9. Alia plays a jack. Dan passes. Lyra passes. Harper plays a queen. Alia plays a king. Dan and Lyra have already passed. Harper a plastic bottle of rum. But removed from that seedy environment it becomes, magically, the perfect game, pitched at just the right level for a ten- and a twelve-year-old and their desperate parents. That is, its rules are simpler to understand than those of hearts, poker, or other adult staples, but its strategy is more complex than grueling little-kid standards like crazy eights, speed, or (shudder) war.

In an intergenerational game of cabbages and kings, adults may do their best, playing the game in a way that's interesting to them. Maybe you're a card-counter, springing your kings and queens on your opponents only when the jokers and aces have been played. Maybe you save your pairs until the last possible moment, then unleash them all in a flurry. But the luck of the draw means that children will win sometimes, regardless of how well or poorly they play, so adults remain interested while kids don't get frustrated. I can't think of another competitive activity in which adults can play at the peak of their abilities and kids can still prevail. Limbo, I guess.

Now, as a grown man, do I *actually* care whether I win or lose at cards

---

plays an ace. Alia passes. Harper can now sweep the cards off the table and start anew, leading a low card for the next round, for which everyone is back in.

Aces are high, but **jokers** are higher—they are the highest cards in the deck.

Runs: If three consecutive cards are played, a run has been created, and any player who plays a card must continue the run. A joker can cut the run short.

EXAMPLE: Alia plays a 4. Dan plays a 6. Lyra plays a 7. Harper plays an 8. Alia *must* play either a 9, to continue the run, or a joker, to win the round and end it; if she can't, she must pass.

Pairs: The person who leads a round may, instead of playing a single card, play a pair of the same card. All following players must *also* play pairs. Players may also lead with three of a kind or four of a kind. In all cases, a player may play a joker to cut this short. If three with my loving family? Of course I do. I want to win. If I must lose, I at least want my wife to also lose. But I admit that the seductiveness of card-playing with my kids goes beyond the pleasure of ascending to kingship and crowing right in their sad cabbage faces. It has to do with my desire, so often thwarted these days, to look at them.

Back when they were babies, we could look at them all the time. There were years of my life when I felt I did nothing *but* look at my children, afraid that if I looked away for even one second, they would be eaten by tigers. But now they disappear into screens and schools, behind closed doors, or out in the world. Even when they're around, I find it difficult to cadge a good long look; it is the plight of the parent of tweens to desire nothing more than to look at his kids in peace and to be rebuffed most of the time by his kids saying, correctly, "Stop staring at me, that's weird."

But around the table, playing cabbages and kings, they're concerned with how to get rid of that solitary six or when to spring the triple fours. They don't notice that I am drinking in the way their faces resemble their

---

numerically consecutive pairs are played, the next player *must* continue the run of pairs.

EXAMPLE: Alia plays a pair of 4s. Dan plays a pair of 7s. Lyra plays a pair of 8s. Harper plays a pair of 9s. Alia *must* play either a pair of 10s or a joker, or she may pass.

Strategy: Low cards are hard to get rid of; high cards are easier. So your goal usually is to use your high cards in hopes of winning a round so that you can lead out one of your low cards that otherwise would remain stuck in your hand. That means you might not play an ace if you know that one of the jokers is still out. Or you might try anyway and cross your fingers! Pairs can be valuable, especially if others don't have them, as a way of clearing out a bunch of cards from your hand at once; for that reason, players will often resist the temptation to split up a pair to play one card as a singleton.

cousins', the ways they express exasperation, their glee at unexpected windfalls. They play cards so differently from each other, befitting their personalities, Lyra in constant protest at the unjustness of everyone else's moves, which turns, in the moment of victory, to benevolent forgiveness; Harper silently and watchfully processing the game and then making a surprising and intuitive play to defeat us all.

We wait out the rain and listen to music and sometimes I can fool them into an honest-to-God conversation. I see them learn from their mistakes, if I'm smart enough to hold my tongue when I see them make one. We've expanded our repertoire into rummy and oh hell, but cabbages and kings is our standard, the game that gets all four of us around the table and, briefly, off one another's nerves.

You might be afraid of playing cards with your kids, scarred from hours spent listlessly trying to cheat your way to defeat in an endless game of war. But on this trip, we figured it out: War is hell. We choose cabbages and kings—an obscene drinking game transformed, via a simple name change, into a delightful family pastime—instead.

Going out: When you play your final card, you're out. If others around the table can play something higher than that card, play continues; if everyone must pass on that card, the person to your left gets to lead the next round.

Endgame: Whoever goes out first is the **king.** Whoever goes out last is the **cabbage.** (It's fun to also declare a vice king and a vice cabbage, with those left in the middle declared citizens.)

The next game: Once the cards are dealt for the next game, the cabbage must give her two highest cards to the king. The king gets to give two bad cards of her choice to the cabbage. The vice king and vice cabbage exchange one card. Citizens don't have to do anything. The cabbage leads the initial round.

Bettering your lot: It can be really hard to escape from cabbagehood! The structure of the game perpetuates inequality, which teaches children a lesson about capitalism.

★   ★   ★

During lunch the clouds roll in, though it still feels like a few hours until rain. There's some not-unusual confusion with the guys at La Isla; as with all appointments in Costa Rica, no one ever wrote anything down, and at first Gerald isn't there. He might be out to lunch or with a girl, his coworkers speculate; reasonable people can disagree on the details. As an exasperated Alia tries to get the story straight first in Spanish and then in English, Harper occupies herself playing with the surf-school puppies. Soon Gerald appears, and he and Harper grab a board, wax it, and troop down to the water.

Lyra's walking around on the beach reading her Kindle and somehow, despite seemingly paying no attention to her surroundings, not stepping in any of the horse poop that litters the high-tide line. When tour guides trot down the beach, leading other horses behind them in a whinnying, shitting herd, they are chased and barked at by multiple annoyed dogs, a comic disturbance that all the people on the beach stop whatever they're doing to watch. Alia and I sit in beach chairs under the palms, her listening to a podcast and me answering emails. Harper's out in the water; as a foaming swell approaches, she paddles as hard as she can but remains perfectly stationary until Gerald discreetly shoves her forward just as the wave arrives. But from there it's all her, and she gets her feet forward with a sprightly hop and balances nicely, arms out, surfing the slow-rolling wave into shore. At the end of the ride she falls to the side with a splash and pulls the board back by the leash, waving happily at me.

It's unclear whether Harper will remain a surfer. She's always been a kid who will get a task in her teeth and shake it until she's worked it out. But surfing is different from learning to tie your shoes. That has a definite end point (your shoes are tied), but you never really *have learned* to surf; you've just, if you're lucky, caught a few more waves than last time. It's really hard to get good at surfing, especially when you're small and neither of your parents are particularly good judges of waves. When *we're* out there instead of Gerald, trying to help her choose waves and pushing her along, her hit rate is roughly one decent ride out of every fifteen attempts, and she gets worn out and frustrated before too long. (As do we.) But God, when she's caught a wave, there's not much I enjoy more than watching her crouching low on the board, her little butt sticking out, biting her lower lip as she flows ashore. I hope she sticks with it.

Thunder rolls in the far distance as Harper returns from the ocean, padding along carrying the back half of the board while Gerald carries the front. From where I'm standing I can see her keeping up a cheery stream-of-consciousness monologue, while Gerald listens politely. It's now about one thirty in the afternoon and sometime in the next three or four hours—it can take a long time for a storm to drift in, here in windless Costa Rica—it's going to start raining. We've already eaten. There's no place to *go*, really. Soon the kids will want to leave the beach, Harper because she's wet and itchy, Lyra because she's never not wanted to leave the beach. So then we go home and...what?

Harper:

When you get on your surfboard in a lot of ways it is pretty boring just sitting there. But once you see a wave, turn around on your board, and start paddling, it is so much fun! As I got on my board looking for a wave I felt excited. As soon as I saw a good enough wave to ride, I quickly turned my board around and started paddling as fast as I could. Once I caught the wave I hopped up onto my knees and slowly went up on my feet, trying to balance while looking where I was going. The first few times I did it I instantly fell, but I was determined to not give up. Over the weeks of living in Costa Rica, I got better at surfing. I wanted to surf all the time! When our friends visited us they wanted to learn how to surf, so the teacher actually told me I could help teach the class. I was so happy!

What I love about surfing is that when you do it you feel so free! I definitely want to keep surfing.

Early in our stay we attempted to combat the empty hours we could foresee filling our days. We called a family meeting at the big porch table to *polder* out a daily schedule. This goal was hampered by Lyra's flat declaration that she did not want us to have a schedule, that anything other than entirely unstructured time would, basically, cramp her style.

"But I don't want the things that we want to accomplish to fall by the wayside, and I'm afraid it will if all our time is unstructured every day," Alia said.

"What things?"

"Duolingo," I said. "Life-skills lessons." We had big goals of teaching them both some basic stuff that we couldn't believe they didn't know, like how to make mac and cheese, how to wash dishes, or how not to leave your gross crusty dried-up toothpaste in the sink. A long negotiation ended with her grudgingly agreeing to a schedule on which FREE TIME was blocked out for hours each day. Soon the kids, like the girl in the Shel Silverstein poem, broke two glasses washing the dishes. Every few days I still step on a shard of glass. By now, overcome by torpor, we've eliminated Life Skills as a scheduled activity.

We load up the car ("Can I pick a song?") and navigate past the Intercultura, waiting impatiently for a horse who's ambling up the road ahead of us. Horses on streets in Costa Rica have the same nonfear of cars that bikers have on the streets of Delft. We stop at the Palí, the big grocery store, for some staples: beans, rice, milk, tortillas, chips, the very bad Chiky chocolate cookies the kids love and I eat out of boredom. For a while we bought *salsa tomate* and we couldn't *believe* how bland it was, and then we realized, oh right, *salsa* means "sauce," we are dipping tortilla chips in tomato sauce.

In front of us in line at the Palí are Pat and his son Noah buying a big old bag of rice. Their family, like ours, do most of their shopping here rather than at the more expensive "gringo market" pitched primarily to short-time tourists. (And the organic market? Hoo boy. Much as I'd like to be a person who shops only at the organic market, we can't afford it for much besides shallots and other hard-to-find produce.) Palí is a strictly business *mercado* stocked with staples, the place where Ticos get rice, beans, plantains, Salsa Lizano for their *gallo pinto*. Its mascot, a *luchadora* in green and red, promises *los precios mas bajos*. (Belying my ode to local businesses in Costa Rica, it's owned by Walmart de Mexico y Centroamerica.)

We chat with Pat a bit as we wait; though there are only two people in line ahead of us, and each has only a small basket of groceries, the checkout process is, as always, protracted. It's not a matter of ineptitude on the part of the clerk but simply a lack of the pretense of uber-efficiency that drives customer interactions in the United States to move at an absurd rate, like a podcast listened to at 1.5x speed.

Not in Costa Rica. Each item is picked up, set down, rotated, scanned with a handheld scanner, picked up again, and placed in the cart. Then the next item is picked up, set down, rotated, scanned with a handheld scanner, picked up again, and placed in the cart. It isn't *slow*—it's a normal speed that, when you first arrive, *feels* slow. Usually I just look at my phone or talk to a kid while I wait; this time, I get to talk to Pat, who's feeling energized, which makes me feel energized. In the annals of Americans-pitching-everything-and-roaming-the-world stories, Pat and his wife, Tiffany, are the gun to our knife fight. What they've done is so much ballsier than what we've done—I admire them and watch them carefully for signs of how our trip might go. In a couple of days, Pat tells me, he's flying out to lock down—fingers crossed—the sale of their boat. "Good luck!" I say as he and Noah head out the door, Pat with the rice over one arm.

The Story of Tiffany and Pat

Tiffany grew up moving all over the country: Virginia, California, Arizona, Texas. "I hated moving because I was a shy child who had trouble making friends," she says. "I always said I would never make my kids move—but being a military family, that wasn't really an option for us." As Pat's air force commitment neared its end, Tiffany enrolled in a PhD program with an eye toward a tenure-track job, a house in the suburbs, stability. She didn't get the exact job she wanted—in a tough market, the best her top-tier University of Texas degree could get her was a precarious spot at Northern Arizona University with the vague promise of a route to tenure someday. They built their dream house in the suburbs of Flagstaff. Pat got a job in NAU's facilities services department. And they settled down, just like Tiffany had always wanted.

They made it two years. Tiffany's fifty-nine-year-old uncle died a long and terrible death from mesothelioma, Tiffany visiting him in Texas when she could. "I was going through that shit," she says, "and Pat was hating going to work. Just hating it." Pat's job was awful; Tiffany felt she was feeling her life slip away in a job she didn't much care for either. "I don't know," Pat joked one day. "I wish we could just, like, sail around the world."

"I think he was being flippant." She laughs. "But I would cling on to anything he showed an interest in, because he just wasn't himself." Research revealed that in fact there were families who lived on boats, sailing from port to port, homeschooling or "unschooling" their children.

Tiffany's dad was already dead at fifty-one. Pat's was dead at fifty-five. "Life is short," Tiffany says. "We're not guaranteed retirement. We've seen that over and over again." In the summer of 2016 they sold everything they owned, left their dream house, drove to Nova Scotia, and bought a catamaran, thirty-eight feet by twenty-one feet. Pat knew a bit about navigation from his time in the air force, but his sailing experience was limited to a weeklong class. After a month practicing on a flat Canadian lake, they sailed out through a series of locks toward the Atlantic. "Within half an hour we got hit by one of the biggest thunderstorms I'd ever seen," Pat says. "I absolutely thought we were all going to die."

The family sailed down the coast and into the Caribbean. They snorkeled off uninhabited Bahamian islands and paid the standard bribes to immigration officers in the Dominican Republic, each payment chipping away at their meager cash reserves. They befriended a robust network of cruisers who used Facebook and WhatsApp to plan meet-ups, share photos, and warn one another about troublesome ports or approaching storms. They met other families who were also escaping civilian life, resetting themselves the way they were. Soon all the food they'd stocked up on in a Florida Costco was gone, so they fished, scrounged, bought as little as they could in port. And they tied up next to mega-yachts, enjoying the same sparkling water their celebrity owners did, the bluest water they'd ever seen.

"The highs were really high and the lows were really low," Pat says. Their living space was tiny—cabins the size of queen beds, a twelve-by-six indoor galley. However, the boat featured a fifteen-foot trampoline from which everyone could bounce into the ocean. None of their friends or family visited them. "Everyone back home thinks we're insane and irresponsible and making a huge mistake," Tiffany says sadly. The boys hated homeschooling and refused to take their parents seriously as teachers. The parents hated the daily debate about whether they had to study. The only one who liked homeschooling was three-year-old Hope, whose insistence that she get to "go to school" with her big brothers was adorable but unhelpful. Tiffany had gotten a job teaching online, which required well-planned navigation in order to access a cell signal whenever she had a class. It wasn't going well. "I love teaching," she says. "I hate teaching online. You know how people are assholes online? That's what the students are like to me."

"If you've got problems in your marriage or in your life," Pat says, "a trip like this won't solve them. It'll bring them into sharp relief." I nod and laugh. Traveling around the world with my family has definitely not solved any of the things wrong with me, that's for fucking sure. I recognize so much of ourselves in Pat and Tiffany, even if their journey is far more adventurous than ours ever was. We, too, viewed this foolhardy jaunt as a kind of family reset, a chance to control-alt-delete the life we'd trapped ourselves in and figure out how to build it back from the ground up. No one told us to our faces that we were ruining our children's lives; instead, other parents told us how brave we were, nodding blithely as they noted they could *never* take their kids out of school for so long. With the exception of our moms, no one in our extended family has visited us anywhere in the world. I know this shouldn't disappoint me—people are busy, life is complicated, traveling is expensive—but it does.

And yes, I'm excited to get back to America. Our easy life in Arlington is looking more and more appealing, in part because all the ways it didn't feel easy are starting to vanish from my memory, supplanted by mosquitoes and nights without babysitting. Sure, we were stressed out and dissatisfied, but still, I had a screened porch, local broadcasts of the Washington Nationals, and a Diet Coke fountain. What was I complaining about?

But it isn't entirely clear we even *can* return to that life as it previously operated. Alia's small, family-friendly firm is merging with a larger firm, one that has no particular incentive to bring back a nonequity partner who's in Costa Rica for some reason. My magazine welcomes me back, but no one is quite sure what I should be doing, least of all me. And when we do return, it's becoming pretty evident that we'll be in the hole. Another reason I identify with Tiffany and Pat: they, like us, are running out of money.

After nine months of sailing around the Atlantic, hurricane season approached, so in May Pat brought the boat into port in Grenada, and the family flew to Costa Rica. "You know the massage school in town?" Tiffany asks. We do; it's where we get thirty-dollar student massages in an air-conditioned room listening to a pan-flute version of the theme from *The Godfather*. Tiffany registered for classes, seeing in massage therapy a path off the academic ladder she'd found herself stuck on, a ladder she'd spent a decade climbing but no longer wanted to reach the top of.

And then, oh God, just to have bathrooms and restaurants. Pat and Tiffany's awed response to their rediscovery of civilization in Sámara was comically opposite to every other visiting American's view of the town's rusticity. Oh, there's only three kinds of cheese in the grocery store? Well, that's three more than they had on the boat. "We hoped we would sail for two years, at least," Pat says. "We thought we might even cross the Atlantic and head into the Mediterranean. But we also wanted to make sure we only did it as long as the kids enjoyed it." When they arrived in Costa Rica, they saw how their children sparked with the addition of school and steady friends to their lives. Now that Harper's found them, she, too, loves nothing better than running around the beach in a pack.

They sold the boat. After Thanksgiving, the family's moving to Portland. "I don't think we found a magic solution to our problems by escaping suburbia," Pat reflects. "But it offered a lot of clarity." Tiffany will teach yoga and give massages. Pat is going to flight school on the GI Bill to fulfill a dream of becoming a commercial pilot. They will be forced by financial straits to downsize and downscale, a complication Pat welcomes. "When we sold the house in Arizona it was full of stuff we'd moved all over the country," he says. "Like, we had a forty-pound bag of sand. We'd bought it in Alaska for whatever reason and then moved it all over Texas and eventually to Arizona." He shakes his head ruefully. "What the hell were we thinking?"

"So what are we gonna do now?" Harper asks hopefully as we pull up to the house, "Paper Planes" blaring on the stereo.

"Boy, I don't know, Harper," I reply. In some ways it is as if our focused, concentrated time together has turned us all into caricatures of ourselves. The heat has burned away our supporting personality traits and we can behave only as we, at our hearts, truly are: I am grumpy. Alia is worried. Lyra wants to be alone.

And Harper wants to be near us, at all times, in all circumstances. She wants to have her screen time in our bed. She wants someone to tell her what the next activity is and then the one after that. She will only use our shower because the upstairs shower, though cleaner and nicer, is too far away from us. Now I ask, "Can you give us a few minutes to get the groceries in and then we can figure it out?"

"Can I help with the groceries?" she says. I pop the trunk and take a few steps back to avoid the stank. Harper grabs three bags and hauls them up to the porch, then says, "Can I have the keys to unlock the gate?"

Beans on the shelf by the river of ants; almost everything else into the overstuffed fridge, where we store all kinds of things we would never refrigerate in America because the refrigerator is bug-free. (Every once in a while when I open it, I see a very lethargic mosquito fly out in slow motion.) "So what are we gonna do now?" Harper asks.

"Harper," Alia says, then takes a deep breath. "Why don't you go upstairs and get your slime stuff." Harper staccato-steps her way up the wooden stairs to her bedroom to collect all the slime accoutrements her blessed grandma brought down from North Carolina. "I took a shower yesterday," Alia whispers to me, "and when I opened the shower door Harper was right there like"—she mimes a prairie dog popping its head out of its burrow—" 'What are we doing now?' "

"What are you saying about me?" Harper calls from upstairs. Then she brings her bag of slime stuff down and sets it on the folding table we've placed at the edge of the kitchen and covered in plastic bowls and food coloring and little plastic beads, all for her.

A few weeks ago, some friends from Arlington came to visit and Harper was in heaven. All she wants in the world are people to do things with her, and here were people who came all the way from America to do things with her for a whole week. Harper made slime with Shira, she swam with Shira, she surfed with Shira, she giggled about how you could see the penises of the horses in our yard with Shira. When one of them needed a shower they took a shower together. When one of them needed to pee they'd announce: "We're going down to pee in the ocean, okay?" Parents and kids all played the party game Celebrity on the porch at night, an activity even solitary Lyra loved, especially when she placed *horse penis* as one of the names in the hat.

But soon after their departure Harper sank into a funk. In Costa Rica we just don't have that many friends. We haven't had any luck befriending neighbor Tico kids—not that many live near us, as most of the buildings around us are small hotels or Airbnbs—and it took us a long time to track down any expat friends. Harper finds joy with Pat and Tiffany's kids, but they're the only children her age she's befriended so far. "What is this trip doing to Harper?" Alia worried the other day. It seems to her, and I can't disagree, that our journey is transforming our children only in that it is turning the cheerful one moody too.

And not just her! Costa Rica is driving home the lesson that Delft taught us, and Island Bay before it: Alia and I, too, are happiest when we have friends around. Not just because it's a break from our kids and not exactly because it's a break from each other. It's more that to focus our attention outside ourselves, our children, and our problems and on others about whom we care a great deal feels as though it enlarges our hearts. We often talk about and think about our family as a team, all of us in it together, and a group of committed friends on whom we can count makes us feel our team is larger even than we knew. We're lucky enough to have several such groups in our lives: our college friends, now mostly living in New York and North Carolina, and two Arlington couples, close friends on our block, with whom we bonded because we all think of ourselves as "the ones who say yes"—the people who, kids' sports or busy workweeks be damned, find a way to grab a drink and hang out. Here in Costa Rica, where we've been slow to make friends, we feel not just alone but lonely in the world. One goal of the trip was for the members of our family to become ballast for one another when we're not surrounded by the structures—school, work, friends—that keep us occupied and give us strength and purpose in Arlington. Sometimes, we've succeeded. Right now, we're failing.

And this is what is starting to freak me out here in Costa Rica: the dreams of this yearlong journey are getting chewed up in exhausted rationalization. I wanted us to get off screens and into the world; instead, we're all staring at our devices, shouting when the rain knocks the internet out. I wanted us to learn to be with one another; instead, Lyra's retreating from everyone and we can't be with Harper for half a day without getting itchy for alone time. I know I must have learned something in Wellington and Delft but I can't for the life of me feel anything other than fraudulent. I'd suspected that moving to paradise couldn't be entirely paradisiacal, but to feel daily my own and my children's failure to appreciate all that is in front of us is getting to be more than I can handle. We're three-quarters of the way through this life-changing journey and it seems as though we haven't changed a bit. And now Harper's coming downstairs and she'll want to do something and I've spent time I could've been trying to relax panicking about whether this entire trip was a huge mistake.

Thankfully, at this exact moment, the next thing to do announces itself in the form of a honk outside the gate. It's the bakers! Oh, thank fucking God for the bakers.

Marianne is Parisienne, a former reporter with *Paris Match;* Dan, her husband, is a bluff Midwesterner who made his nut owning a Mexican restaurant outside Atlanta. She bakes baguettes and sourdough loaves, jars homemade preserves, crafts tarts and pastries. He sells it all at the organic market, along Sámara beach, to hotels and restaurants in town. And sometimes—as when our neighbors the Argentinean B-and-B owners tell him they've got Americans living next door—person to person. Shortly after our arrival, Dan homed in on us with the salesman's predatory instinct: *Oh, these are people who want carbs.* Every few weeks Dan shows up at our gate, calling: "Anyone home?"

Hell yeah, I'm home. I grab a couple of ten-thousand-*colón* bills and walk with Harper out to the road under a sky that's now heavy with clouds building from the mountains toward the sea. Dan is big, mustachioed, wearing the universal retiree's uniform of cargo shorts and sandals. Marianne is wiry, chic, wearing linen and a wry smile. "Whatcha in the mood for?" Dan asks.

In a recent ten-year period, according to Marketplace.org, the number of Americans receiving their Social Security checks in Costa Rica grew by 67 percent. Google *Retire in Costa Rica* and you'll find page after page of articles extolling the country's warm weather, sandy beaches, and affordable housing. Those articles, you'll notice when you read more carefully, tend to come mostly from shady quasi-news outlets with unfamiliar URLs and repeat the same unsupported facts: It's easy to live in Costa Rica on fifteen hundred dollars a month; beachfront property is available for less than a hundred thousand dollars; Costa Rica is a "blue zone" of longevity; the health system is cheap and accessible for American retirees.

Some of this is true, depending on where you end up. Health care in Costa Rica, for example, is modern and affordable, leading to a booming business in medical tourism; the video monitors in the customs line at San José airport play a loop of ads for hair replacement and dental work, and Alia drove to a fancy hospital in Liberia to get a mole removed for a flat hundred bucks. And the Nicoya Peninsula along the west coast of Costa Rica, where we are, does have a lot of centenarians; it was one of the regions highlighted by Dan Buettner in his book *The Blue Zones*, which hit bestseller lists in 2008 thanks to plugs from Oprah and Dr. Oz. The book's conclusions about why Nicoyans live longer do not strike me as revolutionary: They maintain a sense of purpose, cultivate social networks, get some sun, and don't eat too much. Also apparently the water here has lots of calcium in it.

But the influx of expat retirees hasn't necessarily made Sámara a better place for the families who live here. I heard from many Ticos I interviewed that while the retirement boom has brought some new jobs to Sámara, the economic boost hasn't been as dramatic as some hoped it would be. "The Americans are good for jobs!" one local told me. "But not as much jobs as expected." And as retirees buy up the housing stock, they've also pushed a lot of local families out. "It changed a lot," said Odiney, a homemaker who's raised two sons to teenage-hood in one of the few family houses in Sámara town still owned by a Tico family. "Before, there were more families around. But then people start buying houses for so much money, and so families sell and move away from the beach." Many of the Ticos we met lived in surrounding communities and came in to work each day by car or bus.

Odiney, like most local residents, earns money from tourism—in her case, by hosting Intercultura students at about $175 a month. The tide of dry-season tourists raises her boat; the slow but steady infiltration of expats moving to Sámara full-time slowly swamps it. (Her husband, Elbar, is an electrician, who does get work from the home renovations and rebuilds that expats like Marianne and Dan often undertake.) Costs for everything are rising in the area, she said, and her neighbors are changing. "You used to know all the families around. Now you don't know who lives in a house, so the family connection is gone."

As in many coastal towns in Costa Rica, Sámara's character is changing permanently. It was once a tourist town, lived in by Ticos and visited by gringos. Now more and more of the gringos—especially graying ones—stay, sinking money into the economy, raising the cost of living, and transforming the town into something entirely different than it once was. The *sodas* still do brisk business, but they're now joined by coal-fired-oven pizza, fancy sushi, a bar selling microbrews—all welcome additions for the visitor, but all priced at a point unlikely to draw locals to their tables. As lovers of pizza and sushi and microbrews with money to spend, we benefit from this transformation, although we benefit from it less and less as that money dwindles. (It's expensive to spend like you're on vacation every day, even if the place you're in looks like vacation.) But we also recognize ourselves, and people like us, as the cause of this transformation—an uncomfortable moral position, and one that would be tough to maintain if we were to live someplace like this for more than three months.

"I've got bread!" I shout through the window into our bedroom.

"I like bread," Alia answers from under the mosquito net, where she's uploading photos.

Bread bags dangling from each hand, I stop in my tracks on the porch. Harper, close on my heels, bumps into me. "What is it?" she asks.

"Lyra," I say, pointing at the floor. "What is that?"

Lyra, sitting at the little carved-wood kitchen table, looks down. "Ew, what *is* that?" Spread across two tile squares is a lumpy green-and-brown splatter.

She leaps to her feet as behind her we hear the unmistakable scrabbling sound of claws on linoleum. "What is *that?*" Harper cries.

That's a giant iguana, the biggest one I've seen in Costa Rica, stuck in the corner of the kitchen, the folded-up security gate blocking its exit to the yard. It climbs partway up the gate, drops back down to the floor, tries and fails to squeeze underneath, and gives me a panicked look. "That jerk pooped on our floor!" I say.

"Lyra, didn't you notice the giant iguana pooping right in front of you?" Harper asks.

Lyra laughs. "No!"

I'm annoyed at the iguana's decision to relieve himself in the middle of our kitchen, but for the next few minutes we can't stop laughing. Unlike nearly everything else that crawls through our house, the iguana seems too large to be actually upsetting. It can't skitter across your foot or infest your food or swoop down and sting you. It can only scratch plaintively at the gate and crap in frustration. Each time it takes a tentative step toward the wide-open porch from whence it entered our kitchen, we cheer; each time we cheer, the iguana retreats to the hemmed-in corner. Finally it manages to climb the gate, its prehistoric toes gripping the black steel, and as we urge it onward it drops to the ground outside and bolts through the *buenos días* flowers into the yard. The last we see of the iguana, it's bobbing its head in what seems like an attitude of wounded dignity.

Speaking of dignity, I'm cleaning up iguana shit. I carry the utterly revolting trash bag out to our garbage cage, which is literally a roadside cage a foot off the ground that would be emptied once a week by sanitation workers were it not emptied nightly by unknown large animals. When we arrived, the cage was secured by a twistable steel tie; that disappeared, and now it's secured by a binder clip I had in my backpack. The previous two garbage bags I've thrown into the cage now lie ripped open, their contents spilling into the street. In contrast to the picture-perfect ocean side of our house, with its palm trees and dignified iguanas and grazing horses, the street side is a mess, a gravel road festooned with Imperial cans and hot stinking trash, lined with muddy culverts from which swarms of mosquitoes emerge like the helicopters in *Apocalypse Now.*

I think a lot about the ways that life is difficult here. The garbage on the streets, the rain, the bugs, the lack of services, the busted-up roads. I frequently whine about it, in fact. Of course, our money buys us an easier life than that of many local Ticos in some respects, but practically, there's a limit to the comfort our money can buy. (There's also a limit to our money.) We're well-off, comparatively, but not well-off enough to have air-conditioning or avoid bugs or see a movie. (We'd need to be rich.) We're eating mostly the same food as our Tico neighbors and doing the same activities and getting dumped on by the same rainstorms. Presumably we all have the same mysteriously blue arms. What our Americanness buys us, of course, is the opportunity to leave after three months.

So what have I learned about our family and our ability to lead a life that is, for lack of any better term because the Costa Ricans invented the best possible one, *pura?* I've learned we're able to do it only haltingly. I have managed, for example, to get in the ocean almost every day. My kids are certainly not overbooked, even if sometimes their motors can't

Lyra:

I'm a proud advocate for doing as little as possible as often as possible, so Costa Rica was basically heaven except for the mosquitoes and horse penis. I had pretty much no obligations, so I got to laze around, read, sleep, pace on the beach, spend hours on the internet, and write. A lot. It was boring sometimes, but the occasional lethargy was an adequate price to pay for hours of solitude and getting to go barefoot for like five weeks straight.

Sometimes my parents interrupted my solitude to make me go do activities. Swimming was fun on occasion, but I still stick by my belief that the cleanup after swimming outweighs the fun and makes swimming itself a pain. I can't properly enjoy myself if I'm dreading changing out of a sodden swimsuit. Horseback riding was fun, except for that one daredevil horse I got that liked to walk on the very edge of cliffs because it was easier on its hooves or something. If you want a luxurious time, horse friend, go get a pedicure. Meanwhile, keep me away from *any and all precipices.* The chocolate plantation was fun. Chocolate is delicious, so all in all, it was not a wasted trip.

find that lower gear without hitching. Yet we also spend so much of our time trying to wrestle life in Costa Rica into the shape we want, rather than shaping ourselves to fit it. I have not managed to stop stressing out about all the shit I have to do, because I haven't built myself a life in Costa Rica where I don't have all that shit to do. (Dan the baker, for example, has done a great job of building himself a life in which he does only the shit he wants to do. Of course, he's retired.) It's hard to know whether we're focusing on the difficulties of Costa Rica at the cost of embracing the wholeness of our experience because of some congenital inability on our part to see the big picture or because of our relatively short time here. If we were to stay longer, much longer, our whole lives longer, would our emotional metabolisms shift in such a way as to make life here more rewarding?

"Is this rewarding?" I ask Alia as I sit down at the big table on the porch. She's sweeping the area clear of various plastic beads from Harper's slime table, beads that will, no doubt, persist in the Costa Rican ecosystem long after human life is extinguished. In answer, Alia shrugs toward the sea. I take her point: Who would not feel rewarded by this view? The tide is in now, and the waves are rolling steadily across the bay, deep blue capped by crisp white foam as white as a movie star's teeth. A horse is grazing in the yard. In the distance, the natural break-water that protects the bay is wild, waves exploding against the rocks with a near-constant roar. It can feel nearly numbing, honestly, the constant onslaught of beauty you endure living next to the ocean. I should be looking at it, overwhelmed by its glory, every second of every day, but it has become, at times, a kind of screen saver, lovely but unnoticed. (It's similar to how I should delight and revel in the miracle of my children every second of every day, but a lot of the time I'm on the internet instead.)

"I mean," Alia says, "a lot of this isn't rewarding at all."

"No." I sigh. "I don't feel rewarded."

"Maybe *rewarding* is the wrong word," she suggests. "It seems, like, meaningful."

"Meaningful?"

"Sure," she says. "If you're getting a Diet Coke," she adds as I pull a bottle of Diet Coke from the fridge, "could you please pour me one? That would also be meaningful."

I laugh. She leans the broom against the porch railing and sits at the table, facing the ocean, and I pour her a glass of Diet Coke and sit next to her. Lyra is walking her well-worn path along the side of the building; Harper is playing with slime. "So," I say in a way that may seem too on the nose but is in fact appropriate to this compressed "single day" of nonfiction because when you take a trip for the express purpose of changing the big picture of your lives you end up having conversations about the big picture of your lives basically every day: "Meaningful?"

"*I* don't know, I'm not the writer," she says. "But that's what we're looking for, right? Life that has meaning whether it's rewarding or not."

"Life where even the bad shit has meaning."

"Sure," she agreed. "In Arlington, the bad shit is mostly us yelling at our kids about screens and feeling like we're wasting our afternoons. Here the bad stuff is worrying about dengue fever and—"

"And yelling at our kids about screens."

"It's a process," she says with a wry tip of the glass.

One thing I will say for the climate of Costa Rica is that my wife looks particularly great with a tan. We sit quietly for a few moments, watching the waves. The thunder sounds just as far away as it did hours ago; it's just that now it's nearly constant, like the rumbling at a construction site three blocks over.

Alia gets up, brushes her hands off on the seat of her pants, then grimaces. "What?" I ask.

"*Slime!*" she says, shaking her fist at the sky. A wad of slime once splatted on the bench is now stuck to her butt. "Welp, gonna go boil my pants," she says.

"Hey!" I say. "Your arm's blue again!" She looks down and indeed, her right arm is royal blue, the exact shade of the broom leaning up against the—

"Ohhhhh," we both say in unison. She picks up the broom, presses the stick against her bug-sprayed, sweaty forearm, displays the new blue streak.

"We're excellent detectives," she says.

"At last!" I reply. "Resolution!"

While Alia washes her arm and sets a pot on the stove in which to boil her pants, I head to the bathroom. Not to get too grossly specific, but one thing about bathrooms in Sámara is that, due to the fragility of the septic system, you may not flush toilet paper down the toilet. Which means that every bathroom features a small trash can with a lid, which is always filled—sorry, I know—with poop-smeared toilet paper. This I would describe not as a hardship but an oddity; it creates a certain kind of funny intimacy in that no one can keep secrets about this traditionally private matter. Yep, we've all been pooping; there's the evidence. It is also a real testament to how the act of wiping is something we all do on autopilot. Each of us has had the experience of absentmindedly dropping some toilet paper into the toilet, then realizing the error. (It's the Costa Rican equivalent to my New Zealand routine of jingling my keys at the passenger door of the car before remembering I was on the wrong side.) Myself, I just guiltily flushed that toilet paper; that worked fine until suddenly it didn't and the plumbing system went haywire and when you flushed upstairs, the downstairs toilet would erupt as if a depth charge had gone off.

The girls are much more conscientious. Harper came downstairs the other morning and announced that she felt like a real Tico because "I finally got the hang of throwing my toilet paper in the garbage!" Well, what did you do up till now? Alia asked. "Before, a lot of the time, I threw it in the toilet and then had to take it out with my hands and put it in the trash can," she said.

"I do that too," Lyra offered. "It's so gross!"

"But now I don't have to say to myself"—here Harper clenched her fists as if giving a pep talk—"'Okay, Harper, don't forget to put it in the trash can!'" I find it touching that the girls were, on this front at least, so fastidious that they were willing to pluck wet toilet paper out of a toilet. I also hope that they were fastidious enough to wash their hands really well afterward.

When I step back into the kitchen, I'm resolved: We gotta do something. I haven't been in the ocean for a few days even though that was the whole point of living on the ocean, where there are always mosquitoes and where we can't even walk into town without consulting tide tables.

We live in a spot where a two a.m. earthquake led me to call the NOAA's Pacific Tsunami Warning Center in Ewa Beach, Hawaii. (I got their voice mail but saved the number in my phone's contacts as "Tsunami.") So it's time to get in the damn ocean!

"I'm going swimming," I say. "Who wants to come in the ocean with me?" Harper's upstairs changing into her swimsuit before I've finished the question.

"I'm game," Alia says. "My pants are already in this pot."

"Isn't it gonna rain?" asks Lyra.

"It hasn't yet," I say.

"You'll be in the water," points out Alia. "So what if there's also water coming out of the sky?"

Lyra thinks about it. Harper is already standing there in her swimsuit. "I'll come to the beach," Lyra says, "but I don't think I'm going to swim." I open my mouth to complain but before I can, Alia says, "I'm glad you're coming down," so I shut my mouth and we all walk through the gate onto the sand.

When Alia saw the beach on Lake Michigan in Milwaukee, where I grew up—trucked-in sand and waves like bathtub splashes—she looked at me with pity and said, "That was your *beach?*" She grew up working as a lifeguard and spent weeks every summer on the ocean. The first time I swam, truly swam, in an ocean was with her, the first August we went to the Outer Banks, when I was not her husband but merely the only boyfriend she'd ever brought there. In the water she's magical—naturally powerful, decisive. She inhabits the sea in a way that I, here in Costa Rica, am trying—by swimming as often as I can—to understand.

I'm not a natural swimmer. I didn't learn until my teens, and when I'm in the ocean I'm reminded of the fear that kept me out of pools and lakes as a kid. That's especially true at high tide, when the water is opaque and the seafloor is a relentless churn of shells, seaweed, sticks, who knows what, bumping into your ankles with every step. Probably each tickle is not a tentacle or a tooth or a jellyfish's jelly head.

The dark clouds are low and the dark sea is high. Harper and Alia and I float, but the waves heaving themselves toward us are taller than we are. Each wave is a puzzle for me to solve: Jump through it? Dive under it? Ride it? (We bought boogie boards in town, but they were cheap foam numbers that snapped in half after a few rides and now lie abandoned in the yard.) Alia navigates each wave smoothly; I often find, mid-crash, that I've made the wrong choice.

Harper splashes toward me and latches onto my hip, ready to play. "I'll throw you first and then you throw me, okay?" She counts to three, then lifts and pushes me maaaaaybe four inches. I leap like a henchman shot off his perch atop the saloon, flailing a big splash and sticking a single cartoon foot into the air as I'm submerged in the deep roar. When I surface, Harper's already hopping with anticipation. "Now throw me!" I can no longer throw her very far. Soon she'll need to pretend for me the way I pretend for her.

I referee a freestyle race between Alia and Harper; we sing an adaptation of "Despacito" we've been working on called "No Mosquitoes." We tell stories of different oceans we've visited, with or without Harper. ("And when you were in Mexico, that was when Mommy was pregnant with me, right?") We reminisce about the cold water in Island Bay, the colder water of the North Sea at Scheveningen, in The Hague. Here the water, even at high tide, is so warm that only on the hottest days does it feel refreshing. Today it feels like an extension of the heavy, wet, warm air riding ahead of this storm that, despite the thunder, seems like it will never arrive.

Alia points to Lyra wandering on the beach, water up to her ankles. "Do you think we can get her in?" she asks.

"Probably not," says Harper.

"Lyyyyyyyyyyra," Alia calls. Lyra looks up and waves. "Come swimming with us!"

Lyra holds up her arms, shruggie-style. "Lyyyyyyyyyyyraaaaaaaa," I call in my most annoying voice. "Pleeeeaaaasssssseeee!" Harper and Alia join in. Lyra shouts, "I'm not wearing a swimsuit!"

"Just swim in your clothes!" Harper yells.

"They'll get all wet!" she protests.

"So put on a swimsuit!"

"I don't want to!"

"There's no one around!"

"I don't care!"

"Just come in!" I say. "Who cares if your clothes get wet?"

"I don't want to walk around in wet clothes!"

"We can hang them up and they'll dry off!" When Alia says this, I snort; between the humidity and the rainstorms and the heat, our clothes haven't been truly dry for months.

"It's weird to swim in my clothes!"

"Lyra!" Alia shouts. "Don't let the man tell you what you have to wear to swim in the ocean!" Lyra laughs and wades toward us. Alia and I hold our breath at this unlikely sight: Lyra, convinced by us, doing something.

One thing that's kind of fallen out of my parenting repertoire is just plain *playing*—goofing around, wrestling, laughing. We're mostly done with tickle fights and tag and Ho Ho, a game Alia's dad invented in which a kid sits on your knee, you ask her questions, and if she answers wrong, you drop her on her ass. So to have the chance to pick both kids up, toss them into the water, to feel them clinging to my arms, dragging along as I sweep through the waves, to hold hands and dive under a wave, or leap over one—it's a kind of joy that makes up for an awful lot of arguments about bullshit.

Alia bobs a few waves away, watching us. "Your mom told me something," I mutter to the girls as they hang off my hips.

"Oh yeah?"

"She loves to be tackled in the water," I say. "She was like, 'Oh, I hope my girls tackle me,' that's what she said."

"Mommmm..."

After the splashing dies down, Lyra and I go bobbing off into the shallows while Alia and Harper do some wave-diving. "What do you think my husband will be like, Mommy?" Harper asks.

"I don't know," says Alia. "Do you have a type?"

"A type?"

"Is there a kind of man you like? What kind of person do you think you would want to be married to?"

Harper considers the question. They dive together under a big wave, the foaming power churning against their backs underwater, their ears filled with the roar. When they surface, the air is suddenly clear of sound. "Well," says Harper. "I would want him to be funny. And handsome. I wouldn't want him to yell."

Alia is taken briefly aback. "Why would he yell?" she asks. Then she sees me, splashing in the shallows with Lyra. "Oh, you mean like Daddy yells?"

"Yeah," says Harper. "Daddy's funny but sometimes he yells."

Alia laughs. "Harper, when Daddy and I first got married, he didn't yell. Do you think something happened since then that makes him yell sometimes?"

"Ohhh," says Harper. "We got born."

"I think when you marry someone he won't yell at you," Alia says. "He might yell at your kids."

"Will I yell at my kids too?"

"I bet you do." They continue diving under the waves until they are interrupted by me, yelling.

I'm standing thigh-deep when I feel it, a new sensation on my shin, different from the typical blind bumps of sticks and shells and sand. Something wraps around my leg, and *zap*—I instantly feel a constellation of sharp stabs across my calf. "Ow, shit!" I bellow, and before anyone can respond I'm splashing back to shore. "Are you okay?" I hear Alia ask, and through the scorch of my leg I call out, "Something stung me!"

I stomp up the beach toward our house and the rainwater shower. My leg really hurts, yes, but also I'm upset because I've always been able to tell myself that my ocean anxiety was irrational. Today it wasn't irrational at all, and for a wild instant I'm livid that my submerged fear called some creature to us.

And on top of that: We were doing it. We were together, in a moment, creating something as big and natural as the waves. And then it stopped. In the yard I hop back and forth as the rainwater makes its way down the pipes from the roof of the shed to the shower. I don't want to look but I really want to look at the lattice of bright welts sprayed across my leg.

All three of them hurry up the beach to the yard, worried, solicitous, wanting to help. Harper's first, asking, "Are you okay? What happened? What stung you? Does it hurt?" I hold up a hand, as much to hold off the pained retort I can feel bubbling up as to slow her down. I breathe deeply and force a smile that definitely twists into a grimace against my wishes. "Can I just have a minute or two?" I ask.

"Hey, let's get Dad a Diet Coke," Alia says to the kids. "We can give him a minute to feel better."

"Maybe a beer," I reply between gritted teeth.

"Are you mad, Daddy?" Harper asks.

"I'm not mad at you." I wince. "It's just that my leg really hurts."

"Hey," Lyra says, and we all look over to her. She points up. "It's raining."

Plam. Plam. Big raindrops hit the tin roof of the garden shed with a sound like popcorn in a metal pot. Harper scampers into the house with a shriek. Lyra follows her in no particular hurry. Alia stays behind for a moment. "Towel's on the railing," she says.

"Thanks." I show her my leg.

"Oof," she says sympathetically. "That's not great."

"I think it'll be okay. It already hurts a little less." The sounds of the rain are starting to drown out everything else; the ocean, the bugs, all subsumed in a growing static of sharp metallic *pops*, deeper *plunks* on the house's roof, a continuous *shushhh* of palm leaves stirring in the fresh weather. The thunder, grumbling in the distance for so long we'd stopped paying attention, is now clearing its throat to issue fresh complaints.

I pad up the steps to the porch, wrap the towel around my waist, and sit on a bench, leg up. The angry spatter of red across my shin is impressive-looking but the burning recedes as I sit here, breathing deeply.

"Daddy?" Harper pokes her head around the wall of the kitchen. "Can I see your leg?" She's changed into dry clothes, her hair hanging wet and loose.

"Yeah, sweetie," I say. "I'm sorry if I scared you."

"It really hurt," she posits.

"Yeah."

"What stung you?"

"I don't know," I say. "It felt like a plant but I don't think there's any plant that does that, so it must've been some kind of jellyfish."

"That was fun in the water."

"It really was," I say. "I love playing with you."

"Me too," she says. "Until the jellyfish stung you."

Alia joins us on the porch; Lyra has changed into her pajamas and is reading upstairs under the mosquito net. Our family is transitioning to rain mode now, a lazier state even than our typical lazy state, with all four of us occupying spaces within the house, finding activities where we can. I plug in a laptop and turn on a Nationals game, streaming balkily, the players occasionally defaced by digital artifacts. The rain is so loud on the corrugated roof that I can't hear the announcers. Fat-bottomed moths are already stirring in the gloom, stretching their wings, preparing to whump into the lights.

Harper moves over to her slime table; Alia's editing one of the girls' videos of Costa Rica to upload to their YouTube channel and its thirty-seven subscribers. I'm down to one final English-language novel, Maile Meloy's *Do Not Become Alarmed;* the rest of my books have been finished and left, mildewed and swollen, on the Intercultura share shelf. Meloy's novel is about Americans in trouble in an unnamed country clearly based on Costa Rica—one character calls the locale "the Switzerland of Latin America"—and it's been striking seeing the way a good writer like Meloy depicts Pacific beach towns very much like this one. This leads to odd moments of synchronicity. For instance, in the chapter I'm currently reading, a character observes that "the sun had gone down in that abrupt equatorial way, and now it was late," and then I look up and realize that the sun *has* gone down in that abrupt equatorial way, and now it *is* late. The house glows in the streaming dark.

What's most unnerving about Meloy's novel from my perspective isn't the scary story of American children kidnapped by drug dealers; I'm not worried about that for my kids, security gate or no. What's unnerving is the way Meloy doles out misfortune to her characters. For the

Americans, the ordeal is frightening but it never seems truly dangerous. It's the Latinos and Latinas who suffer the real consequences of American parents' inattentiveness—dying, suffering, getting hurt. At the end of the novel, the Americans, all children rescued, board a plane in what seemed to me to be San José airport. One of the fathers observes:

> He kept thinking of old news footage of the fall of Saigon, those last-minute helicopters off the roof. He and his family had escaped, leaving chaos behind them. It was the American way.

Our presence in Sámara isn't getting anyone killed. But it does seem hard to imagine a way that we could live here and make things better for the Ticos whose town we've crashed. Yes, our money is useful to them. Yes, we're single-handedly supporting a robust mosquito population. But what do we really have to offer this community?

I put the book down, pick up a laptop, add the iguana to the Google Doc. While the rainy season has been a drag, the rains themselves haven't been hard to deal with. The storms roll through with monotonous regularity, always the same pounding torrent and frequent lightning. Occasionally the breeze from the mountains is strong enough to blow rain onto the porch; when that happens, we pull down the clothes that are hanging on railings so they won't become *actually* wet instead of their usual state of not exactly dry.

The rain begins to taper off as I start cooking dinner. The lights of our porch illuminate the fence, the palms, the hammock. Something big scurries just out of sight. As the noise on the roof eases, the other nighttime noises take over: The invisible sea. The chirp of geckos, the violin screech of crickets. Play-by-play guys F.P. and Bob and the hum of a baseball crowd two thousand miles away. Sometimes, very late at night, we can hear the exasperated screams of howler monkeys, much like the sound I make when customer service disconnects my call after forty-five minutes on hold. And always, always, overlaying it all, the duck monkeys.

We call them that, though the duck monkeys are really just one of a zillion species of Costa Rican frogs. But after a rain—which, at this point in the year, is all the time—these particular frogs launch into a remarkable cacophony in the puddles around the house, rhythmically quack-shrieking like the offspring of, well, a duck and a monkey. The sound echoes through the jungle every night, an obnoxious constant in our lives. I think sometimes that I will be able to summon forth that sound fifty years from now.

The girls come down for dinner; tonight I've made *gallo pinto* with fried eggs. Ticos eat *gallo pinto*—rice and beans with Salsa Lizano—mostly for breakfast; just as at home in Arlington we often do breakfast for dinner, here we do *gallo pinto* for dinner, because it's easy and filling and we always have the ingredients sitting around. It's about as bland as Latin food can be, in part because Worcestershire-like Salsa Lizano doesn't actually taste very good so we don't use as much of it as you're supposed to. Our home-cooked dinners rotate between bland *gallo pinto,* tasty (but more complicated) arroz con pollo, and quesadillas. When we're out of every fresh ingredient and it's raining too hard to go to Palí, we serve the kids Costa Rican mac and cheese, which tastes the same as Kraft mac and cheese but costs something like ten cents a box. Sometimes when we're feeling exceptionally lazy we just do cheese and crackers—flavorless Costa Rican Colby on what I *now* strongly believe to be the most delicious crackers anywhere in the world, Sanissimo Salmas, which are basically fire-roasted corn chips in a cracker shape (cc: the fine people of the Sanissimo corporation).

We assemble at the big porch table. Lyra reads during dinner; she's reading, for the tenth time, a book she bought for one New Zealand dollar. Harper has questions. "Will you tell me a story about when I was a baby?" she asks.

"Which one do you want?" Alia asks.

"Tell the story about the Lucky Charms," Harper says.

I tell the story about the Lucky Charms, with interruptions. "Well, when you were little, you had a nanny who took care of you—"

"Was this in New York?"

"Yes, in our apartment there. And you were just learning to eat solid food."

"Why did we have a nanny? Why wasn't I in school?"

"Well, schools for babies as little as you were very expensive. It was more affordable to have a nanny."

"Was my nanny's name Merle or Molly?"

"Merle," Lyra says, not looking up from her book. "My nanny was Molly."

"Okay, so I went off to work one day, and I said, 'Merle, we really want Harper to eat solid food today, but she doesn't like a lot of it, so please see if you can get her to eat something.'"

"Was I a baby or a toddler?"

"You were still a baby. So when I got home from work, Merle said, 'Oh! Harper ate a whole bowl of cereal!'"

"But it was your cereal!" Harper can't stop herself from revealing the punch line.

"And I said, 'A whole bowl?'" Harper is now giggling. "And Merle said, 'Yes, a whole bowl of the Lucky Charms.' And I said, 'Oh no.'"

"'Oh no!'"

"'I'm afraid that sugar cereal is not for children,' I told her."

"'It's only for daddies!'"

Alia gives me a raised eyebrow in the direction of Lyra, who, I see, has quietly put her book down on the table. "Will you tell a story about me when I was a baby?" she asks, for just this moment as guileless as she once was.

So we tell the ice cream story, then the walking-up-the-hill story, then the story of the broccoli song. The girls devour these narratives, are annoyed as usual that we don't have more. Despite paying such close attention to these children throughout their babyhoods, we find now that we have a limited repertoire of stories from those years. It's as if ages zero through three were subsumed into a fog of love and panic. It's alarming, the disappearance of those stories, and the thing I love most about this trip is the way that moments from this year are already becoming family lore, retold by children who are finally old enough to contribute to their own tales.

I grab a few *palitos,* or maybe some chips and salsa. The crumbs fall to the floor, where they will be swarmed by ants. We turn on music ("Paper Planes") to drown out the duck monkeys. "Remember," we say, "the muddy hike to the waterfall?" "Remember," we say, "when Lyra took the Wellington city bus to school all by herself?" We deal out rummy or cabbages and kings. "Remember when there was a weta in Lyra's bedroom?" "Remember when Harper snorkeled over an eagle ray?" We slap at mosquitoes. "Remember the big fight we had in Dubai?" "Remember that crazy dance recital?" "Meester Peter?" "The baby turtles?" "The pooping iguana?"

Note: Hundreds of mosquitoes were harmed in the making of this chapter.

HAYS

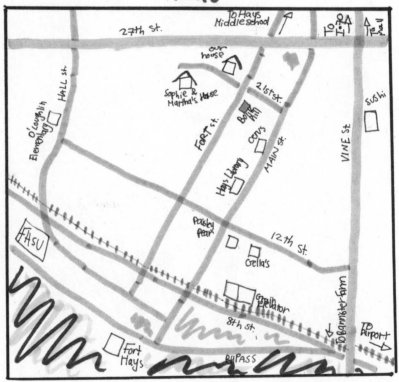

KANSAS

October – December

BRICKS

The flag at the Abraham Lincoln Presidential Library and Museum flew at half-staff. That Monday, the day we started our drive to Hays, Kansas, from Milwaukee — where we'd stopped for a weekend to visit my family and pick up our old Honda, which my mom had been using for nine months — our social media feeds were convulsing with shock about the most deadly mass shooting in American history, the night before at a country-music festival in Las Vegas. We were sick with sadness and shame at what our stupid fucking country had allowed to happen.

The Lincoln Museum is an ideal place to confront those feelings, as it turns out, a celebration of the land of opportunity that is studded with reminders of America's great shames, both historical and contemporary. I MISS ABE said a baseball cap Harper bought in the gift shop; in contrast with the red MAGA hat I'd already seen in a Quick Stop in central Illinois, this hat was jet-black.

Here we were in America. Lyra put on shoes for the first time in weeks to enter the Lincoln Museum, despite her outraged assertion that Lincoln doesn't care about her shoes, he's dead. To appease her we ate lunch at a nearly empty, entirely terrible Chinese restaurant in Springfield, where she ordered that most American of foods, General Tso's chicken. In a hotel room in Macon, Missouri, that night we watched *Wonder Woman,* a celebration of American pluck and a condemnation of the wars it helps make possible, purchased on DVD at the Quick Stop. Harper goggled at the fake-leather couches in the Comfort Inn lobby. "It's so fancy!" she said, likely because before we found the Comfort Inn we'd been warning the kids we might end up staying someplace really gross.

Maybe, as with the Comfort Inn, we would love Hays because it exceeded our expectations. Each time we explained our trip to a Kiwi or a Dutchman or a Tico or the kind of liberal American you tend to run into overseas, we got a certain response when we reached the fourth of our locations. "And rural Kansas," we'd say, and our listener would furrow his brow. The doubt and confusion we saw every time began to inflect our own conversations about our future home. Our Facebook feed was full of comments from friends wishing us the best of luck with our children's upcoming creationist education. At one point I suggested to Alia that we needed to moderate our tone, because our children, echoing us, were starting to say *Kansas* the same way they said *homework*.

Why *were* we going to Kansas? Lots of people had asked us that in the past year. Most simply, it seemed unfair and foolhardy to spend a year trying to find alternatives to our American way of parenting without acknowledging that ours was not the only American way of parenting. Millions of Americans raised children in places other than expensive coastal cities. (For that matter, millions of Americans raised children in expensive coastal cities under vastly different circumstances than ours.) Indeed, the small-town family represents a familiar American archetype, one that's embattled in the modern era but still valorized in the imagination. "Real America" is a place where everybody knows everybody, where life is quieter and calmer, where kids can ride their bikes down Main Street while Mom and Dad sit on the porch.

Presumably Hays, Kansas, wouldn't be exactly like that, although the house we were renting did have a porch. But like chucking it all and moving to the beach, chucking it all and decamping to a small town is an appealing exit fantasy shared by many of my fellow (Fox News voice) *coastal elites.*

Well, it was, once. Between the time we cooked up plans for this trip and the day we departed, Donald Trump was elected, and the gulf between the coasts and the heartland became, suddenly, a subject of enormous—one might say nation-threatening—importance. I'm sure his election looked quite different to Republican Trump voters in Kansas (or in Wisconsin, where I grew up, or in North Carolina, where Alia and I lived for a significant chunk of our twenties) than it did from our perch in dark blue Northern Virginia. But we had long told ourselves that the world, in the words of a playwright whose work I was writing about, only spins forward. On issues of civil rights, humanitarianism, simple kindness, we believed that America was more and more being guided by its citizens' better angels. We found out we were wrong— positive change was not necessarily inevitable; indeed, it could be halted by voters who were not yet ready to leap forward and in fact were actively trying to turn back.

What to do about that situation was a question that consumed us from November 8 to the day we fled the country, just as so many of our compatriots had half joked they would. (Or, in the case of Adam and Marla, two New Yorkers we met in Sámara, actually did—they were about to emigrate to Toronto, taking advantage of Marla's dual citizenship.) To us it seemed that the solution wasn't to leave America but to work to make it the country we hoped it could be. One possible avenue to that result, suggested in op-eds and late-night wine-fueled heart-to-hearts, was domestic migration; some portion of us city dwellers moving to the middle of the country to agitate, activate, and vote. "Go Midwest, Young Hipster," the *New York Times* wrote in October of 2016. "If you really want Democrats to win in Iowa, move there." A few days after Election Day, Will Oremus of Slate echoed the call, scoffing at devastated liberals claiming they would soon decamp to Canada. Moving to a red state, Oremus wrote, "signals that you care about your country and you'd rather fight for it than abandon it."

Now that Alia and I were back in our country, we were eager to find out what such a move, from a blue state to a red state, would actually feel like. In Ellis County, Kansas, Donald Trump won 70 percent of the vote, and we wanted to know whether we could find a place in a community where so many people were on the opposite side in what felt, more and more, like the defining battle of our lives.

Did we think we could change things in our three months in Hays? No. A liberal editor writing about what we fancy East Coasters could learn from humble Kansas families was not likely to win any hearts and minds. But our goal wasn't to swan into Hays like saviors, the way I imagine Brooklyn beardos who buy up abandoned houses in Detroit come off, good as their intentions might be. I wanted to listen and learn from the people we met; I wanted our kids to be friends with their kids; I wanted us to be friends with them. (Surely nice Midwesterners, unlike the Dutch, would be happy to be our friends.) I hoped that by removing the physical distance between us and them we could have at normal volume the kinds of conversations that, in the public sphere and on Facebook, seem to happen only at full shout.

And yes, I wanted to see if things were a bit simpler. Not vacation-simple, the way we fantasized about Costa Rica before that nation's mosquitoes took all our blood. The idea of Hays had always revolved around a different kind of simplicity, a practical one, not a vacation or a dream but an actual life built on the foundation of a community whose values would ease our days and support us when we were down. We wanted to try out an American small town, like Doc Hollywood did, and see if we fell in love.

After the girls went to sleep in the Missouri Comfort Inn I drove to the Walmart to buy a belt to replace the one that had moldered away in Costa Rica. Returning to America was already paying dividends: you could flush your poop-covered toilet paper down the toilet, and when you needed a new belt you could just buy one.

The next morning we woke up early, got in the car, and drove across the Missouri River underneath long, thin clouds stretching in parallel stripes from horizon to horizon. The sun shone through them with glorious radiance. "It really looks like Jesus is gonna step down out of the sky," said Lyra. "What kind of clouds are those?"

"Stratus clouds," Harper said with magnificent confidence. "Weren't you paying attention when they taught us the kinds of clouds at school?" Later, I learned that in fact they were cirrus radiatus clouds.

The last hours of the drive were an agony of scenery-free views and Harper asking nonstop questions about the new house. ("Does it have an upstairs?" "We don't know, Harper.") Hays is halfway between Denver and Kansas City; on a map it dangles off the horizontal line of Interstate 70 like a Christmas light. It has a regional hospital, a university, and about twenty thousand people. Wild Bill Hickok used to be the sheriff; on the corner of Eighteenth and Fort Streets is Boot Hill, where seventy-some-odd Wild Westers got buried with their boots on after various misunderstandings, showdowns, and murders. These days it's a bad year when one resident of Hays gets murdered.

Seen on Google Maps, Hays, like many small towns that have grown into small cities, reveals two separate street grids. The first is the original city map, platted by William Webb at the town's very beginning, about the same time that Delftians were building that third church that isn't old enough for anyone to care about. In the 1860s Hays was the western-most spot on the railroad and Fort Hays was the center of the army's campaign to drive the Native people off their land. This included the Arapaho, Osage, Comanche, and many other tribes who had lived on the land for centuries, not to mention the Delaware and other Eastern tribes who had been forced into Kansas in the early nineteenth century. The streets in this town parallel the train tracks, running from First Street by the fort at the bottom of town to Twenty-Seventh Street up top. Crossing them all is the main street, Main Street, once the only game in town but now struggling to keep its hold on residents' shopping dollars and civic attention.

This two-square-mile town nestles crookedly within the sprawl of a larger city, its grid surveyed by the compass rose but its streets flowering into fractal suburban cul-de-sacs. That city's eyes slide past Main Street to the interstate to the north and Vine Street to the east, which divides the old city from the new and maintains Hays's stock of fast-food restaurants, lube joints, bad pizza, and strip malls. It's on Vine Street that you turn in your cable box, drink a Frappuccino, or see a movie at the multiplex. (The glorious 1950 art deco theater on Main Street is now a rental pavilion visited by a dozen midlevel country singers each year.) On Vine Street, cute places like the café / sushi restaurant flounder amid the Taco Bells and gas stations; on Main Street, dead gas stations get renovated into cute diners.

North of town is a country club and the attendant neighborhood of biggish houses, many of them owned by families who've made their money in oil; farther out, Hays sports a few pockets of new construction. One subdivision, still being built by a company called Covenant, is windswept and mostly bare of trees; the houses stand like desert fortresses, their borders delineated not by landscaping but by mutual understanding. The subdivision is marked by a handsome sign with a line from Matthew: "Seek ye first." It's written in Greek letters, but not in actual Greek, just the Greek letters that sort of look like the corresponding English letters: ΣΕΕΚ ΨΕ ΓΙΡΣΤ.

The houses downtown are humbler and much more charming, ranging from shotguns to big old farmhouses. When we drove into our neighborhood near downtown that first day, Chinese elms arched over the streets, which were all fashioned of red brick. The brick streets are a signature Hays design element, pleasingly old-timey and presumably expensive to maintain; in 2007 the council declared that the city would keep three hundred thousand spare red bricks, about enough to pave five blocks, in stacks at the city's public works department by Al's Chicken-ette on Vine Street. The combination of brick streets and mature trees with questing roots searching for water through the dry Kansas soil means that the surfaces of the roads in downtown Hays have a gently rolling quality, like the ocean the day after a storm.

We parked in the driveway of 201 West Twenty-First Street, a big old Craftsman painted a faded blue with different generations' mismatched additions pointing off in different directions. It had a basketball hoop and a garden gnome. It had an upstairs. Harper shot out of the car. Waving her arms, she ran in great looping circles around the lawn, shouting: "This is the greatest day of my life!"

The front door was unlocked, as it would be every day we lived there. Our friends Sophie and Martha had set a cardboard sign atop a bureau in the living room. On it they had drawn big, friendly sunflowers. WELCOME TO KANSAS, it said.

CHAPTER 8

A Quiet America

Two flights a day took off from the Hays airport, both destined for Denver. There was word that United might add a third flight, to Chicago via Salina; that would change a lot of lives around town. HYS has one gate, one conveyor belt for baggage, one X-ray machine, and two televisions showing Fox News. If you get there fifteen minutes before departure time, you will always make your flight.

Those two CRJ200s return from Denver each evening. In the winter, if you take the earlier of the two flights, UA 5137, you'll descend right around sundown. The plane is usually about half full, so the flight attendant seats all the passengers in the rear ten rows to balance the weight. Seen from the air, the fields around Hays, emptied of wheat and milo, glow gold in the late-evening light, striped by the wheels of combines; the tin rooves of the barns shine as bright as heat lamps. There are seldom clouds. Phalanxes of windmills rotate their arms like Busby Berkeley girls. After the windblown and bumpy landing, you exit the plane onto the tarmac, and if you look up, you'll see a dozen jet contrails. Illuminated from underneath, they slice across the sky, east to west or west to east along the x-axis of flyover. Like most people, the passengers on those cross-country flights will never set foot in Hays. If the federal government, as it occasionally threatens to do, stops subsidizing United's routes to Hays to the tune of $155 per passenger, those contrails will be all Hays ever sees of commercial flights.

Our first afternoon in Hays was spent arranging the few pieces of furniture in the enormous, beautiful house, perfectly placed in downtown

Hays, that we were renting for fifteen hundred dollars a month, less than half the cost of the mortgage on our significantly smaller house in Virginia. The furniture, the dishes, the beds, indeed the house itself were all thanks to our friend Catherine, a playwright with whom Alia and I had gone to college and who'd moved to Hays more than a decade ago when her husband, Carl, got a job teaching philosophy at Fort Hays State. She'd found the house and convinced its owners to let us rent it for only three months, then wrangled loaner furniture from neighbors, gotten a friend to donate her mom's china, bought a few cheap tables at Goodwill, and struck a deal on our behalf with Rent-A-Center for a bedroom set. Our pots and pans were her pots and pans; Lyra's bedroom was decorated with her daughter Sophie's Harry Potter posters.

That afternoon Catherine and her girls stopped by to make sure we had what we needed. She's clever and cheerful and homey with a Georgia drawl left over from her childhood. She was the reason we'd chosen this town—not just because she spoke so winningly of the life she had carved out for herself here in "Hays, America," as she always called it, but because we felt that cracking the social life of a small Midwestern town might be impossible without a dedicated guide. Catherine had often said how much she wished her friends could come to Hays to see what life was like for her; we were calling her bluff and moving in two blocks away.

Catherine's daughters are made from a similar mold as our own: Sophie, the older, is serious, bookish, a little neurotic; Martha, the younger, is funny, headstrong, into sports, a joiner. The difference is that they're two years younger than ours; Martha was in third grade and Harper would be joining Sophie's fifth-grade class, which had been meeting for months already when we arrived. All four girls disappeared to the big playroom upstairs while Alia, Catherine, and I unwrapped dishes and talked in the kitchen. The sounds from upstairs got louder and more joyous until, at one point, Martha burst into the room and froze, eyes wide, as if she couldn't believe she'd been caught having so much fun. "Do you want to go home?" Catherine asked. "Nope!" Martha shouted, then ran away and slammed the door behind her.

On the first day of school, both our children woke up declaring they didn't want to go. "Why do we have to go to schoooooool?" Harper groaned. It had been quite a few months since I'd experienced the low-level exasperation that comes with having a ton to do that you can't get done until you get recalcitrant children fed, watered, and out the door.

"It's too cold!" Lyra declared. She pointed outside, where a prairie wind was blowing leaves horizontally down Fort Street. "Will you drive me?"

"Lyra," I said, "you rode to school in the rain for months in Delft."

"Yeah, but there we had to!"

"I'm not setting a precedent that you get driven to school just because you don't feel like walking."

"Just today?" She batted her eyes.

"If I drive you, will you get ready without complaining?"

"No." She looked reproachful at the very idea. This was America!

She was wearing the Tibetan patchwork jacket and patchwork pants we'd bought at a street market in Amsterdam that together created a real look. "This is what you're wearing on the first day?" I asked as we pulled up to the middle school's drop-off line.

"Yeah," she challenged. "Is there something wrong with it?"

"I guess not," I said. "You remember how to get home?" We'd walked to school the other day, and the sweetest guidance counselor on God's green earth had given her a tour of the building, chatted with her about her likes and dislikes, and then, unbidden, went into the computer system, deleted gym class, and replaced it with art, an action so astonishingly kind I still couldn't get over it.

"I think so! See you later!" Lyra hopped out of the car, swung her backpack over her Technicolor shoulders, and walked up the sidewalk, the wind blowing her hair instantly into a wild tangle. Given the circumstances—new school, new town, seventh grade, she looked like a scarecrow who'd been electrocuted—she seemed remarkably poised. I rolled down the passenger-side window and shouted, "I love you," pretty sure the roar of the wind would swallow my voice, but she turned around and said, "Love you too."

Alia and I walked Harper a block down Twenty-First Street, a block down Ash, three houses down Twentieth Street to the Millers', where Sophie and Martha and Catherine awaited us. "Are you ready for your first day, Harper?" Catherine asked. Sophie smiled encouragingly; Martha was leaping up and down with excitement. As we walked the half a mile to O'Loughlin Elementary, Catherine pointed out various houses: the house they used to live in, where Carl built the porch; the house where Martha takes cello lessons; the house their friend who's the chef at a restaurant downtown has been trying to sell for a year. Our group got larger and larger, fed by other kids and parents making their way down Walnut Street; each mom we met seemed to know our story already. (It was mostly moms.) In her classroom, Harper had a place ready for her, at the same table as Sophie. Sophie had drawn flowers on her name tag. Her teacher was tall and blond and seemed about nineteen years old. "Bye, Daddy," Harper said, and the parents walked back home. "This already feels normal," Catherine said, "but if I stop and think about it for a second, it is still totally surreal. Just, you guys here, and we see each other every day, and we're just sister-wivin' it up."

We dropped Catherine off at her house; she was up against a deadline for a new play reading. "I promise I'll be more helpful in a week," she said, and we laughed because she was in fact so helpful that our entire current circumstance was thanks solely to her. She told us a few places around town she liked to steal internet from, and then Alia and I held hands the two blocks back to our cavernous new house.

That morning I drove around town for quite some time looking for a place to work. Twice I got excited to see the word BOOK on a sign, only to get closer and realize that it said ROOF and it was a store that sold, like, roofing stuff. I finally settled on a combination coffee shop / sushi restaurant that had opened just a week before. Alia walked over later that morning and we shared a lunch table and responded to a week's worth of emails. The café let us stay for several hours after it closed. "Just shut the door when you leave," the owner said. Then we drove home.

Lyra got back in the midafternoon; we saw her walking up Fort Street in the sunshine, her patchwork jacket tied around her waist. A big black dog trotted next to her, made the turn, and joined her in our front yard. We walked out to meet her.

"Only *one person* commented on my outfit," she said indignantly.

"How was school?" I asked. "Did anyone speak Dutch?"

"No!"

"Do we have a dog now?" Alia asked. The dog had plopped down on our porch, panting happily as Lyra scratched its head.

"Yeah," said Lyra. "His name's Zuko. He followed me all the way home from school." The dog was wearing a collar that did, indeed, have the name ZUKO on it, followed by a phone number. While Alia brought out a bowl of water, I dialed. A frantic-sounding woman asked my address, which I had to think about. I had an address again! It took me a moment to sort through the many addresses and numbered streets in my head.

"It's two-oh-one West Twenty-First Street," I said.

"It's the house with Zuko on the porch," Lyra called.

A minute later a beat-up sedan pulled up and a young couple leaped out and ran toward Zuko, who'd been lying in the shade, slurping water. The woman was wearing a Star Wars shirt and was overjoyed. "I've been a sobbing wreck," she said. Her boyfriend shook my hand very seriously and said, "Thank you so much, sir." I felt like a neighbor, just like that.

"Bye, Zuko," Lyra said as they drove away.

"You did a good deed!" I told her. "What else happened at school today?"

"It was fine," she said, and went inside to get her iPod.

"We don't have the internet yet," I reminded her.

"Crap!"

That was the beginning of us meeting everybody in Hays, America, where everybody knows everybody. "We're small enough," our friend Cathy told me, "that there are a lot of connections between families." She gave a few examples. "Our oldest son has a friend who he's known since kindergarten. Her mother taught all my sons science at the high school. Her father is a colleague of my husband. I ran the music academy where she took string classes." Her point wasn't just that she knew lots of parents but that lots of parents knew her kids. "You have plenty of different adults who are connected to your child's life."

By November, four weeks after we got to Hays, none of us—me, Alia, our kids—could walk downtown without someone we'd met honking hello as they drove past. The hello-honk is a distinct phenomenon in the Great Plains, I discovered; while such a garrulous greeting might happen in Arlington, you'd employ it only for very, very close friends and never if there was another car anywhere nearby that might misinterpret your honk. But here in Hays, I got hello-honks not only from Catherine but from the parents of Harper's friends, a clerk at the library, and the mayor of Hays. (After he honked at me, he had to honk at two other walkers farther up the street. It's a lot of work to be the mayor!)

I assumed from the hello-honk that everyone in Hays was friendly. But Andrea, a hairdresser at Redz on Main Street, told me that for a while, she hadn't thought so. "When I came here from Sublette"—a tiny town about three hours southwest—"I thought everyone was so unfriendly!" she said. "The first thing I noticed is that no one waves."

"What do you mean, no one waves?" I asked.

"When you drive past someone they don't wave to you. In Sublette, *everyone* waves."

"So you're saying," I said, trying on this absurd idea for size, "you wave to every single person you drive past?"

"Sure," she said. "It can just be you raise your hand up from the steering wheel, or even just your pointer finger. But you definitely wave."

"Oh yeah, that's true," said Courtney and Abby, two librarians. Courtney was from Grainfell; Abby came from just across the border in Nebraska.

"No one does the wave here," said Courtney.

"Not even the one-finger wave," said Abby.

"Do you still wave?" I asked Andrea.

"No," she admitted. "Now when I see someone wave I think, *Oh, you're small-town.* When I go back to Sublette everyone thinks I'm so mean."

"Where we live, the only wave you'd give is one finger, all right," I said, "but not that finger."

Andrea laughed, then turned serious. "Oh, I don't think I've ever given anyone the finger here. What if they came in the next day to get their hair cut?"

Haysians made frequent reference to this idea that it's important to be nice, since you never know when you'll see a person next. According to people in Hays, the fact that you can't avoid anyone makes everyone more trustworthy. "When people say they're going to do something, they do it," Shaun, Hays's mayor, told me with satisfaction. And a recent transplant, Amanda, who moved from California to teach in the English department at the university, told me that this was one of the hardest things for her to get used to in Hays. "Taking someone at their word is really new!" she said. " 'Oh, you'll just be there when you say you will?' And they always are." Even our internet installer, when we finally got an appointment, arrived five minutes *before* the time—not a three-hour window, a specific time—the dispatcher said he'd be there. I found it unnerving.

For a parent, the smallness of Hays has obvious advantages. The town is safe, boringly safe, 1950s suburbia safe. Other people didn't lock their houses, so we didn't either. Violent crime was uncommon enough, said a professor at Fort Hays who was born and raised here, that "there's stories of, like, so-and-so's secretary got murdered in the 1970s." But everyone knowing everyone had another benefit for a parent, especially a parent of teenagers: Hays is a city of narcs.

If you're a teenager, it is really, really difficult to get away with anything in Hays, America, because someone will see you, and that someone will know exactly who you are because his kid goes to school with your sister, or he goes to your church, or he's your piano teacher, or whatever. While we were in Hays, the parent chatter was all about a group of eighth-graders who'd cut school, took someone's parents' van, and drove for Snoballs at Cervs. Of course some cousin saw them and it got back to Mom.

It's easy to imagine this feeling oppressive to a kid, though all the people I met who'd grown up in Hays talked about their childhoods with great affection. (They were the ones who'd stayed, though.) Certainly I heard from many adults how the village that keeps an eye on your kids is also keeping an eye on you. While we were in Hays, our friends Stacey and Jarrod were closing a deal on an old gas station downtown that they planned to turn into a new home for their medical practices. They hoped to share the news slowly, in part because they needed time to work out the separations from their current practices. But instead, Jarrod said, "We signed the papers on Saturday, and Sunday night I had texts from people asking about it." Stacey laughed, sort of. "People are watching, all the time."

Lyra didn't like it. "Why should everyone know who I am?" she asked one day when we were greeted downtown by someone we'd sung karaoke with the night before. Apparently, I like feeling known. I loved the hello-honks; I liked hearing from other parents that they'd seen Harper and Sophie on their way to the playground. Our second week in town, a reporter for the Hays Post, the online local-news site run by the cable company, interviewed us for over an hour and then wrote a fourteen-hundred-word story. "Family's World Tour to Study Parenting Lands Them in Hays" ran on the home page, complete with a big picture of all of us on our porch squinting at the camera. Alia visited the fitness center, and when she asked if they had three-month memberships, the guy at the counter said, "Oh, are you part of that family from the news?" A couple of days later, both our children received letters at school from Senator Jerry Moran (R-KS) welcoming them to town. One way to view my delight at all these developments is that I appreciated being seen as a part of a community; the less charitable way to view it is that I enjoyed feeling like a big shot.

You don't mind that everyone knows your shit when you're proud of your shit. But kids aren't always proud of their shit; neither are adults. Sometimes a community's less accepting of your shit than it should be.

Were we to live in Hays longer than three months, eventually I would have some shit I didn't want becoming public knowledge.

After Lyra got back from her first day of school, she grudgingly agreed to leave the house again; she wanted the internet. She changed into shorts and a sweatshirt, reflecting the fact that, Kansas-style, it was now thirty degrees hotter than it had been when she'd left for school that morning. We walked down Main Street to the library, which Catherine had advised us was very good. "Surprisingly good," she'd added. The library, a blocky building of the same creamy Kansas limestone as most of the public structures around town, was recently renovated (with the help of a public bond) to look more like the 1911 Carnegie-funded library the city had foolishly torn down in the 1960s. Inside, five out of five cool twentysomething librarians complimented Lyra on her anime sweatshirt.

Where do these amazing librarians come from? I texted Catherine.

They're all English majors, she wrote back. *Those girls don't have anyplace else to work.*

Upstairs was a remarkable YA section, completely packed with kids doing crafts, reading books, playing computer games, and chasing each other around. The Halloween display featured an enormous hand-drawn Babadook. BABADOOK BOOK BOOK, the display read. Lyra walked over to the YA desk and asked about some bad dystopian series; the clerk brightened, said "I *love* that one!," and took Lyra straight to the right section. Lyra made several complicated gestures that seemed meant to convey both that she was dying of joy and that she was finally, after six months in cities that had little to offer to the English-speaking reader, getting the chance to live again.

Vera Haynes was the YA librarian; she'd come to Hays to work as a youth minister, only to have the church that had hired her withdraw the job offer just before she started. "But then this job came up," she said when I interviewed her later. "I applied for it, somehow I got it, and I applied to library grad school the next day." She now studies at FHSU; her fiancé is a librarian too.

The library is one of the few places in town that's open after school every day. On a library calendar crowded with games, activities, quiz nights, coding clubs, there was a big empty stripe down the middle like a highway median. "Oh my gosh, we can't do anything on Wednesday night because that's youth-group night," she said. Even the schools in town don't schedule concerts or games on Wednesday night; no kids would come.

When I spoke with Haynes it was the week of the first of the high-profile #MeToo revelations, and she'd replaced the Babadook display with one featuring books on sexual harassment and assault. RAPE CULTURE, the sign read. "Those books are going fast," she said. "I can't keep them in the building." Haynes seemed unconcerned with whether parents would take offense at the display; she viewed her sole constituency as the teenagers who showed up every day, not the parents who worked till five and then called their kids home. She'd recently instituted a new rule: Even if your parent telephones the library looking for you, the staff will not confirm you're there. "We got a lot of pushback at first," she said, "but the ALA holds that anyone who uses a library should have the expectation of privacy." She nodded: and that was that. It was, I realized, a crucial policy, one that established the YA section (and the library as a whole) as a place that teenagers could trust. Not only not to rat your location out to your mom, but not to tell your parents that you checked out a book about rape culture or being gay. The library would not abandon you in your time of need.

Downstairs in the adult section, I saw the larger role the library played in the life of Hays as an example of what the sociologist Eric Klinenberg has termed "social infrastructure," public spaces that bring together and serve the social needs of broad populations. Older couples learned how to use their phones at Thursday tech support; recent immigrants printed out employment forms; mothers on maternity leave met other parents at Wednesday morning baby storytime. Like the municipal swimming pools I wrote about in Iceland, the Hays Library serves as a town center for families, teens, and the elderly. The Hays Library is a public good funded by a tax levy that the people of Hays voted on themselves, run by optimistic, ambitious twenty-five-year-olds, open to all, a home for teenagers where their parents cannot hassle them. It is glorious. In our three months in Hays, Lyra and I went there almost every single day.

At the library, I got another text from Catherine: *We're at the mayor's new wine bar. Grand opening tonight! Join us.* The wine bar was down the street from the library, so Lyra and I crossed Main, each of us laden with a tote bag full of books. The Paisley Pear was on the corner of Main and Eleventh; the door stood precisely on the corner of the lot, facing the intersection at a 45-degree angle. Tinny speakers above the door played a Spotify playlist that I would get the sense after several weeks was based on the search *'80s roots rock*. You might think John Cougar Mellencamp has just the one song about small towns — "Small Town" — but you'd be wrong. He has a lot of other ones on the same topic, too.

The afternoon sun rendered the windows opaque and so it wasn't until we opened the doors that I realized the wine bar was completely packed. We could enter the atrium but could go no farther, like the final two jelly beans dropped in a full jar. Behind us an older couple opened the door, looked in, and said, "Oh gosh." We wriggled our way over to Catherine and Carl, standing with Alia and Harper next to a shelf of Stonewall Kitchen pancake mixes, the kind that neither I nor you have ever bought from a gourmet market anywhere. The shops of Main Street in Hays were nearly uniformly in this mode: cutesy boutiques of the sort my mom would call "chichi," places to buy Mother's Day gifts (novelty socks, table runners, scented candles), but not where you'd shop every day. They seemed geared toward a fantasy version of Hays as tourism center, one somehow visited by so many leisure travelers that the town needed a dozen such businesses in a three-block stretch.

"How do you know the mayor again?" I asked Catherine.

"Oh, everybody knows him," she said. She said that Shaun, who went to her church, would be appearing—wearing a sash that read MAYOR—in the play Catherine had written to accompany the local symphony's Halloween performance. Before being mayor, Shaun was Hays's first Uber driver. "It's kind of like Stars Hollow here," Catherine said.

"Hey, guys," Mayor Shaun said, making his way to us through the crowd. He was tall and skinny, with an Adam's apple that bobbed excitedly when he talked. He shook my hand with great enthusiasm and said he couldn't wait to see what I wrote about Hays. Then he turned to Carl. "I miss seeing you in the news!" he said. Carl had spent the previous year as the head of the Fort Hays State University's faculty senate in a bitter battle with the university's president, who eventually resigned. Carl's expression made exquisitely clear how much he'd enjoyed being in the news. ("Carl hated the whole thing," Catherine told me later, "but, you know, he really believes in stuff, so he had to do it.")

Soon Mayor Shaun stood in front of everyone and gave a short speech. "It's been real great learning all about wine," he said. Lyra, Harper, Sophie, and Martha went outside during the boring part. When we joined them out on the sidewalk (the speakers playing "Cherry Bomb"), the girls had found a painted rock, one of dozens hidden all around Hays as part of a quirky local project pursued by a number of small towns. "Oh, you're supposed to take a picture and post it online," Catherine said. "Then you hide it somewhere else."

"Ooh, can I hide it?" Harper asked. Martha and Sophie, veterans at finding and hiding such rocks, said she could.

"We'll eat dinner at the good restaurant," Catherine declared, and we walked around the corner to Gella's, the brewery and grill where her friend Manuel was the chef. We all sat down and ordered drinks, and then Catherine grabbed me and we spent twenty minutes going from table to table, saying hi. Catherine introduced me to Manuel, to this professor friend, this couple from her church, that parent at the elementary school. We'd been in Hays only a few days, yet I recognized someone I knew, the saintly guidance counselor from Lyra's school. When I finally sat down, I ate a veggie burger that was so good it became my go-to order for the next three months.

So, yes, we were enjoying Hays. Sure, there was only one good restaurant, but the food was delicious; sure, there was only one library, but it was exceptional. Sure, we had only one friend, but she was the best friend, and she was committed to helping us make more.

"I mean, you're not gonna move here," Catherine said as we walked up Fort Street. Carl was deep in conversation with Sophie; Martha chattered hopefully at Harper, whom she'd identified as a kindred spirit even though she was two years older. Lyra, ambling and thinking, trailed us by a block.

"No, but that doesn't mean it's not appealing," Alia said. The air was crisp but not cold; the stars were not screwing around.

"I complain a lot," Catherine said frankly. "But I also really love it. I love walking home at night. You can really do that." It was clear she meant not just that Hays was safe but that Hays presented her with a life that gave her the leisure time to walk and social engagements that she could walk home from. We dropped off the Millers and kept walking toward our house, two blocks farther.

"What are we doing tomorrow?" Harper asked.

"Well, you have school again," I said.

"Oh, right." She sang a little song to herself, twirling. "I like it here," she said. When we reached our house, Harper took the painted rock and hid it, very carefully, under the root of a tree — so carefully that no one found it again.

Some things we liked about Hays, America:

We liked the big mural at the corner of Thirteenth and Main that featured a bison, some farmers, Bill Hickok maybe, and the words HAYS, AMERICA.

We liked how crazy the weather was, though I expect we eventually would not like it if we stayed there forever. One day my sister-in-law in North Carolina sent me a screenshot of her weather app with the Hays forecast: Thursday rainy and forty-six, Friday high winds and sixty-eight, Saturday sunny and eighty-two. *Weather in Kansas is straight bonkers,* she texted.

We liked that there were parades. So many parades! Our first weekend was homecoming at Fort Hays State, so a parade wended its way down Main Street, crowds of baton twirlers, football players, pep bands. The current homecoming king and queen and last year's king and queen shared a convertible, putting aside any bitterness about the bloody dethroning. A gaggle of Lycra'd dancers ages four to fourteen pranced by, performing a sharply choreographed routine, done up in hot pants, sports bras, and eleven p.m. makeup. "Oh, this dance school," Catherine said. The dance schools were a big deal in Hays; people put bumper stickers on their cars to indicate their allegiance to the dance school their kids attended. According to Catherine there was one demure dance school and two hoochie-mama dance schools; this was one of the hoochie-mama schools. Harper watched in awe.

We liked that everyone went to Cervs, the local convenience store chain. Want bad fried chicken? Get it at Cervs. Want pretty good, locally made flavored popcorn? Load up at Cervs. Want a Snoball, the local equivalent of a Slurpee, as our kids did after sitting in the hot sun watching a boring parade? Stop by Cervs along with every single other kid in town.

We liked how slow the Saturdays were, because we had friends to spend them with. The kids' Snoball cups, dripping bright blue syrup, were stuffed into a trash can at the playground atop other kids' Snoball cups. Every once in a while a kid would approach the trash can and then run away squealing, having stirred up a dozen fat bees that would drunkenly whump into the Styrofoam. Our kids swung on the swings, barely able to work up the enthusiasm to push each other. Catherine and Alia chatted on a bench. My fingers twitched toward my phone but I resisted; instead, I dozed lightly on a tire swing. "This is a real Hays Saturday," I heard Catherine say.

That night Catherine took me over to the Fort Hays campus for a screening of a movie featuring the town. "It's this documentary made for Swiss television in 1976," she explained as we walked through darkening streets. "They needed a regular American small town, I guess, and they picked Hays." The citizens of the city who'd appeared in *A Quiet America* had never actually seen the doc; a samizdat version on Facebook had attracted local attention over the summer before it was taken down on a copyright claim. But now the Hays Arts Council had acquired the rights to the film, and to celebrate Hays's one hundred and fiftieth anniversary, the council was screening it for the town for the first time.

The Beach/Schmidt Performing Arts Center was pretty full; there were probably about six hundred people there chattering excitedly in the few minutes before the show was to start. Extended families occupied full rows of the theater. Soon the lights went down and Brenda, the head of the arts council, bounded onstage for an introduction. "We're just so excited for this movie," she said. "Watch carefully—maybe your parents or your grandparents are in it!" The crowd, predominantly over sixty, chuckled. Before we watched the documentary, Brenda added, she had a special surprise for us: "Just a few years ago, Marc Schindler, the host of the first movie, came back to Hays for a follow-up, which was also broadcast on Swiss TV. We're going to watch that first."

The audience sat patiently through *A Return to a Quiet America,* a portrait of Hays in the present day. "Hays has not changed much," Marc Schindler narrated. At one point, a subtitle described HaysMed, the local hospital, as a "luxury clinic," and everyone laughed. Everyone stopped laughing at the next subtitle, which read, *In Kansas, 17 percent of the population have no health insurance.*

Soon the 1976 documentary began. It featured the same square aspect ratio and the same haircuts I remember from vintage *Sesame Street.* That same narrator we'd just heard, his voice now younger and sharper, described the town almost everyone in the audience remembered with great fondness. A beloved Methodist minister, long gone, got an ovation at his first appearance on-screen. So did several different intersections—beloved intersections, I guess? At one shot of the old downtown, about fifty people said, in unison, "Woolworths!"

In a big city, I realized, you'd have a hard time replicating this event — hundreds of people who all knew one another, who had been here sharing experiences for decades, assembling to see vacation photos of the past. The film mentioned a radio show called *Party Line,* the 1976 version of Craigslist, which allowed people to call in and hawk, live and on the air, whatever they had for sale — flower-bedding material, a tractor, a coffee table. (Even in 2017, there was no Craigslist for western Kansas; the local cable company ran a classified-ad website.) During a wedding scene, while the bride and groom danced to a polka band on-screen, an older couple a row behind us whispered to each other: "Is that Daryl? Daryl and his wife?"

"His ex-wife."

Toward the end of the film, a nighttime scene showed a bunch of cars lined up on Main Street, way more cars than I'd ever seen on Main Street. The auditorium went nuts, cheering and whooping and laughing. All around the room, I heard parents explaining to their children, with various levels of candidness, that once upon a time, cruising was pretty much all there was to do on Saturday nights. The dashboard clock of one old sedan crawling up Main read 12:15 a.m. Every car was full of young people; they drank beer from cans and waved at folks driving in the other direction. "That was us!" I heard from the audience, and I don't think they meant that they actually saw themselves in the scene but that the life they saw on-screen was perfectly recognizable as their own. That was them, and that was them, and that was them. It wasn't me, but to be in that auditorium at that moment was nonetheless to be in a place of great happiness — happiness derived from years of small, shared stories, of the most boring parts of community life.

I thought of something Ian Frazier wrote in his wonderful book *Great Plains,* a description of a feeling he had during a Founders' Day fashion show in Nicodemus, just fifty miles from here, a west Kansas town founded in the nineteenth century by black settlers. "Suddenly I felt a joy so strong it almost knocked me down," Frazier wrote. "It came up my spine and settled on my head like a warm cap and filled my eyes with tears."

Frazier had a theory about joy and the plains. He wrote:

Joy seems to be a product of the geography, just as deserts can produce mystical ecstasy and English moors produce gloom. Once happiness gets rolling in this open place, not much stops it.

Was I idealizing the plains a bit? Sure. But I found a lot to love in the connections between people, the smallness of the town amid the vastness of the land around it, the way everyone was just really, really nice to us. And the geographical austerity of the place had a hold on me. It sure wasn't New Zealand. It was, in its featurelessness, the opposite of New Zealand, a place that, as the journalist Mark O'Connell wrote, has the effect of pummeling visitors into a kind of catatonia with the relentless attack of its vertiginous beauty. "If you don't like getting ravished by views, you have no business in the place," O'Connell declared. "That, famously, is the whole point of New Zealand."

New Zealand is so beautiful that I found it difficult to see myself as a part of its majesty. Kansas, conversely, so lacks ostentatious beauty that it felt easy to sink into its flatness, to feel at one with the endless horizon, as if I'd been there forever. It was both a comforting feeling and a frightening one. It was not at all difficult to imagine what it would have been like to be a hardscrabble farmer here, busting sod in 1880.

I was rereading Frazier's *Great Plains* in anticipation of the monthly book club at the Hays Library. (At that meeting, I would see just how exhausted plains residents are by people like me and our extremely basic ideas of Kansas life. "When I was a girl," one librarian said, "I went on vacation to Florida and another girl asked me how I got there in my covered wagon.") I texted Catherine, who'd also read and loved the book, a passage that was new to me, as it appeared only in the paperback edition's endnotes. It was a letter Frazier had received from a Wyoming rancher after the hardcover edition had been published. It read:

Perhaps you have an overly romantic view of the plains.... But even though you spent a lot of time on the plains, you are necessarily a visitor from the East. The book is something like a Sunday drive through the countryside. From the passing car you can marvel at the beauty of it all, but you can't temper that with the experience of the country's warts and blemishes.

There is a harshness as well as beauty here. Living here is realizing that this huge, beautiful land that can bring so much joy to the soul moves to its own rhythms, not yours. I think this is what makes life here so satisfying for the challenge is to bring your goals and needs into harmony with an environment and land you basically can't change.

In response, Catherine sent me an email:

Kathleen Norris is a poet who moved to her family's farm in North Dakota as an adult. Her two books, *Dakota: A Spiritual Geography* and *The Cloister Walk,* have meant a lot to me out here. In lieu of spending an hour tracking down the quote for you, I'll give you the sentiment in my own words:

One of the things the Great Plains teaches you is the value of scarcity. There are so few trees here that you appreciate the cottonwood in your backyard, as you might a pet or a loved one. You become a fervent lover of trees. You asked me about the leaves changing colors, and I told you they didn't put on much of a show. But as a result, the few leaves in my front yard that give the slightest red hue can make me cry. They seem so precarious and fleeting, the red barely red, mostly brown. I love those crinkled brown/red spots of color more than all the maple trees in Vermont.

She states it much better than that, but you get the idea.

CHAPTER 9

Bloom Where You're Planted

One problem with Hays was that it was so goddamn far from anything. In the Netherlands we loved taking advantage of Europe's density to explore; we were a forty-five-minute cycle trip from Rotterdam, a one-hour flight from London, a four-hour train ride from Frankfurt. Here, Kansas City was four hours straight east, and Denver was five hours straight west. We were finally back in America, yet to get to anywhere else in America required a lot of money and time, as we were reminded in early October when an old friend died in Delaware. Alia flew east—well, west to Denver, then east—to visit his widow. The journey took the better part of a day, and so she combined it with check-ins with coworkers and clients all along the East Coast. There was no way I could fly out too, much as I wanted to, so I stayed in Hays with the girls, feeling, for a week, very sad and very separated from people I loved who, I imagined, needed my help.

Of course, for many people in Hays, the distance from Hays to anywhere else is no barrier to loving their home. It's a *reason* why they love their home. Valerie, a mom of two, told me about how she and her husband had worked fancy corporate jobs "in the city" for a while but returned to Hays because the city just felt too big, too crime-ridden, too hard to make friends in, no place they'd ever consider raising children. I got the impression from her description that Valerie and her husband had lived in Chicago, maybe, or Dallas, until she concluded, with satisfaction, "I think our life is so much happier than it would be if we still lived in Topeka."

The point is that living far away from big cities didn't matter that much if most everything you want and everyone you love was here. That was less true in Hays now than it had been during the twentieth-century dominance of the town's first white settlers, the Volga Germans. These Germans by way of Russia settled Hays in the late 1800s and for the most part stayed right there. Now, native Haysians often left and new Haysians (especially those drawn by jobs at the university or the hospital) often arrived, meaning that many of the town's residents had relatives farther away than, say, Dodge City. But still, most of the people we met had maintained or forged strong friendships and family ties here in west Kansas and resigned themselves to seeing those who had left or those they'd left behind once a year or so. "We FaceTime regularly with friends in Oregon along with family in Mexico," Erin, a translator and mom of four, told me. "Even ten or fifteen years ago that wasn't a possibility."

Erin liked to say that technology altered the small-town experience. Technology also eased the consumer inconvenience of living in the middle of nowhere. What was Hays like before the age of e-commerce? Even now I wondered how people could believe that everything they wanted was here in Hays, a city selling more ROOFS than BOOKS. (Of course, e-commerce is the reason Hays's bookstore went out of business.) A couple of thrift shops and the Friends of the Library shop did sell some good used books; the Friends store was also a great place to buy Criterion DVDs removed from the library's collection nearly unwatched. Otherwise, everyone who wasn't looking for Main Street–style gifts shopped at Walmart or Hobby Lobby. When Alia expressed concern about the political ramifications of shopping at Hobby Lobby, the plaintiff in a recent Supreme Court case allowing corporations to refuse, for religious reasons, to offer contraception to female employees as part of an employer-sponsored health plan, Catherine laughed. "Guys, the only people who work at this Hobby Lobby are sixty-year-old ladies," she said. "They don't need birth control."

There was a small multiplex at the mall where we watched *Thor: Ragnarok* and *Coco,* but it didn't show art-house movies unless they'd won Best Picture or starred enough famous people to fool the AMC programmers into running one screening at 12:35 p.m. (That's when Lyra and I and absolutely zero other people saw *Battle of the Sexes*.) There's a pretty good natural history museum, with a surfeit of prairie fossils and some roaring dinosaurs, but that's about it for museums. There's relatively little art anywhere in west Kansas, although Hays is an hour's drive from Lucas, a weird, great town devoted to folk and visionary art. There used to be a roller rink behind the movie theater, but that closed. Catherine was exaggerating slightly when she said Gella's was the *only* good restaurant; there were three others, though one, the only Vietnamese restaurant in town, closed while we lived there. There were no Indian restaurants, no bagel shops, no Thai food. There was sushi; it wasn't bad.

The difficult project of staying busy in Hays came into focus that week Alia was gone. On Saturday Catherine and I took all four kids out to the natural history museum, which Catherine's children had visited many, many times, as became clear when budding herpetologist Martha sprinted through "Rattlersssss: From Fear to Fascination," ID'ing every snake. ("That's the tiger rattlesnake. It's extremely venomous. It would kill you *really* fast if it bit you.") Then we stopped at Dairy Queen for Blizzards. Then we stuffed all four kids into the back of Catherine's car and drove out to a farm west of town, the kids singing songs from *The Sound of Music* and speculating about their Hogwarts houses. (It's my experience that a lot of people think they are Gryffindors when in fact most of us are lucky if we're Hufflepuffs.) The farm offered hayrides *and* the chance to fling pumpkins across a field with an enormous homemade catapult. To approximate the sound the pumpkins made when they hit the ground, please shout the word "Squash!" while your mouth is completely full of squash.

On the way back to town, Catherine said, "Okay, that's it! You've done all the things there are to do in Hays."

"That's not true!" Martha protested.

"What haven't they done yet, Martha?"

There was a long pause. Then Martha said, "They haven't been to the paint-your-own-pottery studio."

One solution, of course, is to create your own things to do. In Hays, our friend Cathy told me, "If it's important enough, you do it yourself." Cathy, a thoughtful woman with a thicket of densely packed curls, one patch gone dramatically white, was born and raised in our neck of the woods—the DC suburbs—and after a move to Hays more than two decades ago, she has exemplified this motto. She and her husband, a professor in the philosophy department alongside Carl, created for themselves and their three kids the kinds of opportunities they believed were lacking in their adopted hometown. First was a string academy for kids that cello-playing Cathy and her violin-playing husband founded with the help of string students at the university. More recently Cathy established a successful and all-consuming subscription baking business. Every week she prepares and bakes about a hundred and fifty loaves of fancy-ass bread; customers pick them up on Friday afternoon, and the za'atar babka, Nutella-banana bread, or sunflower seed levains are served at various weekend get-togethers. She's filling a niche and defying a stereotype about the Midwest, serving neighbors—even in a "steak and potatoes town," as many described it to me—who love finely crafted food and are willing to pay for it. There isn't much else in Hays for such foodies, though. The farms around Hays are mostly enormous and crammed with wheat, soy, and milo, though a few small farmers bring produce to a summer market. A former restaurant chef named Tim Pfannenstiel founded a clever micro–Blue Apron sort of service, preparing gourmet dinners and meal kits in his home kitchen for pickup by Haysians. One local couple raises bees and has started growing beautiful organic shiitake mushrooms in their basement. The local beef jerky is *exceptional.*

"I'd love it if Hays had a bakery," Cathy said. "A bakery/café!" She shook her head to indicate how far-fetched the idea was. She certainly works hard to fill that void; before she installed a second oven in her kitchen, she was getting up at three a.m. on baking days. Now she has a rule that she won't get up before four.

"That's one of the great things about Hays," she said. "You can really have an impact because there's not so much competition. There are very few bakers in town." She laughed. "If there's something you wanna try, you can do it, and people are really grateful. You may not be the best cello teacher in the world, but people really appreciate what they can't get elsewhere." For her, the smallness of Hays allowed her to try out ideas that in a larger city she might have shied away from attempting, knowing there were already youth symphonies and fancy bakeries. "It's really an opportunity," she said, "to bloom where you're planted."

Catherine, too, had found a way to bloom where she'd been planted, although she also bloomed wherever her plays were produced—London, New York, even my hometown of Milwaukee. But this fall Catherine was producing a new play, and that proved to be my unexpected opportunity to bloom as well.

The fairies were running wild.

It was the first stage rehearsal for *A Fairy Hallow's Eve,* a theatrical piece Catherine had written for the all-volunteer Hays Symphony. Five adult actors would play the rude mechanicals from *A Midsummer Night's Dream,* though in this case, they'd be trying to put on the tragedy of Pyramus and Thisbe for Halloween; a baker's dozen children would play the fairies who disrupt their performance. The symphony would interject musical interludes—a little Mozart as the fairies made off with Peter Quince's scripts, a little Tchaikovsky as everyone danced at the end.

Catherine and the director, Erin—not the Erin who translated and was married to the chef at Gella's but the Erin who ran a dairy farm outside town and taught theater at Fort Hays State—had worked with the kids in a handful of rehearsals downtown at the arts council offices. Harper was a fairy; Lyra had agreed to work as co-production manager alongside Catherine. But this Saturday morning at the Beach/Schmidt Center, Catherine was away on a work trip and Lyra was losing interest.

"Will Catherine be back for part of rehearsal today?" Erin asked Carl, who visibly started. Alia and I knew more about Catherine's schedule this week, it turned out, than he did. I reminded myself, as I'd done about one million times on this trip: other people's marriages and families work differently from ours! "No," I interjected. "She's not coming back until tomorrow." Erin nodded, looked over at the kids in the seats—now bouncing up and down and shouting, in unison, "Look what you made me do"—and walked away without a word.

As rehearsal began and an adult actor flubbed a line, I stepped over to Erin. "Do you need someone to be on book?" I asked. She looked at me and said, "Are you serious?" I saw myself instantly transformed in her eyes from Schlub Dad to Schlub Dad Who Knows Something about Theater. "Here you go," she said, handing me a script.

And that's how I became de facto assistant director of the Hays Symphony's Halloween play.

This was not a long-term appointment; we had only three more rehearsals before the actual performance. But more than a thousand parents and kids were expected to pack into Beach/Schmidt for the show, so there was some urgency to our task. Over the next week, I stayed on book, gave line notes after run-throughs, and supervised long rehearsals in which everything often went wrong. Erin demonstrated admirable patience in the face of an adult actor who liked to direct her costars from the stage, a guest orchestra conductor from Kansas City who treated her with withering contempt, and a mischievous herd of fairies who seemed to expand to fill every available space in the theater.

"I've noticed how good you are helping out with the show," Carl told me one night as we roasted hot dogs in his backyard. "You have a quiet authority." I glowed. Most of the kids didn't, at first, have any idea who I was—I was just the new adult who knew where the props lived—but they did what I said. One ten-year-old, Emmaline, called me Dave all week and invoked my authority at every turn, pleased to seize power by proxy: "Guys, Dave says we have to go stage left!"

The day of the show, as we all sat downstairs, the kids wired on candy, Catherine said, "Emmaline," then pointed at me. "What's his name?"

"Dave," she said confidently. Then, after a pause: "Or, um, something with a D."

"I'm Dan," I said.

"But who *are* you?" she asked. When I said I was Harper's dad, another girl's eyes widened: "So *that's* why you guys always come in together!"

. For the first twenty-two years of my life, I spent more time in theaters than probably anywhere else other than in front of a TV. For years I was in a children's acting company that put on ambitious all-kid versions of adult shows. (*You're a Good Man, Charlie Brown,* sure, but also *The Diary of Anne Frank.* I played Pig Pen and Mr. Dussel.) I worked backstage at our local adult community theater and even, in high school, got a paid gig as a stagehand in a professional company's production of *Shirley Valentine.* Then in college I was a drama major, acting in or directing four shows a year, an absurd level of busyness for an undergraduate to maintain when his friends were, say, going to parties or studying abroad.

And so I knew what Catherine meant as she and I sat stage right folding loose-leaf script pages into paper airplanes for the fairies to launch from the balconies. "God, I still love being in a theater," she said. "There's nowhere I feel more at home." The house was open. Near the curtain, the Beach/Schmidt stage manager was running through the light cues on headset. From the stage, we could hear the honk and drone of orchestra members tuning their instruments.

"Too bad today is like the last nice day of the fall," I said.

She laughed. "I've missed so many beautiful days in theaters, and I don't regret a one."

Me, I hadn't been backstage in a real theater for years. Performing in general fell out of my life when we had kids; it was a frivolity that I felt I couldn't afford to indulge, because it seemed absurd to do something that would take me away every evening yet wouldn't bring in any money. (It's no coincidence that the three times a year I get to sing karaoke, I go a little crazy.) But here in Hays, less than a month after our arrival, I was behind the scenes in a Broadway-size house, an hour from showtime, with a marked-up script and a set of responsibilities to fulfill without which the show could not go on. It happened because my daughter had landed in a show immediately, because no one else knew what the hell to do, and because I was available.

A Fairy Hallow's Eve ran for only one performance, but the theater was indeed packed and raucous, filled with kids who loved the jokes about Bottom's name and the paper airplanes, and with parents who appreciated or at least tolerated the music and the Shakespeare references. Harper got to perform walkovers onstage before a thousand people rather than by herself on our playroom floor. "Is that the *real* mayor?" several children asked me in awe when Mayor Shaun showed up in his sash. And the fairies in my charge hit every cue and didn't miss a line.

After the show, as Harper and her fellow fairies danced around the lobby greeting their fans, I happily gathered up props and put them away. Catherine cleaned up paper airplanes and programs, all crumpled amid the seats, and the set designer collected the big papier-mâché trees to keep in his garage for next year's play. Erin approached me, holding a jack-o'-lantern in each arm, and said, "Thanks for stepping in and taking charge."

"You did a really great job," I said, meaning it; this had been a tough gig. She'd navigated the entire ordeal with great patience and a lot of artistic verve, creating a small delight out of nothing. I was filled with a long-lost sensation, the satisfying post-adrenaline crash of being part of a good show done well. Hays had given me this feeling!

One person who didn't have that feeling was Lyra, whose attention had not been held by her position as co-production manager and who, after skipping most rehearsals, experienced the show from the audience. In the lobby, she seemed a bit at sea. "I wish I had done more," she told me.

I held my tongue; her lack of commitment had frustrated me at every turn, but it wouldn't do any good to remind her of that now. "That would have been great," I finally managed.

In some ways Lyra was treating Hays as she had the other places on our trip, floating along in a little bubble of Lyradom. But, her flaking on the play aside, we saw glimmers of a more mature girl nearing teenagehood. She befriended sweet, goofy Elizabeth next door. She attended a murder-mystery party after school at the library. She lectured Sophie on being more sociable, of all topics. ("LOL, forever," Catherine texted me.)

Was it that Lyra was actually changing or was it that, in a less stressful environment, I could see her more clearly instead of focusing only on her intractability? One Friday night Alia came out to the porch and said, with unveiled astonishment, "Lyra wants to go to the middle-school dance." At that exact moment Lyra opened the door, and we both composed our expressions into a semblance of cool. Lyra wore her cat dress and came home early, reporting inexplicable drama on the part of other kids. But she went!

Yet Lyra occasionally retreated back into her bubble. While Harper liked to tell her Kansas classmates that she planned to attend college at Victoria University in Wellington, where her friends Tracey and Gary said she could stay at their house, Lyra had a line she liked to use on well-meaning adults asking her if she was sad about the upcoming end of our journey. "When I get home," she said, "I'm never leaving our house again."

We had it pretty good in Hays. Our house was so big that there was an entire room used only for Harper's and her friends' gymnastics routines. (She had friends who attended the demure dance school and friends who attended the hoochie-mama dance schools.) The family next door, a recently divorced mom and her five kids, liked to bake cookies and bring them over. Alia had worked out a rhythm with her firm, for now, and she had a steady supply of news stories to vet. She went to yoga with Catherine some mornings; in the afternoons she sewed in the dining room, where she'd set up the Singer Catherine had owned for years but never learned to use. We were accumulating a truly astonishing number of hand-sewn Christmas decorations.

When Harper wasn't cartwheeling upstairs with Molly or Sophie or other friends, she wanted to help Alia sew. In theory, this should have been endearing and fun. The novelist Elizabeth McCracken once joked, "One thing they never tell you about being a parent is that the elevator-button-pushing part of your life is over." ("I like pushing elevator buttons, too, you know," she'd mutter.) Harper had always been a button-pusher and a self-seat-belter and an *I*-wanna-do-it-er. In Kansas, back among the accoutrements of middle-class American life, she seized the opportunity to cook and sew and clean and...and everything. She would have picked out my clothes every day if I'd let her, and in fact every time I wore something she didn't want me to wear, she got annoyed.

Harper's determination to do the things *she* wanted to do was admirable but it also meant that if she set her sights on something *you* were doing, you were no longer doing it; she was. When that was sweeping the floor, a thing neither Alia nor I particularly wanted to do, great! But Alia found sewing on her own therapeutic, so it became stressful when Harper took over the sewing machine and flew into new stitches without asking what actually came next. (Alia liked pushing buttons too, you know.) "I just wanna sew my stupid Christmas bags!" she fumed to me one night. "Do we always have to have so much togetherness!"

Catherine and her girls hung out with us every day, a welcome respite from Smith-Kois family togetherness. Or rather, at this point, they were part of the family, so they were additional family members who helped dilute the togetherness. Carl, a loving father and husband, nonetheless remained just detached enough to serve as both a puzzle and an inspiration. Sometimes we'd go to the Millers' house and he'd greet us from his reading chair, where he'd been straight-up *perusing* the *Confessions of Saint Augustine* or whatever. When I got him to laugh I felt as though I had slam-dunked a basketball. He had no cell phone and therefore we all had to be very clear about where he needed to be and when, and the other grown-ups would often make backup plans with one another in case he got sidetracked at work. In a way, it seemed to me, Catherine, Alia, and I were all *Carl's* sister-wives.

Haysians did not really understand what Catherine actually did for a living. More than one person I met in our time in Hays would hear we were friends with Catherine and Carl and bring up, unprompted, how Catherine sure went out of town a lot for that work of hers. One week when she was overseeing auditions for a new play premiering at a regional theater, a woman I ran into at Gella's observed, "Well, she's away for her writing, I guess. Poor Carl, he's almost raising those girls alone, I think sometimes."

I bristled. "Are you kidding?" I asked. She was not. I'd heard about, but rarely witnessed myself, this kind of gossipy small-mindedness, which carried with it a set of sexist assumptions I was doubly inoculated against as a man and as someone just breezing through town. What I saw was usually straight-faced Midwestern niceness; I never experienced this undercurrent of judgment. (Presumably, they talked about me behind my back—or maybe as a transient, I didn't even reach the threshold as a topic for such gossip.) Yes, Carl handled the girls by himself sometimes. But why shouldn't he? While he did, Catherine made a career for herself bigger than it seemed many Haysians could understand. Anyway, anyone who thought Carl was raising those girls alone didn't know that family very well.

As it happens, in almost every two-parent family we met in Hays, both parents worked. Hays just didn't really have the kind of wealth, for the most part, to enable the stay-at-home-PTA-mom culture that our part of Arlington has. (North Arlington also has plenty of working moms; they tend to be insanely successful, doing things like selling multimillion-dollar homes or running entire departments at hospitals. Those families also often have full-time nannies or live-in au pairs.) But not that many people in Hays had the kinds of jobs that necessitated time away in far-flung places; Hays was not the headquarters for any sprawling corporation, for example, with employees in regional centers who needed checking on. The upside of a work culture like Hays's is that I met very few people who seemed to define themselves by their jobs or whose work ate up their lives. The professors, siding installers, doctors, yoga teachers, real estate agents—even the damn mayor—all seemed pretty content to work their forty hours a week and find other things to do with the rest of their time.

The downside? It's not that ambition wasn't prized in Hays. Jarrod and Stacey were ambitious about building their practice. Vera was ambitious about the library and clearly was positioning herself for bigger things. I met any number of high-school kids whose plans to go to college far away were embraced by their families. And all-American success did make an impact here; those who had created successful businesses or gotten rich off oil had the type of oversize cultural footprint you'd see, I think, anywhere in a country built on such indicators of capitalist triumph.

But there's a certain kind of ambition that bridges the personal and professional, the kind I associate with creative work but that can also manifest itself in the law or government service or many other jobs. It has to do with being known and doing work that other people recognize and care about, doing it not with the goal of being famous but with at least a corner of your gaze on posterity, on achieving some good that lasts beyond the scope of your career. Or maybe it's just about being part of a bigger conversation, the cultural conversation I try to find my way into with my writing or the now centuries-long conversation among the courts and the citizenry and the Constitution that lawyers like Alia contribute to in aggregate. I suppose, though, from someplace like Hays, which bases at least some of its self-conception on standing well outside those conversations, that desire looks self-aggrandizing, immodest.

The longer we stayed in Hays, the nicer everyone was to us, the more it became clear that it would be hard for me to feel at home in this delightful town for the long term. The odd kind of career Catherine has, which mixes stretches of writing at home with weeks in Denver or Milwaukee or San Diego, was mystifying to Haysians—even before you factored in that her product was creative work no Haysian would ever see. *A Fairy Hallow's Eve*? Sure. The Christmas pageants Catherine took over at the Methodist church when she could no longer abide how bad they were? Beloved by all. But *Crooked,* a play that's been performed in scores of theaters around the world, was not going to be performed at Hays High—not enough roles, too much sex talk. (A copy is in the library, in the Kansas Room with other state authors, I'm happy to say, and it's been checked out a total of six times.) "When I try to explain my career to people in town, they usually think I'm making it up," she wrote once. "The idea of someone working in professional theater seems as unlikely as voting for a Democrat." Catherine's career would make perfect sense in Wellington, a city that prizes its quirky creatives in a country that's made enabling people's passion projects a priority. In Hays, she has never made much sense to people who are not her close friends.

Neither would I, if I stayed here long enough. She truly seemed not to care! I'm vain enough to care.

For our kids, Hays was the place in our journey that seemed most like home, of course, especially after Costa Rica, with its lack of American signifiers. They instantly settled into Kansas life, grateful for peers who spoke English, a TV, a library, fast food. We had trouble getting them to notice, really, the ways that Hays might be different from Arlington. Once Catherine asked Lyra what she thought about Hays as compared to home and Lyra, out of nowhere, said, "I feel like here I have cotton in my ears. And it's a little clearer in Virginia." I scrambled for a notebook, scribbled that down, and then asked Lyra, "What do you mean by cotton in your ears?" She shrugged. "I don't know," she said and never spoke of it again.

For us adults, the differences were more obvious, and when I asked Hays parents what they loved about raising a family here, their answers often tracked with what I found notable as well: It's cheap. It's neighborly. It's small and easy to get around; no one ever gets stuck in traffic. "It takes ten minutes to get everywhere!" a professor at FHSU told me. "I don't miss my commute in Kansas City at all." The time you save driving around really accumulates and can have a profound effect. "If you're two hours in your commute, it's hard to come home and read an hour to your kids," Cathy, who runs the subscription baking business, told me. She compared Hays to the Virginia suburbs that we would soon return to. "My sister lives near Manassas. Her husband drives to Vienna every day. That puts a real stress on a family's time." Not to mention on its happiness; a University of Zurich study suggests that a person who drives an hour to work would have to earn 40 percent more to be as satisfied with life as someone whose trip to work is a short walk, like it is for many people in Hays.

Curiously, no one really bicycles in Hays, even though it's as flat as Delft. (Kansas, in general, is really flat; in 2003, three geographers compared Kansas to a pancake in a memorable *Annals of Improbable Research* study and found Kansas to be significantly more flat.) Though the city has a few bike paths marked here and there, the town, like most

American towns, prioritizes cars in its design. It's also really difficult, as I discovered, to ride a bike over bumpy brick streets, in the face of a twenty-five-mile-an-hour prairie wind, or both.

The convenience of everything being a ten-minute drive away is somewhat mooted by the fact that Kansans think nothing of picking up and driving two and a half hours to some other town. For parents, this holds particularly true when dealing with kids who play sports, and the amount of time and energy given to children's sports in Hays was comparable to what we saw in Arlington.

Regular old middle-school sports teams ate up incredible amounts of time for Hays parents and kids because the teams had to travel so damn far just to get to another middle school. Junction City is a four-hour round trip, and that was a common destination for, like, a Tuesday-night basketball game! Hays also had travel sports, and those teams went even farther. The parents I talked to about travel sports echoed what I heard from parents in Arlington: *Oh, we always said we would never do that, but then Maddie's coach said she really needed some better competition, and it's a lot of time but the kids love it, and it's important for them to pursue their passions.* I was as unconvinced in Hays as I was in Arlington, and every time someone turned us down for dinner or a playdate because her kid was traveling to Lincoln for a soccer tournament I felt the same bitter exasperation. I did hear from dissenters, and I appreciated them in Hays just as I did in Arlington. "Our girls were in about as low a level of travel basketball team as you can be on," Ted, who farms south of town, told me. "And we were still spending a thousand dollars a summer!" He shook his head, incredulous. "That's how Americans do family time now—they sit and watch their kids do every damn thing."

In 2008, Hays voters approved a five-year sales-tax increase to build the soccer and baseball complex west of town. That investment in sports was notable, given how reluctant the town had been to similarly invest in education. Haysians like to talk about how good their schools are. Yet on Election Day in 2017, we saw the town vote down a bond that would have replaced two aging elementary schools and upgraded the crowded middle and high schools. "The soccer fields, people got behind those because they could have tournaments, so there was economic benefit with the hotel rooms and restaurants," said Paul Adams, a school board member and the dean at FHSU's school of education. "With schools, voters think, *Well, that's nice, but that's only for people who have children in schools now.*"

Many older Haysians went to school in spartan classrooms, Adams added, and didn't think spending a bunch of money for something nicer was worthwhile. "There is this ethic that, if it ain't broke, don't fix it. You know, 'We will persevere through.'"

We found our children's teachers, all of them graduates of Fort Hays or other nearby colleges, friendly and committed, and the schools themselves welcoming if not particularly rigorous. Our fears about science classes teaching creationism were unfounded. "If you go back ten years or so, that stereotype was closer to reality," Adams said. But in 2006, several pro-evolution candidates were elected to the state board of education, including one representing Hays and west Kansas. Now, said Adams's wife, Cheryl, a science teacher at Hays High and a longtime advocate with Kansas Citizens for Science, the state curriculum is vastly improved, and in Hays, "We try to make sure all our teachers are teaching science as science, and keeping the nonsense and non-science out."

Beyond the quality of the schools, there's a larger problem with being a high-achieving kid in Hays, a problem explained by Cathy, who's raised a couple such kids and who, as a string-instrument teacher, finds herself dealing with others. "The danger of having talented or smart kids in Hays is that they're used to being a big fish in a little pond," she told me. "They're always first place in the music competitions or whatever. First place in western Kansas is nothing! It can be a rude awakening for kids who leave Hays and they learn, oh, wow, *that's* what a real violinist sounds like. Or, wow, that kid is *really* smart, and she took *seven* AP classes." About 5 percent of Hays High students pass at least one AP test; compare that to our local high school in Arlington, where 74 percent of students do. Hays schools, like the town itself, offer its citizens ways to excel. But those ways might serve you best if you didn't have any intention of living farther away than, say, Wichita. For a moment, I had a glimpse of why Lyra might feel as though she had cotton in her ears.

I was buckling my seat belt when I looked up and froze, seeing the pained look on the driver's face. "Don't do that," Ted Bannister told me. "That's embarrassing." I'd already shamed myself when I got into the enormous Ford F-350 pickup, holding the door frame with both hands and hauling myself up as if I were climbing out of a pool. I let the seat belt retract and sat back in a full-width front seat so large I felt like a kid, feet dangling.

Ted's forty-six-hundred-acre farm is an hour south of Hays. His great-grandfather bought the farm in 1906 from a family who thought the land was cursed because their farmhouse had burned down twice. The house that great-grandfather built now bears the signs of generational expansion, each room obviously constructed years apart from the one next to it. "You have another kid," Ted said with a shrug, "you build another room."

As we drove across the farm in that enormous pickup truck, Ted, a lanky, tanned guy with a thatch of blond hair and a killer deadpan, walked me through the business of farming. Ted, his wife, Kathy, and their three kids live in Hays during the school year, then move out to the farm for the summer. The family raises cattle and grows mostly wheat and milo (sorghum), though in recent years a new crop has sprouted on Bannister family land: windmills. Ted drove me out to see a stand of mills, each one two hundred and fifty feet tall and rotating majestically. Power companies pay farmers a monthly fee for the land and pay to improve the access roads. "It's money you don't have to work for," Ted said—crucial in a business dependent on ever-decreasing rainfall and subject to ever-shrinking margins.

Each farm in this part of the country is actually a collection of small businesses, the farmers trying to be as diversified as possible on land that's far too dry to support many crops. ("This is a frigging desert," one farmer told me. ("It's hard to grow shit out here.") The Bannisters' farm is a cattle business, a milo business, a wheat business. They play for both teams in the sustainability game, leasing squares of land to both wind companies and oil companies. If you look across many Kansas farms, you'll see two machines silhouetted against the horizon, moving with similar mechanized stateliness: the derrick pumping up and down, the mill implacably rotating. Ted has diversified the Bannister portfolio further by serving as a representative of other farmers, organizing them to make deals with energy companies to build more windmills.

The farms of western Kansas stand as counterargument to my New Zealand–influenced ideas about local agriculture as a route to a strong local food culture. "Our harvest gets hauled away on semitrucks and gets dumped into the grain elevator with everyone else's," Ted said. "I often wonder if I've bought a loaf of bread with one single grain of my wheat in it." In a recent investigative story in the online magazine New Food Economy, Korie Brown laid out the dire economics of the commodity crops—soybeans, wheat, milo by the ton—that make up most of Kansas agriculture. Between 2003 and 2016, Brown wrote, Kansas wheat farmers increased yields and achieved record harvests. But attaining those record harvests required major investment, and annual farm expenses more than doubled; now that "commodity crop prices have fallen off a cliff," Brown wrote, farmers are barely clearing any money at all. It's "an emergency in the nation's breadbasket."

Why don't the farmers of Kansas grow something more interesting, not to mention less subject to political trade winds and fluctuations in the market, than commodity crops? ("Every cent the price of milo goes down," Ted said, noting how much those prices move according to the trade rhetoric and policies of the Trump administration, "I lose seven hundred dollars on a semi load.") With rural Kansas depopulating by the year, there isn't much of a local market for organic or artisanal foods, so there's little incentive to grow the kinds of produce you might see on the coasts in a CSA or farmers' market. "And anyway," Ted pointed out, "that requires sales and marketing skills, and a lot of us got into farming because we're introverted." Ted's looked into supplying the unexpected boom crops of foodie culture on a national scale, but "niches are easily satisfied. Sriracha is big, but all those peppers are grown by one guy. I thought about chickpeas, but a few suppliers in Virginia take care of all America's needs."

One reason we wanted to stay in rural America for a while was to see what impact farming had on parenting. West Kansas is proud of its farm kids, children who are seen as more hardworking, more resilient, more resistant to the vices older generations always suspect younger generations of—laziness, entitlement, foolishness. "You know, what I've heard is that companies in Kansas City like to hire farm kids and rural kids," one woman told me, echoing a sentiment I heard repeatedly, "because they work harder, more loyally, for longer hours, without complaining." *That sounds terrible,* I didn't say.

For some Haysians who grew up on farms, left, and then returned, the idea of raising their kids in the environment they were raised in was part of the appeal. "We wanted them to have an appreciation for the hard work it takes to farm," Jarrod, a dentist, said of his family's farm just south of town. "We wanted to teach responsibility, work ethic, being a good steward of the land." Ted agreed: "Raising our kids on a farm, we were excited about that: responsibility, adventure, driving when you're a kid."

But it can be hard, parents have found, to really incorporate their children into twenty-first-century farming. "My dad always had things for his sons to do," Ted remembered. "My daughters rarely do anything." Kathy, his wife and fellow farmer, laughed. "Farms are so big now, it's a lot harder for kids to interface with farming," she said. "Ted could learn to drive a tractor when he was a boy because it was a three-thousand-dollar cabless tractor." Compare that with the one-hundred-and-twenty-seven-thousand-dollar sprayer parked on the Bannister farm, ninety feet wide when both booms are extended and GPS-guided; you could see how putting a teenager behind the wheel of that monster might be a bad idea.

"We thought the farm would be much more a part of our lives than it actually has been," Stacey, Jarrod's wife, said with regret. "It took Jarrod a long time to get there." Jarrod's dad had retired and they were in the process of selling off the farm equipment and leasing the land.

"I think they got more out of it than you think," Kathy told Ted.

"Well," Ted said, "they're not scared of cattle."

Rural America still has its fair share of farm kids, of course, children who contribute to the work of family farms and learn responsibility. Indeed, for some farms, the worsening economic prospects of commodity farming mean that children are more necessary than ever. "These kids help," a Wisconsin dairy farmer named Amanda Smith told the *New York Times*. "They're our hired hands." Smith was talking to the *Times* for a story about her six-year-old son, Cullen, whose leg had been mangled by a two-ton loader. Thousands of kids get injured by farm machinery every year in America, and an estimated one hundred are killed.

So farming wasn't necessarily the universally positive influence on rural kids that local folklore might make it out to be. But there was one Kansas farm-family tradition I absolutely wanted our kids to experience: the chance to drive. In Kansas, if you live or work on a farm, you can drive at fourteen. You can drive alone for farm work, and you can even drive your siblings to school. When I was fourteen, I once spent a full weekend with a bunch of my friends recording a cassette tape of our own farts, so the idea of fourteen-year-olds behind the wheel seems bad. But in general, those fourteen-year-olds are not causing problems on the roads of Kansas. According to state highway patrol records, in 2016, fourteen-year-old drivers caused zero fatalities in the state.

On a playdate with Jarrod's daughters, Isabelle and Johanna, Harper and Lyra were galvanized by their stories of "driving" out on the farm. Galvanized in different directions.

Lyra: "I feel absolutely no need to do something that is definitely gonna end in certain death."

Harper: "Can I do that?"

One December afternoon after church, Harper and I headed out to Fairground Road, west of town. I cranked the driver's seat as low as it would go and Harper settled into my lap, giggling uncertainly. It was clear that she had sort of thought I was kidding this whole time. "Okay," I said. "Push this lever down to D. That means when I press the gas pedal, we'll go forward." As we slowly accelerated, the engine's sound was accompanied by a slightly hysterical *Eeeeeee* from Harper. Under our tires, the chalk-white gravel crunched. The road was empty, the sun was bright, a windmill turned slowly in the distance. Harper's back was warm against my chest and her hair tickled my nose. I gradually went faster. Harper kept the car straight.

"How many miles an hour are we going?" she asked.

"Twenty."

She laughed wildly. "I'm only ten years old!" When we got home she told her mom she'd hit a cow, but really she didn't hit anything.

Jarrod and Stacey had returned to Hays to have kids after living in Houston. Everywhere I went, I met other parents who had grown up in west Kansas, left for a while, and then returned. This seemed like one measure of the appeal of raising children here, even if some of those parents still seemed surprised at the turn their lives had taken. "I never thought I would come back to Kansas," Stacey marveled. "I had bigger aspirations for my life."

Yet she, like so many people we met, had come back. Kathy and Ted had returned from Denver. Mary brought her husband back from Charlotte and bought the exact same house on Twenty-Ninth Street that she'd grown up in. "I never thought I'd say it," said Amanda, who returned to Hays after working as a missionary in Honduras and took over her parents' home for disabled adults, "but I am really glad we ended up back in Hays."

In June, the summer wheat crop is ready for harvest, and workers put in fifteen-hour days to get it all reaped as quickly as possible. Each day that harvest-ready wheat stands in a field is another day that the plants can thresh themselves in the prairie wind or seed heads can get knocked to the ground by hail. After harvest, those seeds that fell to earth, planted by accident, bloom into a scraggly late-summer crop. Volunteer wheat, it's called. Most farmers don't harvest volunteer wheat, but it's perfect for grazing. "I set the cows out on that land and they can feed off that for a while," Ted said, pointing to his shaggy blond cattle scattered across a field, making the best of a gift created by happy accident. "That's one reason to grow wheat, even though I only ever break even on it. Volunteer wheat is free."

CHAPTER 10

A Holy Hug

"The girls next door are quite religious," Lyra said when she got home from school one afternoon. "Which I kinda knew already. They asked me if I believed in God."

"What'd you say?" I asked.

Lyra dropped her backpack in the middle of the living room and then, on my look, rolled her eyes and kicked it over to the couch. "I said I wasn't sure. Like, I think there is some deity somewhere"—*dye-ty,* she said, the mispronunciation common for a kid who often read words long before she heard them—"but I don't really follow a church or believe in saints or rites or anything."

"And what did they say to that?"

"They said okay and asked if they could tell me more about *their* beliefs."

Everyone went to church in Hays. If you didn't go to one of the mainline Protestant churches downtown, you went to one of the big evangelical churches nearby, like Celebration, with its sleek website, bearded guitarists playing Christian rock, and coffee bar. The head of the English department? He went to church. The guy singing death metal at karaoke? He went to church. A twentysomething PhD student in geology who studied the actual fossil record and worked at a natural history museum? There he was in our adult Sunday school. "In Kansas," the Princeton scholar and Kansas native Robert Wuthnow once said, "church is the place people go to be good, to know how to do good, to be seen as being good." If you didn't go to any church, it was really hard to fit in.

So we went to church. Specifically, we went to Hays First United

Methodist, a handsome limestone church built downtown in 1948. We chose it, of course, because that's where Catherine and Carl went, so they could introduce us to everyone. I grew up going to a Methodist church in Milwaukee; my recollection is that its doctrine was pretty basic, revolving mostly around making sure people got out in time for the Packers game. Alia attended a tiny Episcopal church, built in 1745, where we got married; a few years later, the congregation was riven by a debate over gay clergy. (The wrong side won, and we haven't been back since our wedding.) When we first moved to Arlington, we joined a nearby United Church of Christ congregation; we liked its progressive politics and the idea of our kids getting some kind of religious education even if we didn't really know about the whole God thing, exactly. It had fallen out of our routine in recent years, sacrificed for Sunday-morning youth basketball games (or more sleep).

But here in Hays we leaped right in. Harper had been raring to go for some time; before the trip, she'd been agitating for a return to our church in Arlington. (She likes dressing up; she likes the sense of occasion; she likes the Bible stories.) Lyra was dubious but agreed to go for the couple of months we would be in Hays. We started attending Sunday services as well as the adult Sunday school led by various parishioners, including, on our first visit, Carl. Being an actual philosophy professor, Carl runs a fantastic scripture discussion. He's knowledgeable, wise, wry. He told the story of Job with comic brio: "And then, after Job acknowledges the power of God and repents, God gives him back his riches and property and his kids! Well, he doesn't get the old ones back, but he gets a new set."

I loved Sunday school. There's something deeply satisfying about setting aside an hour every week to sit around with a bunch of other grown-ups and talk about philosophy, even though I found the language I used was often strikingly different from that used by others. One Sunday, we all sat in an upstairs classroom discussing Joseph's dilemma in Matthew 1:18. He's about to get married, and his bride-to-be, Mary, is pregnant. From the New International Version, the one we read at First United Methodist: "Because Joseph her husband was faithful to the law, and yet did not want to expose her to public disgrace, he had in mind to divorce her quietly." But an angel tells him that, *actually,* the baby is the son of God, so Joseph marries her and raises Jesus as his own. He is *called* to fatherhood, much to his surprise, and finds himself worthy of the role.

The mom and dad of Emmaline—the girl who thought I was Dave during *A Fairy Hallow's Eve*—talked about feeling called to adopt her and her brother from China. An older couple told, through quiet tears, the story of their taking in their son's child, "his goof," because "it's family, and you have to take care of family." That's what they felt called to do.

I thought, *There is no universe in which I would describe a decision I make this way.* A mom at the far end of the table mentioned feeling "called" to have a third child. (If God ever called us to have a third kid, hang up the phone.) Then Stacey, our leader that day, turned to us. "What about you two?" she asked. "You've gone on this amazing journey. Were you called to do this?"

"I've never used that exact language," I said. "It's hard for me to think of our decisions as being driven from the outside that way."

"We definitely felt like the choice was urgent, a thing we needed to do," Alia said.

"Hey." I laughed. "Maybe God opened up a door in the form of simultaneous midlife crises?"

I thought a great deal about this discussion in the days afterward, which is exactly what I want out of church. I was not acting out of a calling from God, I didn't think. But how pleasing to look back now at that snowstorm, which even then I called an *act* of God, and think about how easily it would slot into such a belief were I to embrace it! And called or not, I found it invigorating to think about how to be good, how to do good, how to be seen as being good. I was very conscious in Hays of wanting to be seen as good, much more so than I had been anywhere else. As a visitor from liberal America, I felt a weird responsibility I could only think of as ambassadorial; I wanted to face these people whose singular quality, masking all others sometimes, was their niceness and be nice in return.

The sanctuary was beautiful, all classic dark wood and stained glass, with one blinking fluorescent bulb that wasn't replaced in our entire time in Hays. Services were broadcast on KAYS-FM radio for invalids and truck drivers, and it would have been foolish to expect the pastor to approach his sermons or prayers with Carl's interrogative spirit. He certainly did not. "For those separated from loved ones by miles in this world or the next," the pastor liked to say in Reverend Lovejoy tones, "we offer a holy hug from the Holy Spirit." One day after church, I says to Carl, I says, "Carl, can you go over the scriptural basis for the concept of the holy hug?"

Carl said, "Well,"

Anyway, I loved church. I loved seeing our children wearing the nicest clothes they had left after ten months on the road, squirming during

Lyra:

Full disclosure, the thing I enjoyed most about church were the snacks. I'm not exactly a really religious person — I'm not sure if I even believe in God. I enjoyed giggling over the sentiment of the holy hug, though, and there were worse ways to spend my time. Plus, the cookies really were delicious.

I don't much care for a lot of things that come with the package of being Christian. I don't like how incredibly misinterpreted the Bible is, and this is coming from someone who knows only the vaguest snippets of it. If I can get it right — love people even if they're different from you, hate the sin not the sinner, hey, maybe we should uplift the poor — why can't the guys who have read and analyzed the entire thing? Faith in Hays, however, seemed to get it right. So I didn't really have a problem with them finding something to believe in.

I'm not really down for going to church in Arlington, though. I know I have no power in this family and any statements I make on the topic are null and void (no, I'm not bitter, why do you ask), but I'd rather not. I don't honestly believe in God, not right now anyways, and I'd feel pretty uncomfortable dedicating hours to worshipping Him or singing His praises or baking Him cookies when I don't even think He exists. It was fine in Kansas, because I hadn't really made up my mind about whether or not He was real, and I was doing it for a set time, but going to church carrying all of this disbelief in me would definitely feel like sacrilege.

the boring parts. I loved shaking hands across the pews, saying "Peace be with you." I loved stepping back into the sanctuary after the service while everyone ate Keebler cookies and drank coffee in the fellowship hall and feeling the empty air, as Ian Frazier put it, "vibrating slightly with the suppressed fidgets of children." And I loved the rituals, still encoded in my mind decades later. "How do you *know* this?" Lyra asked during the Doxology. "I'll know it forever," I replied. "Like the Shoe City song."

And forgive me, but I loved teaching my kids what I remembered most of all from church as a child: the delicious pleasure of whispering jokes to your pew-mate during the service. One Sunday we sang the very, very bad hymn "I Want to Walk as a Child of the Light." (You'll find it's number 206 in your United Methodist Hymnal.) " 'I want to *follow* Jesus,' " we sang in verse one. " 'I want to *look at* Jesus,' " we sang in verse two. " 'I want to *be with* Jesus,' " we sang in verse three.

"I want to *high-five* Jesus," I whispered to Lyra. She cracked up, to the point that those with whom we'd recently exchanged the peace looked back at us quizzically. Later in the service, as we were called up for Communion, Lyra tapped me on the shoulder. "I want to *eat some* Jesus," she murmured, pointing at the Communion bread.

On our final Sunday in Hays, Stacey led the prayer at the end of Sunday school. "We're grateful for the time we had with the Smith-Koises," she said, "and for their contribution to our lives, our class, and our community. They've touched us all in their short time here." That feeling I had must have been something like fellowship.

For many Kansans, faith and the church are tied inextricably to politics. First United Methodist lacked the progressive sermons that had drawn us to the UCC congregation in Arlington, though Catherine's Christmas pageant did nod toward current events in its treatment of the Nativity. (In her version, the leads were the innkeeper and his wife, forced to justify their own intolerance of immigrants and refugees. "That was very *timely*," I heard one parishioner say with some concern.) I'd come to

Kansas in part to explore and address the beliefs of a mostly red-state population, yet I found myself, as ever, gravitating toward people — professors, artists, transplants — on my side of what seemed every day a sharper, more unbridgeable divide. During the workday I clicked myself into a frenzy about the state of our country, and then, in my interactions with Haysians, I tried to find a way to bring up politics while still being seen as good.

Maybe that was my mistake. Or maybe the idea of engaging people I'd just met in political discussions without being willing to do it after three beers in a bar was never going to work in this place where everyone who disagreed with me correctly assumed, before I even opened my mouth, what my views were, and saw no point in making a scene. What I found was that each political overture from me was deftly sidestepped by a town full of conversational Barry Sanderses, leaving me grasping in their wake. "Money, religion, and politics, the three things we don't talk about," Jarrod said with a smile.

Sometimes they dodged with platitudes. "That's what's so great about Hays," Mayor Shaun said when I asked him about the politics of his small town. "Doesn't matter whether you're Democrat or Republican, people are just kind." This was a sentiment I heard echoed many times in Hays, this assertion that kindness was universal and rendered political affiliations moot. Republicans, I think, viewed this as a gracious allowance on their part — *See how we acknowledge the good intentions of our opponents* — while I found it enraging. Seventy percent of you voted for Donald Trump! Don't talk to me about kindness!

"Underneath it all," Robert Wuthnow writes in *Red State Religion,* his study of Kansas church and politics, "was the desire to live in a community that upheld both goodness and mutual respect. Goodness was what people strived for in their lives and hoped for in their neighbors. Respect put a human face on goodness. It acknowledged not only differences of opinion but also that people sometimes made bad decisions." It was this sentiment that meant a generally kind person like Jarrod could stand against gay marriage, for example, yet also say, "But that doesn't mean I don't have compassion for those people, and if they needed help I would find a way to help."

"But there's different ways of helping," I said. "You can have compassion and help individuals who need it. But couldn't you also try to enact, you know, systemic change that increases the quality of life for *many* people?"

"That's what's so beautiful about where we live," he replied. "I think we need both of those. If you had all of one but not the other, you wouldn't have the harmony."

I was stymied. "Do you argue with friends about politics?" I asked.

Stacey smiled at Jarrod. "You and Catherine fight about it, but you still love each other."

"Because you need to understand other people's viewpoints," Jarrod said animatedly, "because you never know when you might change someone's mind. To me, that's not living a full life if you're not having that discussion."

"Well, have you ever had *your* mind changed?" I asked.

He chewed it over for a moment. "I think I become more understanding in these conversations, but I don't know that my viewpoint changes."

Kansas was present at the birth of the Republican Party—opposition to the Kansas-Nebraska Act created the GOP—and has voted Republican in thirty-two of the thirty-nine presidential elections in its history. But the longer I stayed in Hays, the more I realized that thinking of Kansas or even Ellis County as monolithically red was reductive and ignored the wide array of progressive political beliefs that I saw in many of the people I met. Sarah Smarsh, who grew up on a farm west of Wichita and is the author of the memoir *Heartland,* has spent years writing about the way that the media and coastal liberals like me tend to characterize flyover country. "Among the 30 states tidily declared 'red' after the 2016 election, in two-thirds of them Mrs. Clinton received 35 to 48 percent of the vote," Smarsh wrote in the *New York Times.* "My white working-class family was part of that large minority, rendered invisible by the Electoral College and graphics that paint each state red or blue."

Clinton's numbers were a little worse than that in Ellis County, but I still came away from Kansas convinced that the undersung political story of the Midwest is not "economically anxious" poor Republicans but Plains progressives like the kitchen workers and farmers and professors I talked to all over Hays. They reminded me of the fierce anti-Reagan activists I'd grown up admiring in Milwaukee, many of them artsy women with conventional jobs who painted and protested on the weekends. "Like 'blue' people find themselves called to do in every 'red' state," Smarsh wrote, "many Kansans were resisting when resisting wasn't cool."

It remains to be seen what effect the gradual browning of west Kansas will have on the area's politics. Hays doesn't have the steady water supply to support the meat-processing industry that's boosted employment in select towns across the Great Plains; as a result, it hasn't experienced the immigration boom that made nearby Garden City, for example, 48 percent Hispanic. Hays is still 89 percent white, whiter than Kansas as a whole. We'd expected that, had in fact joked about going to the whitest place in America. Yet Harper's fifth grade at O'Loughlin Elementary included six nonwhite students out of fifty-three — a small number, yet a higher ratio than the fifth grade she'd return to in North Arlington. The university and the hospital bring pockets of professional-class diversity to Hays, though both those places tend to be first jobs for many, so those populations are fairly transient. (It remains to be seen how the Trump administration's new restrictions on H-1B visas, the program under which most of these foreign-born doctors, in particular, come to rural hospitals like HaysMed, will affect the town's diversity, not to mention its health care.)

"Most years, our kids have had a classmate where their home language was Hindi, Arabic, Chinese, Spanish," said Erin, a Spanish translator and the wife of the head chef at Gella's, the good restaurant. "That was not what I grew up with in northwest Kansas." Erin noted that her family, a cross-cultural mix of Erin's Great Plains roots and her husband's

Mexico City upbringing, was perhaps more likely than some to seek out diversity in their social life. "But really, there's so much more globalization of the small town than there used to be."

The town also has a not-inconsequential population of non-American twentysomethings thanks to Fort Hays State's aggressive recruiting of international students. (The homecoming parade featured not just the cheerleaders and the homecoming court but a float for the Indian Students Association and a full-on Chinese dragon.) But American black and Latino students at Fort Hays can find Hays a shock; one DACA recipient, a sophomore at FHSU, told the Hays Post about her difficulty finding a place to be comfortable in Hays as compared to the vibrant Hispanic culture of her hometown, Liberal, Kansas. That same article quoted two black FHSU students voicing their frustrations about racism and profiling in Hays businesses; when Mayor Shaun posted the article to his Facebook page, the comments were like a caricature of cluelessness: *Now granted I am not in the minority,* wrote one commenter, *but I don't see this in our community. I see people being nice to everyone.*

For many white people in Hays, that was the definition of not being racist: being nice to people. But the way race was ignored by whites in Hays reminded me of the way it was overlooked in the Netherlands. The political scientist Ian Ward wrote that "generalized niceness" serves, in fact, as "a means by which citizens conform to the requirements of unjust social arrangements." What is niceness but Dutch tolerance with a different name, a way of treating others that absolves you of responsibility and foregrounds your good behavior without acknowledging or even seriously considering the role inequality plays in your life, in society at large, or in the history of the place you live? One minority group that's notable in their invisibility in Hays: Native Americans. "The high-school teams are called the Indians," James, an English professor who moved to Hays from California, observed with a raised eyebrow. "There's a big fucking totem pole outside the high school. If we stay here, our daughter will be a Lady Indian. I mean, come on."

Manuel, Erin's husband, feels at home in Hays now, though there have been battles. He won the job at Gella's at twenty-five and was immediately put in charge of a kitchen of fourteen Anglos and one Mexican. "At first, it was a lot of 'What's the special, burritos?'" he said. Now the kitchen is evenly split between white and Latin employees and Manuel regularly meets with investors around town. "Everyone respects him," Erin said proudly. "I did not expect this part of my husband's personality to come out."

"Older people are the ones that are more intense in terms of 'This is our community'; they're not used to seeing too many other cultures," said Manuel. Erin agreed: "I'm sure if you jump to baby boomers or older, there is more resistance, like, 'These are our Volga German Catholic roots.'"

And acceptance comes in other forms for the young people of Hays. On gender, the extremely online teens of Hays are just as uninterested in traditional conformity as their compatriots around the country. "My older kids, no one was out," said Cathy, referring to her two children who recently graduated from college. "No one was trans. Some kids wanted to start a gay-straight alliance at Hays High and they wouldn't let them march in the homecoming parade." But now her youngest son, who's in ninth grade, has out gay and trans friends. Even at Hays Middle School, Lyra found that attitudes about gender and sexuality were evolving as quickly as they were in liberal Arlington. And in places where fundamentalism comes up against these quickly changing social norms, it's sometimes fundamentalism that loses; one fourteen-year-old we met stopped attending Celebration, with her mom's approval, when she found the church's messaging on homosexuality and diversity offensive.

"This is a fairly homogeneous community," Cathy acknowledged. "So if you want racial, cultural, ethnic, religious diversity, if that's important to you, you have to make ways to find that in your community." Over and over I found Hays families who had done just that. They attended Diwali dinners and hosted international students. I was struck particularly by a conversation I had with Amanda, who'd come back to Hays after doing missionary work in Honduras. She and her husband run Bethesda House, the home for developmentally disabled adults her parents founded decades ago. For Amanda and her husband, the six gentlemen who reside at Bethesda House are other lives for their family to share, to make part of their own.

"We teach our kids," she told me, "not that the residents are the same as us but that *we're* the same as *them*. We have disabilities too, it's just that ours are more hidden. My lack of patience, of joy? Of gratitude? My lack of a work ethic? Compare me to them and I'm severely lacking these things." She smiled. We were in the dining room of Bethesda House, a sod house built into a hill, the winter sun streaming through the windows and a fire roaring in the woodstove. This was the table that for decades she and her parents, and now she and her children, have shared with the men she thinks of as her brothers.

And this, of course, is the aspect of the Midwest's worship of "good" that can feel remarkable, moving, even as "goodness" provides cover for so many Americans' vicious political sympathies. When tied to the best of religion, it leads to a beautiful place. "We're followers of Jesus," Amanda said. "We feel that every person is a reflection of good and has an inestimable value." As I steamed about Donald Trump and the Christian right and the way white supremacy seemed to be creeping into the light, as I lost faith in the goodness of so many people, I found it useful to be reminded of the complicated nature of faith and the way that people make for themselves the families and communities they want to live in. No matter where we ended up, if we sought out the kind of family we wanted to be, we could find it.

"When I was growing up, most teenagers around here, the consensus was: Get out of Hays as fast as you can, I wanna experience the world. It never occurred to me that your community is as diverse as you make it." Amanda snapped her fingers. *Voilà!* "It's a gift, it's a huge gift. I never thought we could go back to Hays so we could experience the world."

The Rose Garden is a featureless banquet hall, a high-ceilinged room with a commercial kitchen hunkered on Highway 40 east of downtown. The morning of Thanksgiving, high-schoolers in orange vests directed cars in the gravel parking lot, lining them up under an unexpectedly warm sun. We'd signed up to volunteer at the Ellis County Ministerial

Alliance's community Thanksgiving feast without any real sense of what the event entailed, just out of a desire to find a way to help those in need on the holiday. (Plus, it gave our kids something to do on day two of the eennddlleessss weekend.)

When we got there, Haysians were already pouring through the lobby doors. An overwhelmed woman signed us in and told us we'd be table hosts. Another overwhelmed woman gave us name tags and yellow ribbons and directed us to our team captain, a third overwhelmed woman, who said, "Well, just pick a table, I guess, and then when people come and sit down, you just make conversation and help 'em if they need help."

"So we're just eating food and talking?" I asked.

"Yeah, that's basically it," she replied, looking past us to the next set of volunteers. We picked a pair of tables up near the front of the room, already occupied by early birds who clearly wanted to be as close to the buffet as possible. Harper, Alia, and I sat at one; Lyra sat with her grandmother Maggie, visiting from North Carolina, at the other. At our table were two elderly couples, Frank and Dorothy and Susan and Wes. Frank and Dorothy had been married sixty-two years; Dorothy liked to tell stories about trips they'd gone on, while Frank spent most of his time at the feast in a state of rising anxiety at other tables being allowed to line up before ours did. Susan lived in Plainville and Wes up in Nebraska; they'd met online after both of their spouses had died, "within five days of each other," Wes pointed out. ("Isn't that something!" I said.)

In contrast to the frazzledness of the coordinators, the food-service staff was organized with precision. Enormous steam trays perched on buffet tables behind which a crowd of volunteers in aprons and latex gloves spooned out green beans, mashed potatoes, and piles of pulled-pork-like turkey. Teenagers roamed the banquet hall refilling water and iced tea; every few minutes, a supervisor would emerge from the kitchen bearing, like Rafiki holding baby Simba to the sun, a two-gallon pitcher of steaming gravy. "Just pour that right into my mouth," I said aloud for some reason.

So many tables got in line before ours that I had time to leave, get in the car, drive home, rotate a bunch of pans into and out of the oven, and drive back. When I returned, everyone at our table was eating appetizer pie, which Alia had liberated from the dessert table. At Lyra and Maggie's table, three generations of a family chatted companionably. Shirley, the grandmother, told Lyra about the column she writes for the local paper. It appears the final Wednesday of every month and covers, you know, whatever she's up to. "For instance, I go to the county fair, and then I write about that," she explained.

The crowd was a mix of food-insecure families in need of help—after the meal, bags of donated groceries were handed out at the side of the building—and Haysians who simply wanted company. Catherine and Carl, hosts a few tables down from us, ended up sitting with old friends from their first church who enjoyed visiting with other families for the holiday. Over at the north end of the hall, twenty or so FHSU football players—the ones whose hometowns were too far away for them to go back for Thanksgiving—hulked over their neighbors. Most of them had two full plates of food.

Though in Arlington I occasionally helped cook meals at a shelter, I'd never had a volunteer experience quite like this. The emphasis was not on who was helping whom but on all of these people, a solid five hundred locals, the poor and the fortunate, gathered together. It's not that Arlington doesn't offer such opportunities—I think it's that they're smaller against the backdrop of our enormous community, so I often didn't see them, wrapped up in the responsibilities and stresses of my life there. Here in Hays we had the time to join in, in part because (forgive me, Haysians) there wasn't much else to do.

Cathy, in discussing her concept of Hays as a place where people could bloom, had also described the kind of person who *didn't* thrive in Hays. "The outsiders who come in and then leave after a couple of years—in some cases they aren't putting themselves into the town," she said. "If you really want to succeed, you have to invest yourself. It doesn't mean you only insert yourself into things that already exist. Maybe you're not interested in the Kiwanis Club or the Quilt Guild, so you take your own skills and invest them in the community." Maybe instead of using my big city as an excuse, I should start acting as if I lived in a small one. It seemed to me that this wonderful supper, maybe more than most of the experiences we'd had along the way, closely resembled the life I wanted to live.

What kind of life *did* we want when all of this was over? We had loved things about each of the places we'd been, and yet so many of those things seemed hard to replicate in our own lives. Sometimes that's because they would have required change on a structural level, far above our own spheres of influence: As Alia pointed out whenever I preached the gospel of Dutch cycling, it would take a massive effort on the part of activists and local government for Arlington to create infrastructure like the Netherlands'. But sometimes it's because the things I want, the ways to be a family I love, are contradictory. I want the close-knit community of Hays but also the apartness of Sámara. I want the rugged natural beauty of Wellington but also the rideability of Delft. I want to feel challenge and ambition at work, but not stress. I want my kids to go to a great school, but I don't want to feel the parental and social pressure that often comes with your kids going to a great school. I want our children to be citizens of the world but also to feel close ties to their community. I want to be able to spend time in the country, far away from everything, but also be in a city with art-house movies and plays and museums. I want to choose elements of my life à la carte! What I'm saying I guess is that it would be great to be rich.

Was our goal for our experiences to overturn everything about our old life, transforming us into the perfect, ideally happy family? If so, that was dumb, because surely such an effort would fail. So how *could* this trip make us a better family? I could handle the idea that when this was all done we might wind up living in the same house or even doing the same jobs. But Alia and I were not interested in finding ourselves, a year from now, living the same lives as before, treating our children and ourselves in the same manner, getting stressed out about the same bullshit. We did not want, a year from now, to feel as though our trip might as well never have happened.

The question of how dramatic a change I wanted our lives to undergo came into unexpectedly sharp relief in November, when I started talking to an executive at a Silicon Valley company about a job. I'd known her for a long time and respected her work from afar; she had recently moved to California to take over a project no one, including her, she noted frankly, had quite figured out. I did not understand the project or its goals either but found the puzzles the company was trying to solve fascinating. Which is to say, I had a lot of observations about what the company was doing and what it should be doing, and as I talked on the phone with the executive—let's call her Amy, with my apologies for being vague—I found myself getting more and more intrigued.

My conversations with Amy often happened in the afternoon, after school, so I would spend them walking around our neighborhood in Hays, out of earshot of the kids. Why spur their million questions about a job I might not even be interested in and a move we might never make? But for that reason the conversations acquired a bit of a charged feeling, like a secret relationship, the appeal of which had to do with the intellectual challenge each call posed (as well as, I'm sure, the way that discussing a new job feels in some small way like being courted). The questions I was wrestling with became tied to the experience of walking through the brick streets and gravel alleys of downtown Hays, shielding my earbud microphone from the prairie wind when I spoke, muting my phone when Amy spoke. I was thinking about not just what this tech product could offer the people in her (I presumed) fancy Silicon Valley offices, or in New York or LA or Arlington, but about how this product would affect my life if I were a full-time resident of Hays. How would it help the friends and neighbors we saw every day? Could it do good? Could it be good?

Alia and I talked each night about the job with an anticipatory fervor that reminded me of the way we'd planned this trip, more than a year before. I really liked my current job, but imagine what a lifestyle change this could bring about! Could we love the Bay Area as much as everyone else we knew seemed to? Could we afford the Bay Area? Could the money allow us to make some other changes in our life, allow Alia more flexibility, perhaps? And while we're talking about it—we always came around to asking each other—what kind of money do we think they would pay?

Unsurprisingly, *that* question moved in mere days from the cautious edges of our conversation to the center. I realized that I had no idea what a move to a tech company meant, money-wise. If I continued writing and editing journalism, it seemed unlikely I would ever make *crazy* money, barring an unexpected lightning bolt like some rich dummy founding a magazine and handing it to me. But if I moved outside of the journalism world to an industry like tech—which was famously *not* thrifty—all bets were off, right? Would they be nutso enough to pay me two hundred grand for my writing and editing skills? Three hundred grand? I couldn't imagine such a thing, yet I *could* imagine myself cashing those checks. Couldn't you? It would be easy! Talk about changing your life.

At that Thanksgiving dinner, I was thinking quite a bit about all this because Amy had just told me that she wanted to fly me out for a round of interviews; the company had accelerated the process and now they wanted to hire someone to start around the beginning of the year. "Could you move straight here in January?" she asked. "The company has a lot of support services to help you find a place to live." I was famil- iar with such services from the time that Alia's law firm, when we first moved to New York, recommended a real estate agent who, when she heard the amount we had to spend, laughed long and loud and then referred us to a junior associate at her company.

January. That was so close, and such a real month—a month we already had plans for, the month we were going to return to Arlington and normalcy. Yet California offered so much of what we'd loved on our trip: proximity to the ocean; weather like a perfect spring day in the Netherlands, but all the time; natural beauty to rival New Zealand's, although admittedly a lot of it was on fire. And with that kind of money, maybe we could buy our way into some of the other stuff we wanted.

"I've never flown anyone out of *that* airport before," the company travel agent told me as she booked my ticket from HYS to DEN to SJC. A few days later, as if by magic, there I was: the e-tickets had gotten me on the planes, the vouchers had gotten me into a rental car, my name had gotten me into a nice hotel with paintings of circuit boards on the walls. (It was of course not magic but money, money creating ease and erasing hassles, the way it can when applied by those who know how to use it.) Now I was stuck in traffic, the Santa Cruz Mountains morning-sharp in my rearview mirror. Now I was interviewing with various geniuses. Between meetings, I asked the recruiter babysitting me through the process what she could tell me about the schools around here. "Oh, they're great," she said. "Lots of high achievers, so they're really competitive with the best in the nation. We've got consultants who can help you through the process of finding the right one." My next interviewer asked if I wanted to get outside for this conversation; we ended up walking laps around the office park, the sound of freeway traffic as steady as a river.

At lunch Amy and I went to the company's cafeteria and sat down at an outside table, the sun warm and perfect. We both wore sunglasses and ate delicious salads. In Hays that day, the low was nineteen degrees. Amy told me about the city where she lived with her family. "It's got a real small-town feel," she said. "Kids ride their bikes all over." She had a forty-five-minute window, was sorry we couldn't meet for a drink after it was all over, things were crazy.

The interviews seemed to go great. (Who ever knows?) I spent the afternoon and evening in my rental car crawling through traffic into neighborhoods farther and farther away from the company's headquarters, Zillowing the shittiest houses I saw: Zillow's Zestimate is $1,426,065. Zillow's Zestimate is $2,001,905. Zillow's Zestimate is $1,650,780. When I searched online listings for houses under a million dollars in Amy's city, with its small-town feel, I found a single one-bedroom condo.

When I got home to our actual small town with its actual small-town feel, the girls asked me about my business trip to California. Was this a decision we could *polder*? Cautioning the kids that I didn't know if I would even get a job offer, I told them about the situation. We could maybe have a lot more money. But we would live someplace even more expensive than Arlington, with richer neighbors and classmates, and they'd be going to schools filled with families that were even more intense.

"Would you work more than you work in Arlington?" Harper asked.

"Yes, I think so," I said.

"But you work all the time in Arlington!"

Lyra was sanguine about the possibility. She liked the idea of me working for a company whose products she knew about and understood. "But making money isn't the most important thing," she pointed out.

"That's easy for you to say, Lyra, you have no idea how much anything costs."

"I know how much books cost."

Alia and I talked it over, and over, and over. What, in the end, *was* the story of our family? I didn't know how our newfound love of bike riding, or appreciation for the outdoors, or understanding of one another's differing temperaments, or love of adventure (or lack thereof) would change our family life for the better. Who knew what California would bring on any of those fronts, really? So we didn't know the ways our lives would improve. But we did know the ways they'd get worse: We'd be moving to maybe the only place in America where we could guarantee that the things we *most* disliked about our pre-trip lives—the cost, the competition, the parental craziness, the bubble—would be amplified. Even if Steve Jobs himself flew down from Rich Person Heaven and handed me *five* hundred grand, I wouldn't be able to buy my way out of that story.

So I withdrew from consideration for the job. Amy emailed back that she understood, thanks for my time. Maybe they hadn't been planning to give it to me after all. I'll never know. All I know is that two days later, I was DMing with a friend about every journalist's favorite topic, journalists who escaped journalism, and I was about to tell her my funny story of almost becoming a tech bro when she mentioned the very same company; indeed, the very same department. Someone she knew had taken a job there recently, she said. *They gave her $750K and an interest-free loan for the down payment on a house,* my friend wrote. *Can you believe that?* I don't know that I can properly explain the hot wave of shame and rage and shock and hilarity that struck me at that moment, except to say that my entire field of vision turned bright white as I typed *Wow that's crazy*. I still thought I had made the right decision, which of course was based not on money but on the kind of life we were choosing to lead. But I was astonished at how perfectly my razor-sharp financial instincts had performed once again. Somewhere on the Great South Road in Auckland, both Steves were laughing their arses off.

THE POSADA

On our second-to-last night in Hays, Lyra had a middle-school concert. Up in the balcony of a packed Beach/Schmidt, where fairies had danced to the strains of Tchaikovsky just months ago, Alia and Harper and I settled ourselves in, stuffed winter coats under seats, waved to people we knew. Our next-door neighbor Lori and her crowd filled a row in front of us; her boys squirmed in their seats. The middle school's rumpled assistant principal welcomed us and noted how nice it would be if they didn't have to bus the kids to and from the auditorium to rehearse. (This was universally recognized as a swipe at those who'd voted against the school bond, which would have ameliorated that problem.) The choir director brought the kids onstage in various configurations for an ambitious program heavy on challenging winter-themed music, free of religious overtones. "This next song," he explained before Lyra's choir performed, "has some sections with the altos singing a C, the second sopranos singing a D, and the sopranos singing an E. The dissonance is intentional on the part of the composer."

Our three months in Kansas had been joyously full of music. In part that was because it was now Christmas season. But it was also because Hays, our version of Hays, the Hays we'd made with the friends we'd met, was a place where people made music. After all, the only way to ensure a town this small was the town you wanted to live in was to roll up your sleeves and *make* it that way. The marching bands in parade after parade. The generations of cellists sawing away at Cathy's student recital, from determined little Martha to the polished teens to effortless Cathy herself. A dozen preschool lambs marching down the aisles as Harper's quartet sang "Mary, Did You Know?" in the Christmas pageant Catherine wrote.

After the concert, I waved to my karaoke friend Jarrett, who was in the lobby waiting for his daughter. A few hours later, I saw Jarrett again as I stepped into the Q just as karaoke night was about to begin. "Dan!" my table of friends cried in unison, a *Cheers* moment that made me grin like a dumbass.

I'd become a regular at the Q's karaoke night, taking advantage of the quieter evening schedule Hays offered to come out nearly every week. I wrote the one title I planned to sing on a slip of paper, handed it to the KJ, and bought tater tots and a beer. Wayne, who our table called "the last of the cowboys," stopped by and said hi; he wore a festive red and green bolo with a single sleigh bell at its end. Everyone else at the table sang before me. Jarrett crooned "Let It Be Christmas Everywhere"; Allison, concertmaster of the Hays Symphony, and her boyfriend, Brian, de-problematized "Baby, It's Cold Outside":

Allison: I simply must go.
Brian: Baby, it's cold outside.
Allison: The answer is [*eyes widen*]...uh, maybe?
Brian: [*Laughing too hard to sing*]...cold outside!

I rapped "Christmas in Hollis," a song it seemed, from the general acclaim, that no one in the bar had ever heard before, and headed home after a round of high-fives. We had a lot of packing still to do.

On our final night in Hays I hauled our two remaining giant suitcases and boxes of Christmas presents and a thrift-store chair Harper loved out to the CRV, dodging neighbor kids as they ran in and out of the house shouting goodbyes. Then everyone got in the car, and I drove the crammed Honda to Manuel and Erin's house for the posada, parking with difficulty because I could not see out the rear window.

A bitter wind swept through the front yard, blowing firepit smoke every which way and foiling our attempts to light, with shaky fingers, Advent candles. Neighborhood kids were dressed in Nativity-wear, one as Mary, complete with pregnant belly; Dominic as a shepherd; a kindergartner in footie feline PJs identifying as a barn cat. As observed in Manuel's native Mexico City, a posada includes a reenactment of Joseph and Mary's ordeal, knocking on doors around the neighborhood, asking for shelter, and cruelly being turned away. Here in Hays, where the family has hosted the posada for years, "We don't do the entire traditional thing, getting rejected from house to house," their next-door neighbor Cathy explained to me.

"People would just say, 'Sure, come on in,'" I joked.

"'Door's open.'"

Erin and Manuel joined the kids on the front steps. We sang in call and response. Joseph asks for shelter, and a host rejects him:

JOSEPH

En nombre del cielo	In the name of heaven
Os pido posada	I ask you for shelter
Pues no puede andar	Because she cannot walk
Mi esposa amada	She, my beloved wife

HOST

Aquí no es mesón	This is not an inn
Sigan adelante	Please continue on
Yo no puedo abrir	I cannot open for you
No sea algún tunante	You might be a robber

Huddled together on the Hernandez lawn, we sang—as ordered by the card-stock lyric sheets on which we dripped candle wax—"together with gusto":

Reciban este rincón!	Accept this haven!
Que aunque es pobre la morada	Although the place is poor
La morada	Is poor
Se las d-oy d-e cor-a-zón!	I offer it fr-o-m m-y h-ea-rt!

Manuel, on the porch, raised his hands. "We've hosted this posada for many years," he said. "Each year it seems more and more people arrive. Some years, like last year, we say, well, we just don't have the ability to do it." The crowd was about half Latino, half Anglo. It included his kitchen staff at Gella's, parents of his children's school friends, neighbors, randos like us. Carl and Catherine and Martha and Sophie crowded close to us for warmth.

"This year we tried something new," Manuel continued. "We asked, 'Please bring something.' We worry, will there be enough? But," he said, gesturing in toward the kitchen and its bounty, then putting a hand on his heart, "it's amazing, if everyone bring a little, how much there is."

"Hear, hear," someone called.

"Plus it's cheaper for us," Manuel added. *"Bon appétit!"*

In the kitchen, blue masking-tape arrows directed the crowd to pork tamales, sweet pineapple tamales, steaming posole, mulled cider with sugar cane. The inside seats were crammed full, so I sat on the front porch steps with Catherine, Alia, and Matthew, an FHSU English professor new to town this semester. I introduced him to Cathy, explaining that all his good-bread problems were now solved, then devoured my posole, which was rich with pork and sharp with lime. It almost kept me warm.

Matthew asked how we felt about going home. "I'm really excited," Harper said after some thought, "but sad to leave everyone."

"I'm a little worried," I said. "In February, are we gonna be like, 'Uh, now what?'"

"Well, that's because you're adventurers," Catherine said. "We're not."

"Did you used to be?"

"Yeah, I think so. But now I'm just really comfortable. I'm happy here."

"Catherine," I said to Matthew, "told us once that if we moved to Hays, we'd be bored all the time, but we'd be *so happy.*"

Catherine laughed. "I said *that?*"

"Yup," I said. "We were sitting on our porch in Arlington."

"Had I been drinking wine?" Catherine asked.

"Oh yeah."

We sped east on I-70, the harvest moon set bright in a deep and brilliant sky. The girls sat in the back seat, drowsy in their winter coats, surrounded by everything we'd carried with us. Alia held my hand, looking out the window at dozens of windmills blinking their red eyes in unison. I thought about the song we'd sung. We sang about those who welcome strangers, despite the danger of disappointment or discomfort. We sang in a country battling over whether to welcome strangers or send them away. We sang in a city where our house had been furnished, our children taught, our questions answered, our politics politely ignored by friends who, like the friends of Island Bay and Delft and Sámara, had greeted us and shared their lives. Accept this haven, they'd sung. They offered it fr-o-m th-eir h-ea-rts.

We'd all sung in unison, or as much in unison as a group can when all its members are shivering and singing lyrics only half of them understand to a melody many of them are hearing for the first time. The dissonance, it seemed to me, was intentional on the part of the composer.

Lyra:

What did your dad get wrong about you in the book?

I feel like a lot of my negative qualities were overplayed. I will accept the fact that I am an obstinate, screen-loving girl. But Harper is also an obstinate, screen-loving girl, and that wasn't really shown at all in the book. It just feels like we were stuck into different boxes, Harper as the idealistic, sweet, conformist child and me as the bratty screen-loving precocious jerk. I'd say I got the bad end of that bargain.

What I'm really trying to say here is that I do not entirely dislike my father's portrayal of me but think that it's inaccurate in some ways. It reminds me of two separate conversations, one with my grandparents and one with some of my parents' friends. Both of the conversations included me chipping in to say that I knew about a subject and disagreed with the well-informed adults, and the response I got was "Wouldn't it be nice to be thirteen and know everything?" And in both of those conversations I found myself extremely irritated because everything I was saying was falling onto deaf ears.

"Wouldn't it be nice to be thirteen and know everything?" is a sentence that's not written word for word in the book, but it's written in spirit. The act of disagreeing is seen as an act of arrogance.

I'm not completely stuck-up and stubborn, you know, although I will admit I do my best to be a huge pain as often as possible. Adventure can be fun in small doses. This trip was a really big dose, but somehow I ended up liking it more than anyone—even myself—anticipated.

Thank you and good night.

LOVE AND ATTENTION

We spent Labor Day weekend 2018 in a national park, staying in one NPS lodge one night and another the next and taking a day to tramp between them. The morning of our hike, the girls demanded to know how long I was planning to make them walk. "It's not as long as the tramping in New Zealand, right?"

"It's not *as* long," I said.

The girls had each brought a companion, as our Kiwi friends had suggested, and the six of us squelched our way along an Appalachian Trail muddy from the mid-Atlantic's rainiest-ever summer. On our first rest stop, Harper chugged about half of her entire water bottle. "Are we halfway there?" she asked.

"Harper, we've hiked less than a mile."

"Well, how far is it?"

"Eight miles."

"Eight miles?" This from Alia, in a distinct tone of betrayal.

"We hiked farther than that in Abel Tasman!" I protested.

"Not one of your brighter ideas, Dad!" Lyra said.

We made our way along a ridge, Skyline Drive to our left, the Shenandoah Valley to our right. "Do you hike a lot?" Harper asked her friend Morgan.

"Sometimes," Morgan said. "I like it."

"Yeah," said Harper. "I've pretty much mastered hiking."

To pass the time, Alia posed would-you-rather questions she'd looked up on the internet: "Would you rather... get one free international round-trip ticket a year or be able to fly domestic anytime for free?"

"International!" said Harper.

"What about neither? Can I get neither?" asked Lyra.

"Would you rather live without the internet or without air-conditioning and heat?"

"Air-conditioning and heat," all four kids said in unison.

"It doesn't get *that* cold inside the house," Harper added.

I laughed. "That's because we have the heat on!"

"Oh, here's a good one," Alia said. "Would you rather have a clown that follows you everywhere, one that only you can see and that just stands in a corner staring at you—"

"What?"

"—or have a real-life stalker who dresses like the Easter Bunny that everyone can see?"

"Why did you ask that, Mom? Now I'm gonna have nightmares."

Far to the west, across the valley, thunderheads flickered, but we stayed dry. We passed several overlooks that promised spectacular views but didn't stop. Finally Lyra said, "We have *got* to stop overlooking overlooks."

At one point, Morgan and Sophie and I disappeared up ahead, and Lyra, Harper, and Alia all stopped for a rest. They were hot and sweaty and their backs hurt. "I bet Dad thinks this is fun," Harper said.

"Ugh, he probably does," Alia replied. (When she reported this conversation to me later, she added, "I thought it would be good to express solidarity with them, since we all had a common enemy.")

Lyra nodded. "If we see him at the end and he's smiling, I'm gonna be so mad."

At the end, I was smiling. I'd seen a bear!

While I waited in line to check us into our rooms at the lodge, I sent the four kids down to the café with a twenty to buy the snacks of their choice. (Alia was lying down in the grass outside.) A minute later they all came back upstairs.

"What's going on?" I asked. "Is it closed?"

"No," said Sophie. "The lady won't let us sit down without a parent."

So I went downstairs with them, sat with the kids at a table in the nearly empty café, ordered a pile of snacks and a bunch of lemonades, then told the waitress, sweetly, "I'll be right back!" Then I went upstairs and returned to the line.

Twenty minutes later, when I'd finally gotten our keys and retrieved Alia, the kids were still there, avidly discussing how hot and awful the hike had been. "She didn't like it when you left, Dad," said Harper. "She kept wanting to know where you were."

"Are you the first children ever to come to this popular tourist attraction?" Alia asked.

"In New Zealand," I said, and as if by reflex my kids instantly rolled their eyes, "they would not have cared that you guys were here by yourselves for a few minutes."

"This is America, though," noted Morgan.

The following Tuesday, on the first day of eighth grade, Lyra brought home the papers she'd been given in all her new classes. Some of the teachers asked that parents sign their syllabi to acknowledge that they'd seen the work their kids would be doing over the course of the year. On the syllabus for World Geography, Mr. McDermott noted that the students would be studying plate tectonics, oceans and climate change, European capitals, South American mountain ranges. Alia signed the syllabus and added, beside her signature, *Ask Lyra about our trip around the world!*

A few days later I was paging through the materials in Lyra's take-home folder when I found that syllabus. Next to Alia's cheery message Lyra had scrawled, *No, do not ask me about this.*

We've been home in Arlington a full year now, but acquaintances still ask (after they ask which country we liked best), "How are the kids adjusting to being back?" I laugh, because the kids *adjusted.* They do homework and watch movies and goof off on the internet. Alia was right to worry about math; they have indeed struggled due to missing some crucial lessons, but they are slowly catching up. Harper plays with friends; Lyra draws. Sometimes they are happy and sometimes they are not. Their rooms reveal evidence of the year away: the cute plush French fries that a SWIS classmate sewed for Lyra sit on her windowsill, and the Delftware tile Harper painted occupies a corner of her desk. But when they talk about the trip, it's as a mystifying ordeal they somehow survived, one that scars them to this day. Even now when we ask them to play cards, they demur. "We played *so much* cards on the trip," Harper said only last month. "We just want to do something else."

They've adjusted. We're the ones who are still adjusting. After a year of adventure, a return to routine offers comfort but can feel a little wan. It hasn't helped that Facebook has been constantly reminding me of all the cool stuff I was doing just one year ago today. Oh really, I was eating gelato on a bridge over a picturesque canal? Well, fuck you, Facebook Memories, today I'm itemizing expenses and mopping our flooded basement.

I put a great deal of pressure on myself for the trip itself to be transformative. I hoped that writing all this down, doing my best to chronicle all that we experienced, would help us come out at the end of the trip with a determined plan of action—a set of dramatic changes we could make to our lives so that, two or five or ten years from now, we would view our journey around the world as a turning point. In that respect, I totally failed. We have generated no to-change list. We have not moved to New Zealand, even though we loved it so much. We have not quit our jobs to sell smoothies on the beach. Maybe we'll do those things someday; for now, we still live in Arlington, stare at our phones too much, and drive everywhere.

Alia and I set out on this journey dreaming that the places we were going were medicine for our ailing American souls, a medicine that— when taken in just the right dose—could solve everything. But a place never solves anything. All of us live our lives moving through all kinds of places; if we're lucky, we do it with the ones we love by our sides. Those places come and go. What is critical about those places is our relationship to them while we're there and how we bring each one with us to the next. In a thousand little decisions and a few big ones, in late-night conversations and workday text chains, Alia and I are still probing the experiences we had and the ways of life we saw, still thinking about what it means for our family.

And so the changes in our lives since the trip have been modest ones. Inspired by the volunteering we did in Hays, we've organized monthly service outings at work and at home, preparing and handing out food to migrant workers and families in need with organizations like A-SPAN and Martha's Kitchen. We've become more devoted to the friends we'd left here, people whose support throughout the trip made us miss them dearly and whose loving welcome when we returned made Arlington seem more like home than it ever had before. Our time explaining America to foreigners has made us more political; we've brought the girls downtown to shout about Brett Kavanaugh and gun control, and Alia mailed scores of handwritten postcards to swing-state voters this election season. Inspired by Tracey's netball league, I finally found a weekly "advanced-beginner" pickup soccer game run by the county. In six months I have not yet scored a goal, but I *have* been nutmegged so flagrantly that I fell down and bruised my ass. I love it so much.

We've been going to church. Not every Sunday, not yet, and Lyra thus far has begged off. We've tried out a couple of friends' congregations around Northern Virginia. The nearby Episcopal church was awfully stuffy, and the service lasted almost an hour and a half, though Harper liked the youth group. At a big Presbyterian church in McLean, the music was catchy (electric guitar, drums) but the priest, an alarmingly handsome Scotsman with one of those Broadway headset mikes, talked a *lot* about how the power of prayer would bring us everything we needed. So we haven't quite settled on a place.

And while I'm no Troublesome Amsterdammer, I've made a conscious decision to ride differently when I bicycle in Arlington. I pedal like a Dutchman — confident, no helmet, taking up my fair share of the street. I spent many an afternoon this year trundling along the quieter parts of my neighborhood, a couple of cars lined up behind me as I approached an intersection. I enjoy playing big on the road, and making drivers recognize that I belong in that space just as much as they do.

Alia came back from the Netherlands convinced both that a bike-oriented city was her dream and that Arlington could never become such a place. I'm less certain it's impossible. After all, as I learned, Holland was turning into a country of cars before a handful of devoted activists enacted a radically transformative change. When I asked the cycling advocate Chris Bruntlett, coauthor of *Building the Cycling City: The Dutch Blueprint for Urban Vitality,* how I could best push my city into making real change, he had one simple answer: "Run for office!" I'm not there yet, but I joined my local cycling activism group and attend as many city-planning meetings as I can.

One real dividend of our year away has been discovering that now, on regular-size vacations, we travel very smoothly as a family. The kids are practiced in airports and undaunted by unfamiliar transit systems. And Alia and I have learned the value of letting the children weigh in on our plans—yes, yes, *polder*ing the decisions—and building in events that are specifically for them. That's why, before that Appalachian Trail hike, we gave them an afternoon at a water park, and that's why, on vacation to France this fall, we ended up doing the most uncool thing we've ever done: we spent our first night at Disneyland Paris.

We were in Paris because fares were cheap and because Tracey and Gary had invited us to meet them. (We're the ones who say yes.) But before the Pompidou and the bistros and the moonlit cruise down the Seine, we celebrated a cold and rainy Halloween riding Space Mountain and Blanche-Neige et les Sept Nains. Disneyland Paris is basically the Magic Kingdom with more smoking. The costumes the mostly French patrons wore to the Halloween party were incredible; the transit situation was a shambles. The experience was a real mix of what Disney does well (create family magic) and what the French do well (dress beautifully, make everything as difficult as possible). The result was the four of us standing in the rain forty miles outside Paris at one thirty in the morning, our cell phones signal-less, no cabs, trains, Ubers, or hotel rooms to be found. The whole night was a series of absurd disasters, all of them weathered with patience and good humor by our kids, who had somehow turned into wonderful travel companions.

(Eventually, we bluffed our way past a couple of security guards into a hotel lobby where a front-desk clerk grudgingly called us a local cab.)

So: Volunteering. Traveling. Riding without a helmet. What does all this add up to? A life that's not too different from what it was before we left. The third question everyone asks is "Well, how did the trip change your life?" For a while, I'd chuckle and say, "Buy the book!" But the truth is, that's the question we've wondered about too, and only recently have I started to come to a satisfying answer.

My dad isn't a particularly vivid character in my junior-high memories. In part that's because in those years he was pulling away from us, on his way out of a marriage that wasn't working. In part, I'm sure, that's due to my own childhood solipsism. He's certainly become much more real to me in my adult life, and I frequently wish both that I'd opened my eyes more and that he'd been more willing to put himself in front of me when I was little.

For the year we traveled around the world, everyone in our family was, for better and for worse, very present in one another's lives. There were days I wished they were a little less present. I'm *certain* there were days that Alia or my kids wished they were away from me. (How many times in one year must a child see her father walking around in his underpants, scratching himself?) But that year was a chance for all of us to see one another more clearly. In Greta Gerwig's movie *Lady Bird,* a teacher reads Lady Bird's college application essay and observes that she really seems to love her hometown, Sacramento. Lady Bird, who up to now has thought of nothing other than getting *out* of Sacramento, says, "I guess I pay attention."

"Don't you think they're the same thing?" asks her teacher. "Love and attention?"

I live with three remarkable women, and for the past two years—as we took the trip and as I've written this book—I've been given the gift of time to pay more attention. And they, too, have had the chance to pay attention to me, to us, to all of us. To our family. There's a reason that a guidance counselor recently observed that Lyra and I banter with each other like a comedy team. There's a reason that, when Alia or I drop something, Harper now says, "You're screwing up!"

We learned on this trip that you can't actually change your kids but your kids change nonetheless. Harper and Lyra are eleven and thirteen now, eons away from the nine- and eleven-year-olds they were when we left. I can't even express how different they are from two years ago today, the day we landed in Auckland. Lyra recently found some drawings she did in Delft and dismissed them as the work of an immature artist. Harper now fits into Lyra's hiking shoes from New Zealand. At thirteen, Lyra struggles with anxiety and writes stories I can't even understand and is in rehearsals for a devised theater project and collects crazy buttons. At eleven, Harper bakes amazing brownies and keeps a perfectly organized homework planner and cries bitterly when even mildly criticized and has impeccable taste in sneakers.

And Alia and I have changed too. The purple streak Alia put in her hair at Kinki Kappers has faded to blond; she's doing pro bono work for refugees; she's cooking up a crackpot scheme that will definitely make us hundredaires. I taught college writing classes this year; I finally like Steely Dan; I no longer bring my phone to bed with me. I fail the people I love all the time and feel the terrible pain of hurting them, but I am getting better at recognizing my triumphs as well.

The trip didn't change our life. The trip was our life, and it remains our life, forevermore. The trip didn't change how we are a family; we are a family, and we were all changing, the whole time. For that year, we each got to be the scaffold around which the others grew. The miracle of the trip was that we were all together to notice it. The miracle of the time after will be that we still do.

There is no way for any of us ever to tell the story of 2017 without the others being wonderfully, awfully *there*. When Harper or Lyra gets to college—no way we can afford to send both, sorry girls, battle it out—she'll be sitting in her dorm room late one night with a Diet Coke or a joint or a bowl of popcorn getting to know her friends, and her roommate will ask, "What's your family like?" and that daughter will cough, laugh, wave her hand in the air. At that moment she'll grow just a tiny bit more in a direction we helped to determine. "Oh God," she'll say. "This *one* year—"

Arlington, Virginia
January 4, 2019

Acknowledgments

We're tremendously grateful to everyone who supported us before, during, and after the trip. We're *especially* grateful to everyone's amazing kids.

Ashley and Kevin, Rachel and Matt, Karen and Dave, Jennifer and Duane, Jill, Patti and Greg, Abbie and Justin, Leslie and Greg, Jessica and Andrew, Anne and Chip, Maia and David, Lisa and Kevin, Mimi and Nik, Rebecca, Maureen and Austin, Meghan and Joe, Gwen and Mike, Claudia and Carson, Tammy, Caroline. Our parents, siblings, and in-laws.

In Iceland: Regina and Henry, Katrin, Eliza and Guðni.

In New Zealand: Tracey and Gary, Bronwyn, Sarah and Olly, Fiona and Regan, Frankie and Eddie, Helen, Janet, Nicola, Alison and Darren, Richard, Quintin, Raewyn, Emily and Rowan, Kirsty and Dean, Anna and Andy, Fareen, Natalie and Al, Kate and Jeet, Veronica and Pete, Miranda, Pip and Brent, Alma. Island Bay School and South Wellington Intermediate. Lucy Johnston at Education New Zealand. Chris Price at the International Institute of Modern Letters. Shaun Wilson at Radio New Zealand. Dylan Reeve, David Farrier, Eleanor Catton, Taika Waititi. Brew'd Island Bay.

In the Netherlands: Lindsay and Ferdinand, Elizabeth and Jeff, Sarah and Aaron, Elizabeth, Renee and Bas, Alaa, Shaun and Bouke. De Eglantier. Wim Bot at the Fietsersbond. Michele Hutchison. Mark O'Connell. Postkantoor.

In Costa Rica: Gustavo, Teresa and Gerardo, Tomás, Mercy and Canuche, Marla and Adam, Tiffany and Patrick, Javi. Kelvin and everyone at Intercultura. Lo Que Hay.

In Kansas: Catherine and Carl, Stacey and Jarrod, Lori, Erin and Manuel, Cathy and Doug, Allison and Brian, Erin, Kathy and Ted, Jarrett,

Amanda, Shirley, Shaun. O'Loughlin Elementary and Hays Middle. Hays First United Methodist Church. Hays Public Library. Cristina Janney at the Hays Post. Gella's.

If you don't appear above, it's because you were even *more* important than everyone else but I didn't want to embarrass you.

Thanks to those who read the manuscript and gave valuable notes and advice: Alia Smith, Ashleigh Young, Belle Boggs, Catherine Trieschmann, Jonathan Farmer, Liam Callanan, Lyra Kois. Thanks to Alia Hanna Habib, Vanessa Mobley, Reagan Arthur, and everyone at Little, Brown.

Also: Teachers and staff at Discovery Elementary and Williamsburg Middle. Levine Sullivan Koch & Schulz and Ballard Spahr. Will Dobson at NPR. Sasha Weiss and Willy Staley at the *New York Times Magazine*. The NC State creative writing program. Isaac Butler.

The people of Slate dot com were tremendously supportive throughout this project. I'm very lucky to work at a great magazine with such kind people: Laura Bennett, Benjamin Frisch, Rachelle Hampton, Aisha Harris, Rebecca Lavoie, Josh Levin, Steve Lickteig, Lowen Liu, Ayana Morali, Marissa Martinelli, Laura Miller, Willa Paskin, Gabriel Roth, Dana Stevens, Julia Turner, Carvell Wallace, Forrest Wickman, Jessica Winter. Extra thanks to my forever cohost Allison Benedikt and our *Mom and Dad Are Fighting* listeners.

Special thanks to the Virtual Crib.

Alia, Lyra, and Harper: I love being on your team.

About the Author

DAN KOIS is an editor at Slate, founding host of the podcast *Mom and Dad Are Fighting,* and a contributing writer to the *New York Times Magazine.*